LITERARY CRITICISM AND CULTURAL THEORY

Edited by
William E. Cain
Professor of English
Wellesley College

A ROUTLEDGE SERIES

LITERARY CRITICISM AND CULTURAL THEORY

WILLIAM E. CAIN, *General Editor*

POETIC GESTURE
Myth, Wallace Stevens, and the Motions of Poetic Language
Kristine S. Santilli

BORDER MODERNISM
Intercultural Readings in American Literary Modernism
Christopher Schedler

THE MERCHANT OF MODERNISM
The Economic Jew in Anglo-American Literature, 1864–1939
Gary Martin Levine

THE MAKING OF THE VICTORIAN NOVELIST
Anxieties of Authorship in the Mass Market
Bradley Deane

OUT OF TOUCH
Skin Tropes and Identities in Woolf, Ellison, Pynchon, and Acker
Maureen F. Curtin

WRITING THE CITY
Urban Visions and Literary Modernism
Desmond Harding

FIGURES OF FINANCE CAPITALISM
Writing, Class, and Capital in the Age of Dickens
Borislav Knezevic

BALANCING THE BOOKS
Faulkner, Morrison, and the Economies of Slavery
Erik Dussere

BEYOND THE SOUND BARRIER
The Jazz Controversy in Twentieth-Century American Fiction
Kristin K. Henson

SEGREGATED MISCEGENATION
On the Treatment of Racial Hybridity in the U.S. and Latin American Literary Traditions
Carlos Hiraldo

DEATH, MEN, AND MODERNISM
Trauma and Narrative in British Fiction from Hardy to Woolf
Ariela Freedman

WRITING THE CITY
Urban Visions and Literary Modernism
Desmond Harding

THE SELF IN THE CELL
Narrating the Victorian Prisoner
Sean Grass

REGENERATING THE NOVEL
Gender and Genre in Woolf, Forster, Sinclair, and Larence
James J. Miracky

SATIRE AND THE POSTCOLONIAL NOVEL
V. S. Naipul, Chinua Achebe, Salman Rushdie
John Clement Ball

THROUGH THE NEGATIVE
The Photographic Image and the Written Word in Nineteenth-Century American Literature
Megan Williams

LOVE AMERICAN STYLE
Divorce and the American Novel, 1881–1976
Kimberly Freeman

FEMINIST UTOPIAN NOVELS OF THE 1970s
Joanna Russ and Dorothy Bryant
Tatiana Teslenko

DEAD LETTERS TO THE NEW WORLD
Melville, Emerson, and American Transcendentalism
Michael McLoughlin

THE OTHER ORPHEUS
A Poetics of Modern Homosexuality
Merrill Cole

INTIMATE AND AUTHENTIC ECONOMIES
The American Self-Made Man from Douglass to Chaplin
Tom Nissley

REVISED LIVES

Walt Whitman and Nineteenth-Century Authorship

William Pannapacker

Routledge
New York & London

Published in 2004 by
Routledge
29 West 35th Street
New York, NY 10001
www.routledge-ny.com

Published in Great Britain by
Routledge
11 New Fetter Lane
London EC4P 4EE
www.routledge.co.uk

Routledge is an imprint of the Taylor & Francis Group
Printed in the United States of America on acid-free paper

10 9 8 7 6 5 4 3 2

Library of Congress Cataloging-in-Publication Data
Pannapacker, William.
    Revised lives : Walt Whitman and nineteenth-century authorship / by William Pannapacker.
        p. cm. — (Literary criticism and cultural theory)
    Includes bibliographical references and index.
    ISBN 0-415-96870-4
    1. American literature—19th century—History and criticsim. 2. Identity (Psychology) in literature. 3. Religion and literature—United States—History—19th century. 4. Literature and society—United States—History—19th century. 5. Whitman, Walt, 1819–1892—Criticism and interpretation. 6. Group identity in literature. 7. Ethnicity in literature. 8. Sex role in literature. 9. Self in literature. 10. Autobiography. I. Title. II. Series.
PS217.I35P36 2003
810.9'353—dc21   2003014636

For Teresa, Rebecca, and Jessica

Contents

LIST OF ILLUSTRATIONS ix

ACKNOWLEDGMENTS xi

INTRODUCTION xiii

CHAPTER ONE
Revised Lives:
Self-Refashioning and Nineteenth-Century American Autobiography 3

CHAPTER TWO
Politics, Poetics, and Self-Promotion:
Walt Whitman and Abraham Lincoln 19

CHAPTER THREE:
"He Not Only Objected to My Book, He Objected to Me":
Walt Whitman, James Russell Lowell, and the Rhetoric of Exclusion 49

CHAPTER FOUR
"What Is a Man Anyhow?":
Whitmanites, Wildeans, and Working-Class "Comradeship" 105

CHAPTER FIVE
A Question of "Character":
Visual Images and the Nineteenth-Century Construction
of "Edgar Allan Poe" 129

NOTES 145

SELECTED BIBLIOGRAPHY 179

INDEX 193

List of Illustrations

Fig. 1. Walt Whitman, c. 1855. From *Leaves of Grass* (1855).   xiv

Fig. 2. Walt Whitman, c. 1863. Alexander Gardner, Washington, DC, from Horace Traubel, *With Walt Whitman in Camden*, Vol. 1 (New York: The Century Company, 1905), 363.   xv

Fig. 3. Walt Whitman, 1881. Bartlett F. Kenny, Boston. Library of Congress.   xvi

Fig. 4. Frederick Douglass, 1845. From *Narrative of the Life of Frederick Douglass, An American Slave* (Boston: Anti-slavery Office, 1845).   8

Fig. 5. Frederick Douglass, 1855. Frontispiece to *My Bondage and My Freedom* (New York: Miller, Orton & Mulligan, 1855).   9

Fig. 6. "The Meeting with Whitman." From W. D. Howells's *Literary Friends and Acquaintance* (New York, 1902).   78

Fig. 7. Walt Whitman, c. 1860. From *Leaves of Grass* (Boston: Thayer and Eldridge, 1860-61).   84

Fig. 8. Edward Carpenter in his late twenties. Carpenter Collection photographs 8/6, courtesy Sheffield City Council.   116

Fig. 9. Edward Carpenter at age 43 in 1887. Carpenter Collection photographs 8/24, courtesy Sheffield City Council.   117

Fig. 10. Edward Carpenter on right, John Johnston on left, and George Merrill standing. Carpenter Collection photographs 8/53, courtesy of Sheffield City Council.   124

Fig. 11. Edgar Allan Poe, the "Ultima Thule" daguerreotype (1848). Courtesy American Antiquarian Society.   128

Fig. 12. Oliver Leigh's "swelled head" Poe. From Oliver Leigh,
Edgar Allan Poe: The Man, the Master, the Martyr
(Chicago, 1906).   131

Fig. 13. Edgar Allan Poe, the "Whitman" daguerreotype (1848).
Brown University Library.   134

Acknowledgments

I
T IS DIFFICULT TO LOOK AT ANY SCHOLARLY PROJECT OF LONG DURATION AND not see the shifting of an author's interests and influences. This book began as a seminar paper in 1991, and, from the perspective of more than ten years, I can see that scholarship is a form of self-representation, and the author of the first chapter is not the same as the author of the last one. Even in the most carefully revised work, some dissonant voices inevitably break through the harmony that the author wishes to create. *Revised Lives*, in this sense, is a serial autobiography, a series of snapshots of the author and the critical context in which he was writing.

I was born in Camden, New Jersey, and grew up in Philadelphia. I think it is partly a sense of place that stimulated my interest in Benjamin Franklin, Edgar Allan Poe, and Walt Whitman. But it was not until I was a thousand miles away from my birthplace, a graduate student in English at the University of Miami, that Peter Bellis and Joseph Alkana helped me ask the questions that would produce the first stages of this project. Under their guidance, I studied autobiography as a genre, wrote a version of the chapter on Whitman and Lincoln, and became interested in the politics of literary reception. Although I left Miami for Harvard University in 1993, the topic of self-refashioning in response to larger cultural developments shaped much of the research I undertook for my dissertation in the History of American Civilization Program, where I benefited from the influence of Sacvan Bercovitch, David D. Hall, Alan Heimert, Werner Sollors, and, most of all, Lawrence Buell. Looking back, I can see that the best parts of this project are those that attempt to extend and combine their seminal research on American religious history, literary culture, and the historical contingency of the "American Self."

This project also reflects the positive influence and contributions of the following colleagues, correspondents, friends, and family members: Daniel Aaron, Kenneth Carpenter, Natalie Dykstra, Donald Fleming, Ezra Greenspan, Robert Gross, Jay Grossman, John Guillory, John Hench, Mary Kelley, David Klooster, Joann P. Krieg, Mason Lowance, Christine McFadden, Meredith McGill, Gertude

Pannapacker, David Reynolds, Michael Robertson, William Spengemann, Roger Stoddard, Kathleen Verduin, Shirley Wajda, Michael Winship, and Paul Wright. My research assistants Jane Bast and Sarah McKluskey were unfailingly helpful as I reviewed and updated the manuscript for publication.

I am grateful to the Mrs. Giles Whiting Foundation for a Whiting Fellowship in the Humanities, which provided a year of support while I was a graduate student in 1998-99. I am also indebted to the Harvard University Graduate School of Arts and Sciences, the Harvard Graduate Society, and the Program in the History of American Civilization for providing fellowships and grants in support of my doctoral program. Additional support—in the form of substantial monetary awards while I was a graduate student—was provided by the William Harris Arnold and Gertrude Weld Arnold Prize Committee, the Helen Choate Bell Prize Committee, the Bowdoin Prize Committee, and the Phillip Hofer Prize Committee, all of Harvard University.

In addition to providing me with an academic home and generous colleagues, Hope College has supported my scholarly activities with two faculty development summer grants (2001, 2002), underwritten by the Mellon Foundation, and a research fellowship (2003–07), underwritten by the Towsley Foundation of Midland, Michigan. For their confidence in the value of my work (and willingness to invest institutional resources in it), I am grateful to James Boelkins, James Bultman, Jack Nyenhuis, William Reynolds, and Peter Schakel.

For their kind assistance, I am pleased to thank the staff of the following institutions: the American Antiquarian Society; the Barnum Museum in Bridgeport, Connecticut; the Boston Public Library; the Bridgeport Public Library; the Houghton Library, Harvard University; the Library of Congress; the New York Public Library; the Schomberg Center for Research in Black Culture; the Walt Whitman House and Museum in Camden, New Jersey; the Bolton City Library, England; and the Sheffield City Library, England. Quotations from the manuscripts of James Russell Lowell are used by permission of the Houghton Library. Photographs are used by permission of the American Antiquarian Society, Brown University Library, and the Sheffield City Council. Earlier portions of this book were published in the *Harvard Library Bulletin* and *Mapping Male Sexuality: Nineteenth-Century England,* edited by Jay Losey and William D. Brewer.

I am grateful to William E. Cain, for selecting this project for Routledge's *Literary Criticism and Cultural Theory* series, and to Paul Foster Johnson, Associate Editor, who shepherded *Revised Lives* from manuscript to publication.

This book is dedicated to Teresa Jenkins Pannapacker and our two daughters, Rebecca and Jessica, who put everything into perspective.

Introduction

"Dream delivers us to dream, and there is no end to illusion. Life is a train of moods like a string of beads, and, as we pass through them, they prove to be many–colored lenses which paint the world their own hue, and each shows only what lies in focus."

—Ralph Waldo Emerson[1]

I N THE SECOND APPENDIX TO WHAT HE WAS SURE, THIS TIME, WOULD BE THE final edition of *Leaves of Grass* in 1888, Walt Whitman looked back over his long career as the self-proclaimed "American Bard":

My Book and I—what a period we have presumed to span! those thirty years from 1850 to '80—and America in them! Proud, proud indeed may we be, if we have cull'd enough of that period in its own spirit to worthily waft a few live breaths of it to the future![2]

In his final statements about *Leaves*, Whitman expresses the central duality of his life-long project: the reciprocal relationship of self and national representation in a period of rapid change—and by implication the impossibility of representing either completely (or even satisfactorily) for very long. Each attempt to fix a specific identity was subject to reconstructions of national identity, the changing structure of the literary field, and appropriations by unanticipated communities of readers.

Whitman's ongoing attempt to construct a coherent textual identity out of historical fragments ("Specimen Days") mirrors the process by which a continually reconstructed "Myth of America" imposes a coherent meaning over a continent of indeterminate significance. Adrift in a sea of books, manuscripts, newsclippings, and photographs, the aging Whitman humorously complained, "I meet new Walt Whitmans every day. There are a dozen of me afloat. I don't know which Walt Whitman I am."[3] As the extensive textual and visual record of Whitman's life shows,

Figure 1. Walt Whitman, c. 1855. From *Leaves of Grass* (1855).

by the late 1880s there were several Whitmans in circulation: the surly, sensual workman of 1855 (Figure 1); the tough, maternal "Wound-dresser" of 1865 (Figure 2); and the jovial, benevolent "Good, Gray Poet" of the 1880s (Figure 3).[4] As Whitman told his biographer Horace Traubel, "It is hard to extract a man's real self—any man—from such a chaotic mass—from such historic debris."[5] *Leaves of Grass* was not a book, according to Whitman, but the man himself; "It is I you hold, and who holds you," he writes in the concluding poem of the 1860-61 edition.[6] It was this edition on which Whitman first used a butterfly motif on the spine and on the concluding page of the book, suggesting that the "man" he presented was evanescent—not a fixed identity, but a cyclical process in which the "self" is reborn many times, though each moment seems like the culminations.[7]

In this sense, Whitman is representative of the American cultural tendency towards reinvention; the nation too had undergone dramatic changes during his lifetime. Whitman's expansions and revisions of *Leaves* and his accompanying personae were prompted by moments of national transformation; new editions of the book responded to national disintegration in 1860-61, followed the turmoil of the Civil War in 1867, the Centennial Exposition and the end of Reconstruction in 1876, continued through a period of accelerating urban and industrial growth, in 1881 and 1889, and concluded just before the World's Columbian Exposition and the closing of the frontier in 1893. Though continuous in many ways, each version of

Figure 2. Walt Whitman, c. 1863. Alexander Gardner, Washington, DC, from Horace Traubel, *With Walt Whitman in Camden*, Vol. 1 (New York: The Century Company, 1905), 363.

Leaves offered a different construction of the author they claim to represent. Through his writings, Whitman ultimately became a spectator to his own life, which was inseparable from the life of the nation in the nineteenth century.

As Whitman produced successive editions of *Leaves*, the renegotiation of his identity (both as individual and representative), was affected not only by historical events; the generic options available to Whitman also changed as relationships between low and high forms of literary self-representation shifted, as regional literary cultures coalesced into national and international markets, and as new technologies for self-representation such as photography became available.[8] Moreover, this process was complicated by his reception by several communities of readers, each of whom wanted a "Whitman" who embodied their own cherished social, political, and aesthetic agendas.

The many editions of *Leaves of Grass*, together with companion volumes of prose autobiography such as *Memoranda During the War* (1875) and *Specimen Days and Collect* (1882), dozens of publicly circulated photographs and engravings, and three "biographies" of Whitman at least partially written by Whitman himself provide an extraordinary example of the fluidity of the nineteenth-century American self and the means of representing it. While Whitman's self-representational writings are unusually extensive, his life-long project was not unique; well-known contemporaries such as P. T. Barnum, Frederick Douglass, and Abraham Lincoln, along

Figure 3. Walt Whitman, 1881. Bartlett F. Kenny, Boston. Library of Congress.

with a few dozen lesser-known figures, were engaged in a similar process of public self-revision, though not always in strictly autobiographical genres. Lincoln's speeches, for example, are a series of autobiographical statements—constructions of who Lincoln is and what he represents—as much as they were attempts to articulate the historical context of Civil War America. Moreover, as the nineteenth-century reception of Edgar Allan Poe demonstrates—perhaps even more tellingly than the example of Whitman—the author himself may be viewed by the reader as a text or "character" to be interpreted through his writing but also through the visual "texts" in circulation. The author or self becomes, in effect, a site of interpretation for both the larger culture in which the author—increasingly alienated from the version of the self once it is documented—typically participates as long as he or she can.

Most broadly defined, self-refashioning reveals the alienation of an author from an earlier construction of his or her identity as that identity ceases to conform to the exigencies of the present. This alienation is more likely to occur when the subject constructs a public identity at a relatively young age, when the subject achieves a radically altered social position, when society itself changes and the self is no longer responsive to the larger context, when new technologies for representing the self emerge, and when an identity has become subject to misreadings and misappropriations.

In the United States during the nineteenth century, the definition of the "self" and how one translates that self into a textual form were in a state of perpetual change and contestation. Indeed, the question of who was entitled to write an autobiography—in short, who was entitled to call himself an "American"—had to be faced by all of the figures in this study. The larger pattern of nineteenth-century autobiography in the United States is the relation of this textual form (the factual prose narrative of an individual's experiences and consciousness) to rapid class mobility—the expansion of a literate "middle-class"—which caused the convergence the "high" and "low" forms of autobiography.

Rather than a chronicle of the official events of state or sordid adventures, the American bourgeois autobiography emerges from a deeply rooted religious tradition: spiritual self-examinations and conversion narratives, a vast, largely unpublished genre often represented by examples such as Augustine's *Confessions*, John Bunyan's *The Pilgrims Progress*, and Jonathan Edwards's *Personal Narrative*. A major theme of the essays in this book is the role of religious impulses in ostensibly secular activities—how religion infuses politics, literature, celebrity, sexuality, and even photography. At the most basic level, the impulse to reshape the self through writing has its roots in the tradition of the spiritual conversion experience: the task of explaining how one came to hold one's beliefs. Although American civic culture became increasingly secular through the nineteenth century, American autobiography sustained the template of the spiritual journey, replacing the "Celestial City" with the attainment of bourgeois status through the mastery of the self via the conquest of all attributes—immorality, poverty, alien ethnicity—that refute one's status as an American. From the beginning, American autobiography—indeed, much of American literature—has been a reciprocal process of self and national definition in the context of an apocalyptic vision of world history.

American autobiography's centripetal tendency, grounded in the interconnected ideologies of capitalism and Christianity, is complicated in the nineteenth century by an ambiguous relationship to a nation fragmented into different regional communities. In response to rapid changes in the national identity before and during the Civil War, both Whitman and Lincoln reconstruct their public personae by abandoning the absolutist rhetoric of the early careers and moving towards poses of moderation and acceptance of diversity of opinion as they struggle to become more inclusive, "Representative Men." In response to the suffering of the Civil War and the need to unify irreconcilables into a single national identity, both men adopt a rhetoric of reconciliation that enables them ultimately to become embodiments of a contradictory national culture, and, in the case of Lincoln (partly through the agency of Whitman), the central figure in the civil religion that overlaid the older Christian vision of a specifically American role in the unfolding of providence.

Additionally, in the effort to reach or represent a diverse national audience—rather than narrow regional or sectarian niches—sometimes authors elude precise self-definition; instead, they define themselves by opposition to other authors, who are typically reduced to iconic stereotypes. Enmeshed in a network of larger influences (most importantly, the shift of publishing capital from Boston to New York and the emergence of a large "middle-brow" readership), the contradictory elements of Whitman's life-long project of self-representation threatened to compromise his status as a "poet" while not promising a compensating popular readership. The contrived rivalry between Whitman and Lowell was part of a larger means of promoting Whitman as a "high literary" figure by claiming for him the status of a censored, excluded author (evoking the religious tradition of martyrdom or redemptive self-sacrifice) even as other supporters promoted him before middlebrow audiences (including Lowell on one occasion) as the nationalistic celebrator of Abraham Lincoln, a role he cultivated for twenty-seven years. If Whitman helped to make Lincoln the central figure in the American civil religion, Lincoln and Lowell made Whitman into the central figure in the American literary canon.

In the last decade of his life, Whitman's home in Camden, New Jersey became a site of pilgrimage for young male writers, particularly in England, who were struggling to construct a new concept of "manhood" in the wake of the industrial revolution and the breakdown of the old social order. These men, whom I divide into "Whitmanites" (Edward Carpenter and the Bolton Whitman Fellowship, sometimes called the "Whitman Church") and the "Wildeans" (Oscar Wilde, Aubrey Beardsley, and other "Aesthetes"), looked to Whitman as a spiritual guide who could help them construct alternative masculine identities. Foremost among the English Whitman admirers, Carpenter, a former minister, underwent a conversion experience and decided to base his own identity on Whitman's working-class masculine persona and his relationships with working-class boys. Carpenter's writings and evangelical mission suggest that Whitman's persona as much as his poetry had a significant influence on late-Victorian social progressivism in England. However, the alternative social roles for men suggested by Whitman were inherently unstable when appropriated by middle-class admirers in a different cultural context; ultimately, they tended to reinforce the social hierarchies that progressives like Carpenter claimed to oppose. As much as the various images of Whitman competed for legitimacy, the political agenda suggested by his developing poetry and persona was subject to revisions Whitman himself probably would never have sanctioned.

Undoubtedly, the impulse to reconstruct authorial identity is directly related to the inability of the author to control the reception of his or her self-representations. Indeed, efforts to control one's identity through self-refashioning often complicate the reception of the identity by introducing a confusing multiplicity of images over which competing factions struggle for interpretive control. Throughout the nineteenth century, the reciprocal relation of self and nation and competing models of authorship (rooted in religion, national, or ideology) were further complicated by the emergence of new scientific methods for reading visual images made available by rapid developments in photography. The daguerreotypes of Poe, for example, became "objective" phrenological and physiognomic evidence in efforts to construct a unified, consistent author from the fragmented identity produced by changing technology, the proliferation of texts and images, and by competing interpreters trying to establish a uniquely American literary tradition. Specific images, such as the famous "Ultima Thule" daguerreotype of Poe, became icons, which were consulted as source of mystic information about the hidden "character" of the subject.

Although there was a strong normative tendency towards the middle-class success narrative—the secularized story of adversity overcome—self-representation in the nineteenth-century United States, with its fluid class structure, relative variety of official institutions, proliferating cultural fields and sub-fields, religious fluidity, and changing representational technologies, was inherently unstable. Ultimately, every effort at self-representation—no matter how much an author regulated it by repeated acts of self-refashioning and generic modification—became subject to the appropriations of readers. The readers were, in turn, seeking to define their own identities and support their own beliefs in relation to the struggles of earlier writers to understand who they were and what they believed in a rapidly changing, unpredictable historical context.

REVISED LIVES

Chapter One
Revised Lives
Self-Refashioning and Nineteenth-Century American Autobiography

"I should have no Objection to a Repetition of the same Life from its Beginning, only asking the Advantage Authors have in a second Edition to correct some Faults of the first."
—Benjamin Franklin, *The Autobiography*[1]

SCHOLARSHIP ON AMERICAN AUTOBIOGRAPHY DURING THE LAST FORTY YEARS IS itself a rags-to-riches narrative; interest in the subject has expanded rapidly since the early 1960s. The focus of the New Criticism on the formal analysis of poetry, drama, and the novel tended to push autobiography to the margins of literary studies, leaving it to biographers and historians. Stephen Shapiro was certainly over-stating the case in 1968 when he called autobiography a "Dark Continent," for American autobiography had already begun to be mapped by two major bibliographies.[2] Since the mid-1970s, however, autobiography in general and American autobiography in particular have become the subjects of intense scholarly activity.[3] The notion of autobiography as a strict representation of biographical facts has all but disappeared, but the debate concerning the degree to which autobiography is distinct from fiction has continued in numerous books and essays.[4] Many studies have related the theoretical concerns of autobiography more specifically to American literature and culture.[5] Meanwhile, the efforts of scholars to recover and interpret representative texts by African Americans have contributed significantly to the renewed interest in first-person narratives as documentary evidence rather than as a species of fiction.[6] More recently, comparable efforts to reconstruct the traditions of women's autobiography have been undertaken successfully.[7] Within little more than a quarter-century, then, autobiography has become one of the most active fields of literary theory and American cultural studies.

Most literary scholars acknowledge that autobiographical writing flowered in mid-nineteenth-century America through the convergence of the influences of spiritual self-examination, an expanding middle class, rising literacy rates, an expanding literary marketplace, Romanticism, popular democracy, individualism, and a belief in the reality and autonomy of the self. As evidence of this convergence, the more comprehensive bibliographies demonstrate that the decades of the so-called "American Renaissance," 1831–1860, were a period of particularly intense autobiographical writing (see Tables 1 and 2). This efflorescence was stalled for about thirty years by the Civil War and its aftermath (a sustained period of relative extro-spection that corresponds loosely with literary realism), but the antebellum growth in autobiographical writing resumed in the 1890s, and it is probably accurate to say that the American autobiographical tendency has continued to expand (with brief hesitancies) until the present.

Table 1. Autobiographies published in the United States, 1801–1900.[8]

Decade	Autobiographies Published	% of Total
1801–1810	5	1.0
1811–1820	3	0.6
1821–1830	11	2.4
1831–1840	25	5.4
1841–1850	31	6.7
1851–1860	62	13.5
1861–1870	44	9.6
1871–1880	55	12.3
1881–1890	89	19.5
1891–1900	132	28.9
TOTAL	457	100.0

Table 2. Ratio of autobiographies published by decade and United States Population at end of each decade, 1801–1900.[9]

Decade	Autobiographies Published	U.S. Pop. at End of Decade	Ratio of Persons to Autobiographies (in thousands)
1801–1810	5	7,239,881	1,448
1811–1820	3	9,638,453	3,213
1821–1830	11	12,866,020	1,170
1831–1840	25	17,069,453	683
1841–1850	31	23,191,876	748
1851–1860	62	31,443,321	507
1861–1870	44	39,818,449	905
1871–1880	55	50,155,783	912
1881–1890	89	62,947,714	707
1891–1900	132	75,994,575	576

It is not surprising that so vast a field has been subject mainly to macro-level theorizations of the genre as a whole or micro-level explications of a few sub-genres. John Cawelti and Sacvan Bercovitch, for example, have examined American autobiography as a ritual of national consensus, a celebration of the "self-made man" and the "Myth of America"; while Lawrence Buell has emphasized the heteroglot complexity and generic variety of American autobiography.[10] Buell, William Spengemann, and Jeffrey Steele have also expanded the definition of autobiography by examining generic hybridity within the so-called American Renaissance in such works as *Walden, Leaves of Grass,* Emerson's essays, and *The Scarlet Letter.*[11] More recently, considerable research has focused on slave narrative; though a much-needed corrective for previous critical blindspots, these studies have tended to over-emphasize the separateness of African American traditions from other forms of nineteenth-century self-representation. And full-length studies of American autobiography have tended to conclude with the *Autobiography of Benjamin Franklin*—the end of the tradition of spiritual autobiography—or begin with *The Education of Henry Adams*—the supposed beginning of the modern fragmentation of the self. As a whole, therefore, the subject of nineteenth-century American autobiography has been treated unevenly. It has been subject to sweeping ideological interpretations; it has been theorized in relation to the development of the genre as a whole; discontinuous portions of it have been given intensive treatment; and it has been bracketed by more comprehensive studies of the eighteenth and twentieth centuries. Still it seems remarkable that amid this explosion of scholarship, the ideologically and theoretically significant practice of *self-refashioning,* in all its multi-generic variations, has been largely ignored except in the case of a few individual figures.[12]

Many nineteenth-century writers wrote multiple autobiographies, substantially reshaping their identities with each revision. Frederick Douglass, the most studied case (see note 10), published his *Narrative of the Life of Frederick Douglass, an American Slave, Written By Himself* in 1845, which he revised and expanded into *My Bondage and My Freedom* in 1855, and finally completed as his *Life and Times of Frederick Douglass* in 1881, only to revise it yet again in 1892.[13]

Douglass's multiple autobiographies, impressive as they are, are less extensive than the compulsive revisions of the showman and circus promoter, P. T. Barnum, who published an autobiographical novella called "Adventures of an Adventurer" in the New York *Atlas* in 1841, which he later revised and expanded into the *Life of P. T. Barnum, Written By Himself* in 1854. This autobiography was drastically transformed and extended into *Struggles and Triumphs* in 1869, which Barnum supplemented up to 1875. *Struggles and Triumphs* had become so long (875 pages) that an abridged version (314 pages) was published in 1876, which Barnum continued to supplement until his death in 1891. Near the time of his death, he arranged for his wife, Nancy Barnum, to write "The Final Chapter" of his life. He also arranged for the publication of an adulatory biography, carefully revised from his autobiography by Joel Benton from the first into the third person.[14]

Patterns of revision comparable to those of Douglass and Barnum have been followed by such diverse nineteenth-century figures as William Wells Brown, Stephen Burroughs, Mary Chesnut, Davy Crockett, Elizabeth Custer, Laura Smith Haviland, William Dean Howells, Henry James, John Marrant, Mark Twain, Booker T. Washington, and Noah Webster.[15] If the conventional boundaries of auto-biography as a prose narrative are expanded to include hybridized literary forms, the political oratory of Abraham Lincoln and the poetry of Walt Whitman—the writings of two men who presented themselves as "representative Americans"—can be added to this list.

Although they are nearly exact contemporaries, Frederick Douglass (1818–1895), P. T. Barnum (1810–1891), and Walt Whitman (1819–1892) seem an unlikely cluster for comparison, for they have generally belonged to different realms of scholarly investigation. Their most obvious similarity is the paradoxical quality of their initial self-representational projects. At the outset of their public lives they were all marginal, oppositional figures: a runaway slave and abolitionist of racially mixed parentage; a barely legitimate showman of dubious social origins and questionable ethics; and a self-declared "national bard" who never marries, never settles into a steady job, and survives largely through the kindness of friends and relatives. While all three figures seem to stand outside mainstream nineteenth-century American culture, the current of Douglass's *Narrative*, Barnum's *Life*, and Whitman's *Leaves* flows in the opposite direction by transforming them into national character types: the Literate Slave, the Yankee Businessman, and the Free Worker. Each is a species of the "self-made man," and each comes to endorse the individualism so characteristic of nineteenth-century American public discourse.

Though the bulk of Barnum's 1855 *Life* describes the means by which the showman hoaxes the public on an ever-grander scale (liquor, lotteries, Joice Heth, the Feejee Mermaid, Tom Thumb), it ends with a domestic idyll called "Home, Sweet Home": "I am at home, in the bosom of my family; and 'home' and 'family' are the highest and most expressive symbols of the kingdom of heaven."[16] Barnum's narrative begins like the *Memoirs of Stephen Burroughs* (1798), a noted Yankee rogue, but it ends with an affirmation of domesticity; the wandering boy from a broken home in the backcountry ultimately reaches the Celestial City of his own construction, a vast, Byzantine mansion called "Iranistan," suggestive of Youth's air-drawn castle in Thomas's Cole series of paintings, *The Voyage of Life* (1842). Ultimately, Barnum attributes his triumphs to American characteristics as much as to his own initiative; he expresses this neatly in his dedication: "To the Universal Yankee Nation, of Which I am proud to be one." Barnum's *Life*, writes one British critic, "would scarcely claim a notice here, if regarded simply as a literary effort; but it is a *representative book*."[17] By 1867 American critics like Richard Grant White would acknowledge, with some elitist irony, that Barnum "is the representative man, and his museum is the representative 'instit∞tion' of this country."[18] Like Mark Twain—another "representative American"—the showman would later brag that a letter addressed to "P. T. Barnum, America" would easily reach him.[19]

Similarly, Douglass's 1845 *Narrative* details how the former slave managed to overcome systematic exclusion from the advantages of middle-class domestic life (a birthday, a mother, siblings, marriage, and literacy) and ultimately becomes a complex symbol of American individualism. Perhaps the most famous lines from Douglass's 1845 *Narrative*—"you have seen how a man was made a slave; you shall see how a slave was made a man"—describe the basic narrative structure of masculine self-representation in the nineteenth-century United States. Douglass's determination to fight Covey the "nigger-breaker" to the death, if necessary, does not dwell on the personal and racial specifics of the confrontation; instead, it is the moment in which a generalized "slave" becomes a generalized "man." In the process of becoming a "man," he abandons the name "Bailey" for "Douglass," a name taken from the history of Scottish resistance, proclaiming himself nothing less than a direct heir of the unfulfilled promise of the Enlightenment and the American Revolution.[20]

Most overtly of the three, Whitman proclaims himself the long-awaited American bard in the prose preface to the 1855 *Leaves*. Throughout his career, Whitman's poetic persona strains at being the embodiment and mouthpiece of the ordinary American: "No sentimentalist, no stander above men and women or apart from them." As shown earlier, the first of Whitman's many frontispieces, presents him not as a poet but as a common workman.[21] The Whitman of the first "Song of Myself" is a living symbol of the motto, "E Pluribus Unum": "Walt Whitman, an American, one of the roughs, a Kosmos."[22]

The initial self-representations of Barnum, Douglass, and Whitman all demonstrate a centripetal tendency to emphasize their representativeness of some broad segment of America, if not the nation as a whole, and seem—at first glance—to affirm rather than deny the potential inclusiveness of the American system as each becomes a "Representative Man." This paradoxical duality of individualistic representativeness is, of course, characteristic of antebellum civic discourse, which may elevate an individual to heroic proportions provided that the individual is an embodiment of the heroic qualities of the common people. In *Representative Men* (1850), for example, Emerson praises figures such as Goethe and Napoleon as exemplifying the superior qualities of the civilizations that produced them; "The genius of humanity," Emerson writes, "is the real subject whose biography is written in our annals."[23] Each of these figures presents an account of the subject's ability to apotheosize American types through personal struggle *within* the existing social, political, and economic order. They are reformers rather than revolutionaries. These celebrations of the "Self-made Man," then, may be read as exceptionalist endorsements of the American consensus view of unlimited social mobility through individual effort, an inclusiveness that can even stretch to accommodate the huckster, the drifter, and the hounded slave. Just as Barnum presents himself as the "Universal Yankee" and as Whitman claims to incarnate the American people *en masse*, "Douglass," according to his contemporary James M. Smith, "passed through every gradation of rank comprised in our national make-up, and bears upon his person and upon his soul

Figure 4. Frederick Douglass, 1845. From *Narrative of the Life of Frederick Douglass, An American Slave* (Boston: Anti-slavery Office, 1845).

everything that is American." For all his protestations against American social injustice, Douglass was "a Representative American man—a type of his countrymen."[24]

This process is nicely encapsulated by the changing visual iconography of Douglass. Daguerreotypes from the 1840s present Douglass as an overwhelming physical and moral presence who almost seems to crack the photographer's glass plate with the fierceness of his gaze and the urgency of his demands. A Scotsman who saw Douglass in 1846 said, "he seemed a buirly fellow, ane I shouldna like to hae a tussle wi o' him either feeseecally or intellecktually [sic]."[25] In the frontispiece to Douglass's 1845 *Narrative* (Figure 4), however, he appears resolute, hopeful, even romanticized, but certainly not powerful or threatening. His racial features are softened and his imposing body fades harmlessly into outline. He is not the insurrectionary Nat Turner feared by Northerners and Southerners alike; Douglass reclines with hands folded genteelly upon crossed legs, and his eyes seem to gaze above the reader, perhaps at changes safely in some distant future. Similarly, his signature appears formulaic, lacking individuality, as if it is conforming self-consciously to the rules of proper penmanship—just as the ideal slave will conform to the rules of polite society. Douglass's next autobiography, *My Bondage and My Freedom* (1855), presents an engraved image of him that conforms much more closely to the photographic record (Figure 5). This time Douglass looks formidable, even dangerous as he gazes directly at the reader with clenched fists on his open lap. His signature too, presented below the engraving, is considerably more individualized. The difference

Figure 5. Frederick Douglass, 1855. Frontispiece to *My Bondage and My Freedom* (New York: Miller, Orton & Mulligan, 1855).

between the two frontispieces is so striking, that one must question whether Douglass had control over his representation in the 1845 engraving or, whether this change in his appearance was deliberate and tactical. Was Douglass portraying the greater urgency of the abolitionist cause in the 1850s, after the passage of the Fugitive Slave Act (1850) and after *Uncle Tom's Cabin* (1852) in which he was a partly fictionalized character? Was he writing for a more militant audience? How did Douglass—and the larger culture of his readers—construct and reconstruct "Frederick Douglass" over that decade and for what reasons?[26]

Despite the initial efforts of Whitman, Barnum, and Douglass to appear culturally representative, none of their initial publications were treated as endorsements of mainstream values. Indeed, quite the opposite is true in general. In the *Delaware Republican* of 12 December 1845, for example, A. C. C. Thompson calls Douglass's *Narrative* "a ridiculous publication, which bears the impress of falsehood on every page."[27] In the March 1855 issue of the *Harvard Magazine*, an anonymous critic writes of Barnum's *Life*, "Not since Rousseau and his *Confessions* has anyone dared with such deliberate effrontery to insult the world by offering to its inspection so unblushing a record of moral obliquity."[28] Of the three, Whitman received the harshest criticism; reviewing the 1855 *Leaves*, Rufus Griswold found "it impossible to convey any, even the most faint idea of its style and contents, and of our disgust and detestation of them." Griswold, calls Whitman a "monster" and accuses him in Latin of being a practitioner of "the love that dare not speak its name."[29]

All three men were attacked not only in the press; each experienced the physical violence of the democratic masses they supposedly represented and sometimes celebrated. Barnum had been "in imminent personal peril" at the hands—and pitchforks—of angry townspeople more than once in his early career as a promoter, and his American Museum was nearly burned during the New York City Draft Riots in 1863.[30] Douglass's first experience of free labor was a shipyard beating that nearly cost him his life; shouts of "'Kill the damned nigger! Kill him! kill him!' echo through Douglass's career."[31] At an anti-slavery lecture in Indiana in 1843, Douglass's arm was broken by a mob of "roughs" of the sort apparently celebrated by Whitman's persona in *Leaves*.[32] It is possible that Whitman, too, had been the target of violence; according to David Reynolds, in 1840 a mob in Woodbury, New York, may have tarred and feathered the future poet and ridden him out of town on a rail.[33] As chapter three of this study examines, Whitman's entire career as a poet is characterized by collisions with civil institutions and public authority. The hostile reception frequently accorded each of these figures seems to demonstrate that, for all their efforts to portray themselves as representative Americans, their personae were not unambivalently accepted as such.

The mutability of authorial identity in the nineteenth century suggests, in particular, that representative selfhood enabled writers to construct a self in accord with pre-defined social categories (business man, freedman, worker, etc.), but it also enabled these writers to attack the existing social, political and economic order by exposing the exclusions and hypocrisies of its universal claims of freedom. These writers construction of themselves as ideal types allowed them to express their resistance as a *collective* voice against social inequities. They were not just speaking for themselves but for all Americans. At some point each of these figures aligns himself with the rhetoric of the "Declaration of Independence" only to show how their nation has failed to live up to its ideals.

Whitman, for example, claimed to have published the first edition of *Leaves* on July 4, 1855, suggesting that *Leaves* was a reassertion of the ideals of 1776, which Whitman articulates in the tone of a frustrated Free Soil Democrat who is outraged by the possible expansion of slavery into the West: "Through me many long dumb voices,/Voices of the interminable generations of prisoners and slaves/ . . .And of the rights of them the others are down upon."[34] Similarly, when Douglass revised his 1845 *Narrative* into *My Bondage and My Freedom* in 1855, he restored the passages regarding the tyrannical imposition of slavery deleted from the "Declaration" in his own revised declaration; his struggle with Covey, like that of the American revolutionaries with George III, was "repelling the cruel and unjust aggressions of a tyrant."[35] Outside of the autobiographies, Douglass asks more pointedly in 1852, "What to the Slave Is the Fourth of July?," in which he explicitly references the foundational text of the American system, highlighting all the more the irony of the mere existence of "An American Slave." Even Barnum, probably the least marginalized of these figures (and certainly the most upwardly mobile), begins his 1855 *Life* by saying that he made his "debut" when "Independence Day had gone by" and "the cannons had ceased to thunder forth their remembrances of our National Anniversary."[36] Barnum presents himself as born in a post-heroic period, one in which nostalgia for the Age of Washington conceals unbridled economic opportunism—perhaps ironically symbolized in Barnum's own *Life* by his blockbuster sideshow exhibitions of Joice Heth, a toothless, profane slave-woman, advertised as the nurse of the infant Washington; and later, Tom Thumb, a bawdy midget who posed in costume as the "Father of the Country."[37] Had Barnum been born in a different time, he implies, he might not have needed to engage in such "humbugs," which the public seems to applaud as bravura performances of entrepreneurial virtuosity.

The self-constructions of Barnum, Douglass, and Whitman, then, are complicated by the tension between their social representativeness and their exclusion from the right of social representation. The basis of this tension was directly related to the conflicts inherent in nineteenth-century American autobiography as a developing genre. Unlike most "literary" genres, autobiographical writing in the nineteenth-century United States was not entirely a gentry-class product; it did not require any professional commitment or specialized training. Autobiographers, as a whole, need not be members of intellectual and artistic coteries, and they need not even be particularly well educated or well connected, though many were. Unlike poetry or the novel, autobiographical writing was a genre accessible in different forms to statesmen and thieves alike, but there were clear divisions within the genre as a whole. The paradoxical rhetoric of heroic representativeness enabled writers from an expanding literate middle class to assert their right to participate in (and inadvertently to hybridize) a textual practice heretofore defined, on the one hand, by the "autobiographies," "lives," and "memoirs" of statesmen, generals, and bishops; and, on the other, by the "narratives," "adventures," and "confessions" of slaves, sailors, and criminals. It is partly this ongoing tension within modes of self-representation and the corresponding generic forms available to Douglass, Barnum, and Whitman that forces them perpetually to renegotiate the balance between the conflicting sides of their public personae as the relationship between genres and identity constructions develops through the nineteenth century.

Perhaps the most significant connection between Douglass, Barnum, and Whitman, among others, is their life-long construction and reconstruction of their public personae through various self-representational projects. Most generally stated, self-refashioning reveals the alienation of an author from earlier constructions of his or her identity. Revisers, perhaps more than other autobiographical writers, express dissatisfaction with the self-text relationship.

Even as the pen moves across the page, the "I" of the previous sentence becomes increasingly discontinuous from the self in the present; the "I" becomes an historical construct, an impersonation, a fiction that should be in the third person but usually remains in the first. This essential flaw in the genre (shared conceptually with the memorializing function of the personal icon, and later, the photograph) is particularly problematic when the subject becomes a public figure at a relatively young age, as Douglass, Barnum, and Whitman all did. Ideally, an autobiographical work should be written just before death, when the self has less potential to change and alienation from the textual self become less likely. The first autobiographical works of Douglass, Barnum, and Whitman were acts of public self-creation; subsequent writings could only revise what had been created. All three figures were partially trapped at an early age by the meaning they had prematurely assigned to their lives.

Even at the outset of his public life in 1845, Douglass perceived the gulf between himself and the self of only a few years earlier, "You must not judge me now by what I then was—a change of circumstances, has made a surprising change in me. Frederick Douglass, the *freeman*, is a very different person from Frederick Bailey, the *slave*."[38] In 1855, Barnum seems to have fully identified with the self presented in his *Life*. In the face of strong moral censure he responds, "I would not this day change a line or word in the entire volume were I to re-write it."[39] Ten years later, however, an increasingly wealthy and respectable Barnum—now an elder Universalist and temperance advocate—could not so easily identify with the trickster Barnum of 1855; he writes, "I have *striven* to *do good*, but (foolishly) stuck my worst side outside, until half the Christian community got to believe that I wore horns & hoofs."[40]

This expression of alienation from previous versions of the self comprises a number of more specific overlapping and sometimes contradictory reasons for revising an autobiographic work: to increase the appearance of verisimilitude by selecting different past events to suggest the antecedents of the desired present persona; to increase the relevance of one's past to new social, political, religious, and economic commitments and interests; to separate oneself from a previous collaborative or otherwise externally "contaminated" autobiographical work; to transform the style of one's autobiography from vulgar colloquialism to more literary styles of presentation as one advances socially; to adapt new technologies such as photography for replicating and disseminating a more immediate self; to redefine one's understanding of the relationship between the public and private identities; to conform with or distance oneself from changing ethnic, racial, religious, sexual, or class-based social formations; to alter one's relation to other imagined communities such as a nation, a region, or an emerging literary marketplace niche; or to adapt one's self-representations developing autobiographical genres.

The most vexing problem of autobiography studies—and genre studies in general—is reaching a definition of the genre itself. Few definitions of autobiography remain satisfactory for very long. Quite often, we are left with a definition that makes everything autobiographical or makes nothing autobiographical. On the one hand, all texts are inherently autobiographical in the sense that they reflect the discourses emanating from a specific self. On the other hand, no text is autobiographical because the self is constructed out of various social discourses. Apparently in resignation, Paul De Man observes, "the distinction between fiction and autobiography is not an either/or polarity"; in short, the distinction is "undecidable."[41] Although critics such as De Man and Roland Barthes have indefinitely postponed the definition of autobiography as a genre, one should not conclude that autobiography is therefore indistinguishable from fiction. No doubt, autobiographical identities—to the extent that they are retrospectively arranged into some kind of meaningful order—are pre-determined to some degree by available discourses, particularly as they are regulated by genre categories. But as we have seen, autobiographical writings are inherently dialogic, to use Mikhail Bakhtin's term, and contain alternative, and even subversive, discourses that actively undermine the bourgeois drift of representative selfhood built into the structure of nineteenth-century autobiographical genres.

Of course, all genres are inherently unstable. A genre is never uniform at any given moment, and it changes unevenly over time and place, sometimes increasing in its availability to a population, sometimes becoming associated with certain professions and not others, sometimes merging with or incorporating other genres, sometimes spinning off new forms (see Tables 3a and 3b). It is particularly difficult to speak authoritatively about autobiography in the early-nineteenth century, for example, because genres were diversified by partially autonomous and/or overlapping subcultures—races, classes, genders, ethnicities, religions, professions, languages—within the United States, to say nothing of extensive international influences. Although the rules of a genre are perpetually contested by different groups, there are usually some rules which are generally agreed upon by all but the most experimental or marginal practitioners, particularly as a literary culture becomes more homogeneous (as was the case in the post-bellum United States).

Table 3a. "High" and "mixed" genre titles of published autobiographical writings in the United States, 1801–1900.

Decade	Autobiography	Life	Memoirs	Sketches	Recollections	Reminiscences
1801–1810	0	2	0	1	0	0
1811–1820	0	2	2	1	0	0
1821–1830	0	4	0	3	0	0
1831–1840	0	6	7	3	0	2
1841–1850	3	13	2	4	1	2
1851–1860	8	24	5	3	3	1
1861–1870	5	13	6	4	3	0
1871–1880	10	16	3	4	6	6
1881–1890	15	25	0	4	10	9
1891–1900	14	30	3	6	10	17
TOTAL	55	135	28	33	33	36

Table 3b. "Low" genre titles of published autobiographical writings in the United States, 1801–1900.

Decade	Incidents	Confessions	Story	Narrative	Adventures
1801–1810	0	0	0	0	0
1811–1820	0	0	0	0	1
1821–1830	0	0	1	1	1
1831–1840	0	2	2	4	3
1841–1850	0	0	1	9	4
1851–1860	6	2	1	3	6
1861–1870	0	2	4	2	1
1871–1880	6	0	2	4	6
1881–1890	4	0	4	0	4
1891–1900	1	2	7	1	3
TOTAL	17	8	22	24	29

Patterns of growth and decline in autobiographical genres (such as the steady growth of "reminiscences" from 1870 to 1900 and the decline of "narratives" in the 1880s, shown in Tables 3a and 3b) seem to reinforce the position taken by Philippe Lejeune and Elizabeth Bruss, among others, that autobiography is generic "pact" or "contract" between the writer and the reader, both of whom have certain expectations about what one is producing and the other is consuming.[42] The most obvious contract is that an autobiography has some basis in history, as opposed to the novel, which may contain autobiographical elements but makes no claims regarding the faithful representation of historical or biographical events. The naive reader does not object when Frederick Douglass takes liberties with his experiences in his novel, *The Heroic Slave* (1851), but that reader might take exception to inconsistencies and omissions in the *Narrative*, which may suggest that the autobiographer is not "sincere" about the link between self and text and has, consequently, violated the contract.

This autobiographical contract—useful as it is—is complicated by the instability of the rules; there is no guarantee that a writer and reader interpret the contract in the same way, particularly when they are separated by time, place, and cultural difference. Moreover, the contract may be confused by contemporaries with similar coexisting contracts; it may be corrupted by incompetence or intentionally breached, or there may be experimental or hybridized works in which the contract is uncertain. The multiplicity of autobiographical forms in the nineteenth century suggests that the rules were in contestation, particularly with respect to the relationship between high and low forms. One result of this contestation is the tendency of autobiographical writings to mutate into different subgeneric forms, even when the author ceases to exert any control over the textual product. An autobiographical work can be written according the rules of one subgenre, but, over the course of century, it might drift like continent into an entirely new literary hemisphere.

   The variability of the title of Benjamin Franklin's "autobiography" in the nineteenth century is a case in point. Franklin wrote sections of his fragmentary autobiography at odd moments in the late eighteenth century; he never used the term "autobiography," and each section was written for different reasons.[43] Franklin's autobiography was not cobbled together into anything resembling its present form until the 1840s. Franklin's memoir was surely the most widely disseminated American life narrative in the nineteenth century, but it was published in such heterogeneous forms, under such different titles, that it is difficult to define what one means by "Franklin's autobiography." The work's textual history is extremely complex; it was adapted in dozens of variably priced editions for different audiences at different times. As shown in Table 4, from 1791 to 1820 Franklin's fragmentary writings were most often titled the "Life" of Benjamin Franklin. In the 1850s, however, "Life" was displaced as the most common title by "Memoirs," which was the title of the original French publication of the first part. About a decade before this interlude of "Memoirs" in the 1850s, the title "Autobiography" was assuming a larger portion of genre representation. By the end of the nineteenth century, all other titles had nearly disappeared, and "Autobiography" became, and remains, the most common title for Franklin's life-writings.

Table 4. Genre categories of Benjamin Franklin's life-writings, 1791–1900.[44]

Decade	Autobiography	Memoirs	Life	Narrative	Reminiscences
1791–1800	0	1	10	0	0
1801–1810	0	1	8	0	0
1811–1820	0	3	13	0	0
1821–1830	0	1	4	0	0
1831–1840	0	1	2	0	0
1841–1850	4	0	1	2	0
1851–1860	6	11	4	3	0
1861–1870	1	0	0	0	0
1871–1880	0	0	3	0	1
1881–1890	6	0	1	0	0
1891–1900	7	0	2	0	0
TOTAL	24	18	48	5	1

   In the early nineteenth century, the term "autobiography" must have seemed like a pedantic neologism, but, as the term became more common and Franklin achieved "Founding Father" status, the decline of the high-caste association of "autobiography" and increasing popular access to previously elite genre categories intersected in the 1840s and 50s. At that time, "autobiography" probably retained vestigial connotations of its origins, but it was beginning to be appropriated along with "life" by middle-class (or middle-class aspirant) writers as a more suitable term than "narrative," which was increasingly reserved for ex-slaves, or "adventures," which became the province of sailors and other low-caste writers.

Set against this background of generic evolution in the nineteenth century, the self-representational projects of writers such as Douglass, Barnum, and Whitman become increasingly dialogic, both internally, as their own sense of alienation from former identities prompted revision, and externally, as developments in the genre itself called for revised approaches. Overall, the process of revision created at least two paradoxes in understanding the self-representational projects of the each of these three figures: first, each was initially an outsider to the mainstream culture, but their earlier publications tended to present a representative self, albeit one who protests the failures of the system to live up to its avowed ideals; second, as they became increasingly institutionalized and celebrated by the culture as a whole, their self-representations became less exemplary and more individualized. Again, this was partly the result of their own personal development and partly the result of shifting genre expectations.

For example, Frederick Douglass, the elder statesman of the *Life and Times* (1881, 1892), while still a representative self-made man to some degree, is considerably more individualized, more detail-specific, than the generic escaped slave of the 1845 *Narrative*. Douglass no longer wishes "it to be imagined that I am insensible to the singularity of my career, or to the peculiar relation I sustain to the history of my time and country."[45] Consequently, *Life and Times* is a less unified work than any of his previous autobiographies, for, by the final edition, Douglass does not revise the work as a whole for consistency but merely adds a supplement to bring it up to date. Similarly, the P. T. Barnum of the final editions of *Struggles and Triumphs* (1884, 1889) is no longer the protean, generalized Yankee huckster of 1855; rather, he becomes a self-indulgent moralist chronicling his public services in regular supplements to what has become, like Douglass's *Life and Times*, a "full-dress" autobiography, one which covers the events of a prominent individual's life from birth to old age with as much factual detail as possible. Such works emphasize the distinctiveness of their lives rather than their qualities as representatives of a large group people.

As a group, Douglass, Barnum, and Whitman drift from their early proclamations of representativeness to more self-assured if sometimes contradictory individualization in their autobiographical projects from the 1840s and 50s to the 1890s. This change was partly the result of their changing status; they began their careers as unknown figures who wrote themselves into public personae, but by the 1890s they had become cultural institutions who could command public interest in their own right rather than as reflections of the national culture. In each case, it was the story of the author-celebrity, rather than politics, entertainment, or aesthetics, that became the focus of their final publications. The political urgency that energized and motivated the antebellum autobiographies of Douglass, for example, had abated somewhat by 1881 and 1892, when the former slave was appointed a representative of the United States government. By the 1880s, the reprobate Barnum of the

1850s had become a proprietor of the "Greatest Show on Earth," and, like Whitman, Barnum began to soften his image by presenting himself as "The Man the Children Love."[46] And Whitman, who had been fired from his clerkship in the Department of the Interior in 1865 for being the immoral author of an indecent book, was considered for a Civil War pension by the United States Congress and feted in New York City by the likes of Andrew Carnegie in 1887 as we shall examine.

Yet, unlike Douglass and Barnum, who by the early 1880s became satisfied with the autobiographical narratives they had constructed, Whitman experimented with self-representation right up to his death in 1892.[47] Of the three figures, Whitman is unquestionably the most complex. Like Barnum and Douglass, Whitman fell into the pattern of internal revision and supplementation of *Leaves of Grass,* which continues to expand with appendices of autobiographical prose such as "A Backward Glance o'er Travel'd Roads," and "Good-bye My Fancy," as well as new poems ranging from the indirectly autobiographical "Prayer of Columbus" to the trivial poem, "My Canary Bird." But the multiplicity of Whitman's efforts at capturing a contingent self in an historical context goes beyond the efforts of Douglass and Barnum to preempt biographers in assigning an "official" meaning to their lives. Whitman, for example, urged three of his acolytes to write three substantially different "biographies," which he edited for "accuracy."[48] The evolution of genre, the development of the nation, shifts in literary taste, the multiplication of images that circulated among communities of readers—none of these were impediments to Whitman's self-representation; they became irreducible elements of it. Through all the changes of Whitman's persona and the context that shaped it, he ultimately never sought to impose a fixed meaning on his existence or the nation's, and he strongly resisted those who attempted to impose a singular meaning on either.

Chapter Two
Politics, Poetics, and Self-Promotion
Walt Whitman and Abraham Lincoln

I. "I AM LINCOLN'S MAN"

IN THE 1880S WHITMAN SAID, "LINCOLN IS PARTICULARLY MY MAN—PARTICULARLY belongs to me; yes, and by the same token, I am Lincoln's man: I guess I particularly belong to him; we are afloat on the same stream—we are rooted in the same ground."[1] Both opposed the expansion of slavery, but they were not abolitionists. Both were committed to free labor and territorial expansion, but the preservation of the Union was more important than either. Both revered the heroes of the American Revolution, particularly Washington; neither adhered to any religious sect. They shared working-class origins, and each adopted the rhetoric of Jacksonian populism. Their literary styles were both influenced by the Bible, Shakespeare, Thomas Paine, and Robert Burns; both also tapped the vitality of American vernacular speech, political oratory, and drama. Lincoln even seems an incarnation of the poet-redeemer described in the 1855 preface to Whitman's *Leaves of Grass*, and Whitman himself would later imply that they were comparable types: "Lincoln gets almost nearer me than anybody else."[2] At the root of Whitman's development and transformation is his relationship to the tumultuous political culture of the United States before and during the Civil War.

Ironically, Whitman, the "political poet," disliked most politicians and political parties. Despite the compromising, all-embracing rhetoric of *Leaves of Grass* (1855), "The Eighteenth Presidency!" retains the fighting words and rhetorical strategies of Whitman's earlier editorials: "The President eats dirt and excrement for his daily meals, likes it, and tries to force it on The States."[3] In an effort to define what sort of people become politicians, Whitman writes of "pimpled men, scarred inside with the vile disorder, gaudy outside with gold chains made from the people's money."[4] Yet, Whitman also describes his ideal Presidential candidate, a man crafted in the image of his own persona as "one of the roughs":

I would be much pleased to see some heroic, shrewd, fully-informed, healthy-bodied, middle-aged, beard-faced American blacksmith or boatman come down from the West across the Alleghenies, and walk into the Presidency, dress'd in a clean suit of working attire, and with the tan all over his face, breast, and arms; I would certainly vote for that sort of man.[5]

When Lincoln was nominated as the Republican candidate for the nineteenth presidency, he must have seemed the real-life counterpart to Whitman's idealized President. In addition to their similar political views, Whitman seems to have perceived, at first only intuitively, a comparable foreground in their struggles to find public voices. Both emulated the American bourgeois success narrative in their efforts to rise from the poverty and obscurity of their births to positions of social prominence. Whitman's origins were working-class, but, inspired by the pamphleteers of the American Revolution and the heroic sermons of Carlyle and Emerson, he launched a career in radical political journalism and hoped to become a famous orator. Lincoln, also inspired by the glories of revolution and heroic self-reliance, emerged from a semi-literate family to become a small-town lawyer and politician with opinions as decidedly clear-cut as Whitman's. Lincoln's public aspirations were, perhaps, most obvious in his 1838 "Address Before the Young Men's Lyceum": "Let every American, every lover of liberty, every well wisher to his posterity, swear by the blood of the Revolution never to violate in the least particular, the laws of the country; and never to tolerate their violation by others."[6] In both cases, their dogmatic faith in the political values they ascribed to the American Revolution (and perhaps a comparable sense of their own potential for personal greatness) led to an uncompromising "political religion" that often failed to cultivate an appreciative audience; indeed, they often alienated more people than they attracted. Partly as a result of this certainty, by 1849 both Whitman and Lincoln had suffered traumatic professional failures that threatened to silence their public voices. In response, they began to develop an apparently more compromising means of expressing their ideological convictions, which became increasingly ambiguous and seemingly more inclusive.

On the brink of their emergence into a larger public sphere, both Whitman and Lincoln faced the necessity of becoming "Representative Men," of modifying their black-and-white radicalism, even superficially adopting the perspectives of their opposition, if they were to retain and expand their public voices. Walter Whitman becomes "Walt Whitman, an American, one of the roughs, a kosmos," advancing his populist politics as ideologically neutral, with all differences mystically harmonized within an all-inclusive self, and he creates a poetic form avowedly intended for the common reader rather than the well-educated.[7] Similarly, Abraham Lincoln becomes "Honest Abe," the "Railsplitter"; he abandons the legalistic fustian of his early prose and adopts a Biblical cadence and simplicity comparable to Whitman's poetry. Unlike the obviously alienating rhetoric of early speeches like the "Lyceum Address" in 1838 and his "Speech on the Sub-Treasury" in 1839, President Lincoln's "First Inaugural Address" attempts to harmonize the discordant voices of a divided

nation in a chorus directed by his own interpretation of the Constitution as a statement of federal authority over the rights of individual states:

> The mystic chords of memory, stretching from every battlefield, and patriot
> grave, to every living heart and hearthstone, all over this broad land, will yet
> swell the chorus of the Union, when again touched, as surely they will be, by
> the better angels of our nature.[8]

Thus, and in other speeches through the Civil War period, Lincoln sustains an
inclusive public voice by embodying a Union that he transforms from a voluntary
association into a mystical entity from which deviation is a sin against the sacred
martyrs of the American Revolution.

Although these personal and rhetorical similarities may have been grasped only
intuitively by Whitman in a backward glance before Lincoln's election, his identification with Lincoln during the Civil War became quite conscious and probably
influenced the rhetoric of Drum *Taps* (1865). Although the two men had never
done more than exchange nods (or so Whitman claims), Whitman wrote in 1863,
"I love the President personally,"[9] for Lincoln seemed a genuine manifestation of
Whitman's invented self; he represented the apotheosis of Whitman's utopian, democratic vision. Not only does Whitman love the President, he writes in 1863, "I
more and more rely upon his idiomatic western genius."[10] Whitman's identification
with Lincoln was also reinforced by a parallel development in the rhetoric of both
men who sought to represent a united country in the midst of sectional conflict.

During the Civil War, the rhetoric of Whitman and Lincoln changed from confident certainty to an uncomfortable ambiguity based upon an acceptance of internal contradictions. Lincoln's "Second Inaugural Address," for example, acknowledges that the dogmas of the quiet past are inadequate to the stormy present: "let us
judge not that we be not judged."[11] Likewise, at the center of *Drum-Taps* Whitman
formulates a new rhetoric of compromise: "was one side so brave? the other was
equally brave."[12] By the end of the war, both Lincoln and Whitman had abandoned
their polarizing rhetoric, even when such rhetoric appeared to offer compromise, as
in *Leaves of Grass* and in the "First Inaugural Address." Both the "Second Inaugural"
and *Drum-Taps* are less aggressive, more receptive, gray rather than black-and-white.
Each moves away from the exclusive, absolutist principles of their earlier rhetoric by
acknowledging ideological opposition as honorable and possibly right, and, if
wrong, tolerable within a Union that can accommodate diversity of opinion. The
persona of Lincoln changes in many minds from a "Black Republican" to the mid-
wife of "a new birth of freedom," and Whitman becomes the "Wound Dresser,"
transformed from "one of the roughs" to a "Good, Gray Poet."

After Lincoln's assassination, Whitman's poetic task of self and national reconstruction would be dramatically altered by his relationship to the President, the corresponding shift in his rhetoric, and his desire to appeal to a larger audience. Soon
after its initial publication, *Drum-Taps* received an addendum mourning the loss of

the nation's spiritual father, "Memories of President Lincoln." Like much of Whitman's work, "Memories" is a mixture of innovation and opportunism, both honoring the man for whom he felt a strong kinship and capitalizing on an out-pouring of public grief and fascination. As Roy Basler observes: "Whitman saw the possibility of this binary relationship with Lincoln, perhaps not clearly at first, when so strongly drawn to admire the President . . . but surely and purposefully when, fol-lowing the assassination, he set about writing the two most famous of his poems, "O Captain! My Captain!" and "When Lilacs Last in the Dooryard Bloom'd."[13]

While "When Lilacs Last in the Dooryard Bloom'd" attempts to complete the healing of deep personal and national wounds without submitting to the conven-tions of traditional elegy, it is followed by the most uncharacteristic of all Whitman's poems, "O Captain! My Captain!" Rather than a song of the self, "O Captain!" seems a song of subordination, obediently following every previously rejected poet-ic convention: regular meter, rhyme, and stanza pattern, along with a rather trite poetic conceit—everything conducive to its immediate success as popular verse.

"Memories of President Lincoln" demonstrates Whitman's growing conciliation with the demands of the post-war literary marketplace. Although Whitman later claimed to dislike it, "O Captain!" was a calculated critical and commercial success. Referring to the poem, one contemporary critic writes, "If everything else Whitman wrote could be buried at the bottom of the sea the world would be better off."[14] Unlike any earlier poem, "O Captain!" constructs a bridge to a popular audience by submitting to its limitations. F. B. Sanborn's review in the *Commonwealth* seems to articulate this motive quite plainly: "The complaints made of his earlier poems, that they were coarse and immoral in passages, will not apply to this little volume [*Drum-Taps*] . . . It will do much, we are confident, to remove the prejudice against Mr. Whitman in many minds."[15] Among the converted was William Dean Howells, who wrote that Whitman had "cleansed the old channels of their filth," and poured in a stream of blameless purity."[16] In subsequent years, Howells would become an important defender of Whitman against the critiques of more established poets such as James Russell Lowell.

It seems Whitman's experiments in self-creation finally succeeded with a major segment of the public when he enclosed his persona within the halo encircling the martyred President. "Death enshrined the Commoner," observes Daniel Aaron, and "Whitman placed himself and his work in the reflected limelight."[17] It was a project that had developed intuitively, for the most part, from political, rhetorical, and per-sonal parallels Whitman perceived between himself and Lincoln, but it became an increasingly conscious plan of self-promotion as "O Captain!" became canonized, and, through two decades of newspaper articles and lectures, the poet came to be associated with and regarded as an authority on Lincoln. Appreciation came slowly to his other works, but Whitman seems to have reached the same conclusion as William Barton, a biographer of Lincoln, came to in 1928: "The common people have never cared for Whitman, and there is no present prospect that they ever will. But they understand and love Lincoln . . . the common people believed in him and his theories of democracy."[18] Whitman supporter Edmund Stedman was convinced that Whitman's lecture, "The Death of Abraham Lincoln," was the medium required to reach a larger audience. And, by the time of the Madison Square Theater performance of 1887, Whitman himself believed that he could only be popularly accepted in his own time for work he regarded as mediocre and conventional—for "O Captain!" rather than for "Lilacs." The "Death of Abraham Lincoln" and the reading of "O Captain!" had become an unalterable public ritual; Whitman could not jeopardize a potential triumph by defying the conventional expectations of his audience.

II. POLITICAL RELIGION AND REVOLUTIONARY MARTYRDOM

According to Allen Grossman, "Walt Whitman found his truth, and the unity of his world, precisely at the crisis of contradiction where Lincoln found disintegrative instability."[19] Although their positions appear contradictory at times (particularly between 1855 and 1863), there is no fixed principle of exclusion in Lincoln's rhetoric, nor is there a consistent principle of inclusion in Whitman's prose and poetry. Rather, Whitman and Lincoln are most often characterized by internal tension and movement. As Whitman observes in *Leaves*: "Do I contradict myself? / Very well then I contradict myself, / (I am large, I contain multitudes.)"[20] Therefore, a basis for comparison between Whitman and Lincoln may well be the rhetorical inconsistencies that emerge early in their careers from tensions inherent in their larger cultural context.

The early rhetoric of both Whitman and Lincoln emerges from the contradictions of a post-heroic age that longed for revolution while it guarded the status quo, from tensions between religious certainty and free-thinking, and from a conflict between personal ambitions and the demands of the literary and political marketplace. As a consequence, both Whitman and Lincoln develop comparable public personae, decreasingly certain, as they advance from political positioning as exclusive, often radical extremism in their early speeches and journalism toward inclusive representation as embodiments of universal values in Whitman's *Leaves of Grass* and Lincoln's speeches as President.

Whitman (1819-1892) and Lincoln (1809-1865) grew up when living memory of the Revolution was rapidly fading, to be replaced by a tension between a romantic longing to renew the violent, egalitarian struggle for liberty and a conservative desire to support and defend the political status quo. Whitman's father, an acquaintance of revolutionary pamphleteer Thomas Paine, indoctrinated his children into the worship of the Founding Fathers and Jacksonian Democracy—he even named two of his sons George Washington Whitman and Thomas Jefferson Whitman. As a small child, Walter was supposedly thrust into the hands of General Lafayette when he visited Brooklyn on July 4, 1825. This event would assume increasing importance for the older Whitman, who wrote of himself, "he not only saw, but was touched by the hands, and taken a moment to the breast of the immortal old Frenchman." In another account of the event, Whitman receives a still more symbolic benediction from the old revolutionary: "[Lafayette] gave me a kiss and set me down on a safe spot." [21] Before long, the emerging writer would be enlisted in the ranks of the radical Jacksonian Democrats as poet, novelist, journalist, and platform orator. Predictably, Whitman's oration in 1842 before a Democratic rally of possibly fifteen thousand invokes the red-hot fires of revolutionary strife:

> We are battling for great principles—for mighty and glorious truths. . . . The guardian spirit, the good genius who has attended us ever since the days of Jefferson, has not now forsaken us. . . . Again will she hover over us, encouraging us amid the smoke and din of battle, and leading us to our wonted victory.[22]

Just as Whitman urged his contemporaries to resume the struggle and sacrifice of the past, Lincoln would come, after many years of comparable development, to participate in the rhetoric of romanticized Revolution: "The probability that we may fall in the struggle ought not to deter us from the support of a cause we believe to be just."[23] Lincoln couldn't claim the personal blessing of any revolutionary hero, but his early rhetoric (and some of his speeches as President) frequently attempted to translate the sacrifices of the Revolution into renewed dedication to his own political interests. All through his youth, Lincoln was exposed to the frontier celebrations of American independence and the stump speeches of aging veterans, and his early reading included the leading figures of the Enlightenment and the American Revolution. He came to worship the Founders, particularly the deified Washington of Mason Locke Weems: "Washington is the mightiest name of earth," Lincoln said in an early speech, "To add brightness to the sun, or glory to the name of Washington, is alike impossible. Let none attempt it. In solemn awe we pronounce the name."[24] As a young man, Lincoln dreamed of defending a Union he feared would be dissolved by sectional conflict; in his "Address before the Young Men's Lyceum" (January 27, 1838), Lincoln's jeremiad contrasts the Founding Fathers with the degenerate citizens of his time:

> We, when mounting the stage of existence, found ourselves the legal inheritors of these fundamental blessings. We toiled not in the acquirement or establishment of them—they are a legacy bequeathed us, by a once hardy, brave, and patriotic, but now lamented and departed race of ancestors.[25]

In both cases, the politics of Whitman and Lincoln are characterized by a tension between a nostalgia for the past and an appreciation for the comparative security of the present, the agrarian idealism of Jefferson and the egalitarian pragmatism of Jackson. Lincoln's political oratory reflects Jeffersonian ideals even while it appeals in many ways to the hardscrabble origins of the Jacksonian populists. There is also a tendency at this early stage in their careers for the flexibility demanded by politics and journalism to be subdued by the rhetoric of religious dogmatism. However, this is not to say that sectarian religion alone forms the basis for Lincoln's or Whitman's political ideology. Religious rhetoric is used for specific political purposes, in effect,

a "political religion" based on a view of the American mission as sacred and the frag-
menting of the union as sacrilege. This secular creed pervades much of Whitman's
and Lincoln's early work; it lies, for example, at the center of Lincoln's "Lyceum
Address":

> As the patriots of seventy-six did to the support of the Declaration of
> Independence, so to the support of the Constitution of Laws, let every
> American pledge his life, his property, and his sacred honor . . . let it become
> the *political religion* of the nation; and let the old and the young, the rich and
> the poor, the grave and the gay, of all sexes and tongues, and colors and condi-
> tions, sacrifice unceasingly upon its alters.[26]

Just as Whitman appeals to the "Last of the Sacred Army" in his early poetry, prose,
and platform oratory, so Lincoln appeals to the suffering of the Revolution to solid-
ify the Union in a new declaration of loyalty solemnized by universal sacrifice.
Caught between their idealistic desire to form a more perfect union by re-enacting
the sublime sacrifice of the revolutionary martyrs and their pragmatic desire to
escape the blood and suffering of renewed conflict, Whitman and Lincoln resolve
the tension in the intense and uncompromising rhetoric of an ideology that assumes
the orthodoxy of a religion applied to specific political goals.

As an editor for sensationalistic newspapers, Whitman's early journalism was
confined to a simplified polemical rhetoric that reflects both his "political religion"
and the requirements of the medium in which he worked. Anson Herrick and John
F. Ropes, the politically independent owners of the *Aurora*, hired Whitman as their
editor in 1842 because of his rising political and literary profile in New York. He
was the author of the successful temperance novel *Franklin Evans* (1842), and he
had recently given a noteworthy speech before a large Democratic rally. It was in this
new position with the *Aurora* that Whitman stumbled upon subjects, styles, stances,
and strategies to which he would later return in *Leaves of Grass*. Penny presses like
the *Aurora* were politically one-sided, but Whitman's editorials were more than
biased; they frequently made vicious and fanatical personal attacks that went beyond
the broadest boundaries of editorial decorum. As Whitman himself admitted, "the
'rora has a bad habit of calling people names":

> We have in America many literary quacks. . . . If they are lucky enough to get
> into the chair editorial, thereby obtaining a chance to puff themselves directly
> and indirectly, they straightaway give themselves great airs, and imagine they are
> very important characters . . . this enormous baboon . . . this witless ape [Park
> Benjamin, editor of the *New World*, for whom Whitman had once worked]
> . . . . He has lately degraded the very name of literature by a series of clap traps
> and low vulgar tricks to advance the interests of his paper.[27]

Despite his sensationalistic criticisms of former employers and fellow journalists
alike, Whitman himself was never above making nativist slurs to reinforce a politi-

cal point: "[S]hall these dregs of foreign filth—refuse of convents—scullions from Austrian monasteries—be permitted to dictate what we must do? The bulwark of truth—the "unterrified democracy," ruled by tattered, course, unshaven, filthy, Irish rabble!"[28] Although he lacked inclusive poetic sentiments, the young Whitman already demonstrated a facility with catalogs that itemized what groups were to be excluded from his vision of America.

Subscriptions to the *Aurora* increased during Whitman's editorship, but the paper's owners endeavored without success to "tone" Whitman's editorial voice. Responding to the complaint of another paper, Whitman took pride in his tactlessness, as if it were a characteristically American virtue: "We never intended to mince matters—to stop for honeyed words—to crust the wholesome dose we administer, with sugar—to be polite unto filthy vice—to stand on ceremony with a traitor—or to treat a traitor with dainty punctilio."[29] Within a month of this editorial, one of Whitman's frustrated employers wrote, "There is a man about our office so lazy that it takes two men to open his jaws when he speaks," but it appears that the owner's disapproval resulted more from his inability to moderate Whitman's writing than any problem with deadlines.[30]

About two months after he began, Whitman was fired from the *Aurora*. Before long, he was insulting the *Aurora* and its owners in the *Evening Tattler*, another New York paper. During the next eight years Whitman worked for at least ten more papers in New York and Brooklyn before coming to a position on the *Brooklyn Daily Eagle* in 1846-7. He worked for the *Daily Eagle* for nearly two years until, once again, his vitriolic politics collided with the interests of his employer. After a brief stint with the New Orleans *Crescent*—from which he was again fired—Whitman returned to Brooklyn in June 1848, determined to make a success of his own paper, the *Brooklyn Freeman*, whose revolutionary motto was "Liberty, equality, fraternity." Only the first issue of the Freeman survives, "But," observed the *Advertiser*, "like all hot headed ultras, he [Whitman] awards no 'liberty' unless they belong to the 'spirit of progress'; as for 'equality' 'twould be ridiculous for foreigners to claim such a privilege."[31] By August Whitman was speaking at Democratic meetings in Brooklyn, and he was elected as one of fourteen delegates to the Buffalo Convention, but the *Freeman* went out of business when Whitman's candidate lost and readers lost interest. For the most part, Whitman's career as a full-time political journalist was over by 1849. He had a reputation as being intractable, unreliable, and shiftless. Unable to hold a position, he had created a number of influential enemies in the press and in government, and he seemed to have lost faith in the political system with which he been embroiled for almost a decade.

The young Lincoln was also prone to polemical writing that descended to the level of personal attack. In 1837, Lincoln engaged in a journalistic battle with an Illinois official, James Adams, that went on for weeks: "[Adams] is all as false as hell, as all this community must know. 'I will only say that I have a character to defend as well as Gen. Adams, but I disdain to whine about it as he does."[32] Lincoln occasionally lost control of his own rhetoric, allowing his "political religion" to overpower his reason and alienate the audience from whom he sought support. On a relatively insignificant fiscal matter, Lincoln's "Speech on the Sub-Treasury" (1839) concludes:

> Many free countries have lost their liberty; and ours may lose hers; but if she shall, be it my proudest plume, not that I was last to desert, but that I never deserted her. I know that the great volcano at Washington, aroused and directed by the evil spirit that reigns there, is belching forth the lava of political corruption . . . while on its bosom are riding like demons on the waves of Hell, the imps of that evil spirit. . . . Broken by it, I, too, may be; bow to it I never will. . . . I swear eternal fidelity to the just cause.[33]

Like Whitman, Lincoln sometimes publicly cast himself as a hero, another Washington, eager for martyrdom in some high place, standing alone against vast, demonic forces arrayed against holy democracy and the virtues of the Founding Fathers.

Perhaps the most lurid example of Lincoln's partisan errata, one that altered the tone of all his future political wrangling, was his satire of James Shields, the state auditor of Illinois, in 1842 (the same year that he attempted to publish a pamphlet concerning his religious views and the year of his irreverent "Temperance Address"). Lincoln published a letter in the *Sangamo Journal* under the *nom de plume* of "Rebecca," a simple country woman, who not only attacked Shields's politics but his integrity: "Shields is a fool as well as a liar. With him the truth is out of the question, and as for getting a good bright passable lie out of him, you might as well try to strike fire from a cake of tallow."[34] Outraged, Shields demanded a duel, much to Lincoln's embarrassment. And within a few days, arrangements had been made for Lincoln and Shields to fight it out with the weapon of Lincoln's choice, "Cavalry broad swords of the largest size."[35] At the last moment, however, Shields was persuaded to accept Lincoln's recantation of the insult. Having narrowly escaped a potentially fatal incident, Lincoln never again used personal attacks or vicious satire to make a point.

As a lawyer and a budding statesman, however, Lincoln was often required to reduce staggeringly complicated issues to the artificial simplicity of opposites, thus clarifying otherwise ambiguous differences between himself and other candidates. Like Whitman's editorials, Lincoln's political speeches, prior to his campaign for President, reflect "a legal grammar (Blackstonian) adapted to political use, the structure of which was based in the Aristotelian laws of thought-identity, non-contradiction, the excluded middle."[36] As with Whitman, much of Lincoln's political rhetoric concerned the expansion of slavery in the West, and his platform initially reflected a moral simplification of the complicated social and political machinery represented by his opponent, Stephen A. Douglas: "I do not understand his declaration that he cares not whether slavery be voted down or voted up."[37] Feigning the confusion of the ordinary voter, in the famous "House Divided Speech" (1858), Lincoln removes the gray-area of compromise by reducing the complex differences between

North and South to a simple binary opposition in which one half, the utilitarian or morally righteous half, would be preserved, and the other half subsumed: "I do not expect the Union to be dissolved—I do not expect the house to fall—but I do expect it *will* cease to be divided. It will become all one thing or *all* the other."[38] Under these terms, the choice between Lincoln and Douglas becomes a black-and-white referendum for or against slavery.

Much of Whitman's and Lincoln's early discourse, with its revolutionary ideology, religious certainty, and simplified binary oppositions, is unproductively exclusive, particularly when it designates proponents of the opposing position as heretical transgressors of a political religion sanctified by the blood of revolutionary martyrs and reaffirmed by renewed acts of heroic self-sacrifice. As Whitman learned, it is a dangerous editorial technique, for it is vulnerable to political change and often alienates more readers than it attracts. Likewise, it can be costly for a politician seeking a plurality of voters to place oneself on the political fringe (to say nothing of the potential for creating mortal enemies). As a result, both Lincoln and Whitman suffered a series of setbacks that culminated, for both men, in the nearly ruinous year 1849, which ultimately marked a transition in their rhetorical styles.

Caught in a tension between representation of established interests and the egalitarian doctrine of his "political religion," Lincoln became embroiled in a controversy over the legality of the Mexican War. His speech before the House of Representatives (January 12, 1848) was a political disaster:

> There is but *claim* against *claim*, leaving nothing proved, until we get back of the claims, and find which has the better foundation. . . . If I should claim your land, by word of mouth, that certainly would not make it mine; and if I were to claim it by a deed which I had made myself, and with which, you had had nothing to do, the claim would be quite the same, in substance or rather, in utter nothingness.[39]

Although Lincoln advocated what he believed was a popular position, the mass of opinion was divided and leaned more toward war; thus Lincoln was left without a majority of supporters among the popular constituency on which he depended. His speech was ignored in the Capital and denounced in Springfield. In Illinois there were angry public meetings, and one of their resolutions stated, "Henceforth will this Benedict Arnold of our district be known here only as the Ranchero Spotty of one term." William Herndon, Lincoln's law partner, said in an 1887 letter that in 1849, Lincoln was "politically dead," and Lincoln himself "thought his political fortunes were ended forever."[40] After the next Presidential election, Lincoln was offered the position of secretary of the Oregon Territory—exile, in effect. He returned to Springfield in 1849, assuming that his political career was over.

After this event, Lincoln seems to have gone through a period of indecision and depression from which he would not recover until 1854. When Lincoln finally emerged from this moratorium," observes Dwight Anderson, "he did so with a revolutionary vengeance, identifying himself not with Washington, the father of his country, but with Jefferson, the revolutionary son."[41] Confident in his own authority and destiny for greatness, but thwarted by the failure of his political rhetoric to cultivate sufficient support, Lincoln modified his discourse to become a viable candidate in the late 1850s; he adopted more inclusive-sounding rhetoric that remains, however, ultimately authoritarian, typically labeling his stance on controversial issues as "self evident truth" and deriving his authority from canonized political icons and the absolutism of religious orthodoxy.[42]

In the same year that Lincoln's political fortunes appeared to be over, Whitman's career as a political journalist also came to an abrupt end. During the next five years, while working in the family carpentry business, Whitman began to turn to poetry as a means of imposing order and meaning on his life. He published a group of four bitter, political poems in the New York *Tribune* in 1850: "Song for a Certain Congressman," "Blood-Money," "Wounded in the House of Friends," and "Resurgemus." Although the poems anticipate the poetic form of *Leaves of Grass*, they retain the tendency of his journalistic writings toward name-calling: "Doughfaces, Crawlers, Lice of Humanity . . . Muck-worms, creeping flat to the ground, A dollar dearer to them than Christ's blessing."[43] Only one of these poems would be included later in *Leaves*, "Resurgemus":

> Liberty, let others despair of thee,
> But I will not despair of thee:
> Is the house shut? Is the master away?
>   Nevertheless, be ready, be not weary of watching,
> He will surely return; his messengers come anon.[44]

Whitman, like Lincoln, began to refashion himself as an idealized revolutionary martyr, and he would eventually criticize his early journalism and speech-making as "Come-day go-day palaver . . . what I really had to give out was something more serious, more off from politics and towards the general life."[45]

Confident in their destiny for greatness, but shaken by their failure, Whitman and Lincoln experienced a crisis that profoundly altered their exclusive qualities of their rhetoric. Despite their uncompromising extremism and Olympian certainty, both men, although separated by hundreds of miles and an even broader gulf of personal experience, would simultaneously undergo the first of a series of transformations in the 1850s from the polemical style of their earlier discourse to become the authors of the among the most celebrated examples of egalitarian inclusiveness in American literature.

III. INCARNATING THE NATION

In addition to the tensions embedded in their political religion, Whitman and Lincoln, both possessed of a sense of personal destiny, were caught between different values that contributed to their failures in 1849 but also led them, after periods of prolonged reflection, to adopt more ambiguous rhetorical strategies that concealed ambition and authoritarianism, giving many observers the impression that both men incarnated the nation—that their personal achievements were representative of the people en masse.

Conceiving of himself as a successful artist in the aristocratic manner ill-suited Whitman for the indignities of economic hardship. In 1840, while working as a schoolteacher in Woodbury, New York, Whitman wrote his friend, Abraham Leech:

> Time, put spurs on thy leaden wings, and bring on the period when my allotted time of torment here shall be fulfilled. Speed, ye airy hours, lift me from this earthly purgatory; nor do I care how soon ye lay these pudding-brained bogtrotters, amid their kindred earth. . . . Never before have I entertained so low an idea of the beauty and perfection of man's nature, never have I seen humanity in so degraded a shape, as here.—Ignorance, vulgarity, rudeness, conceit, and dullness are the reigning gods of this deuced sink of despair.—The brutes go barefoot, shave once in three weeks, call "brown cow" "breown ke-ow."[46]

This pretentious, condescending, and Anglophile Walter Whitman couldn't seem more at variance with the Walt Whitman who emerges in 1855 as "one of the roughs . . . no stander above men and-women or apart from them," and who proclaims "What is commonest, cheapest, nearest, easiest, is Me."[47] What remains at the core of Whitman's rhetoric and personae, although increasingly concealed, is a private sense of superiority to his audience and subject matter: the literary man slumming, the bohemian whose unpretentiousness is a pose. Whitman identifies with yet removes himself from the nonchalant readers of hack journalism to whom he must appeal for political and literary acclaim. Despite his avowed admiration for the common folk, he could never privately count himself as one among them:

> You do not know, my friend, nor can you conceive, the horrid dulness of this place. . . . The next you hear of me, I may possibly be arraigned for murder, or highway robbery, or assault or battery, at the least.—I am getting savage . . . do for pity's sake forward something or other to me soon, in the shape of mental food.[48]

Whitman's sense of future greatness is shared by the young, self-aggrandizing Lincoln who, as early as 1838 in the "Lyceum Address," reveals himself as a "towering genius":

> Many great and good men sufficiently qualified for any task they should undertake, may ever be found, whose ambition would aspire to nothing beyond a seat in Congress . . . towering genius disdains a beaten path. . . . It thirsts and burns for distinction; and, if possible, it will have it, whether at the expense of emancipating slaves, or enslaving freemen.[49]

As a young man, Lincoln is not self-deprecating character into which fiction and hagiography later made him; the famous description of Jefferson Davis as "ambitious as Lucifer" would not seem inappropriate for Lincoln as well. His secretary John Hay later said, it "is absurd to call him a modest man. No great man is ever modest. It was his intellectual arrogance and unconscious assumption of superiority that men like Chase and Sumner could never forgive."[50] One year later, Lincoln's "Speech on the Sub-Treasury" prophetically reiterated his sense of fitness for the trials of history:

> If I ever feel the soul within me elevate and expand to those dimensions not wholly unworthy of its Almighty Architect, it is when I contemplate the cause of my country, deserted by all the world beside, and I standing up boldly and alone and hurling defiance at her victorious oppressors.[51]

As with Whitman, a sense of self-anointed messianic destiny pervades Lincoln's rhetoric; he would render the heroic image of his own martyrdom regularly in times of political crisis until the last days of his presidency.[52]

Leaves is often interpreted as an inclusive work, one that fills the void in Lincoln's exclusive political rhetoric.[53] The root of this supposed inclusiveness may be Whitman's conspicuous adoption of Emerson's transcendental formulation of a spiritual democracy. Just as in "The American Scholar" Emerson proclaims, "Books are for the scholar's idle times," Whitman proclaims, "You shall no longer take things at second or third hand . . . nor look through the eyes of the dead . . . nor feed on the spectres in books, / You shall not look through my eyes either, nor take things from me, / You shall listen to all sides and filter them from yourself."[54] Yet, this is the beginning rather than the end of the book that contains "Song of Myself." Ultimately, Whitman does not abdicate the role of mediator: "You will hardly know who I am or what I mean, / But I shall be good health to you nevertheless, / And filter and fibre your blood."[55] Whitman suggests that he will teach the reader to develop an independent and possibly superior poetic sensibility: "I am the teacher of athletes, / He that by me spreads a wider breast than my own proves the width of my own, / He most honors my style who learns under it to destroy the teacher."[56] In the end, however, Whitman resists the possibility of an unmediated experience: "I teach straying from me, yet who can stray from me? / I follow you whoever you are from the present hour; / My words itch at your ears till you understand them."[57] Just the poet ultimately becomes fertilizer for the grass—part of its substance—the poet will "filter and fibre" the reader's blood. The text, in effect, is a instrument for the conversion of the reader to a Whitmanian sensibility.

The apparent inclusiveness of *Leaves* results, in part, from Whitman's attempt to camouflage a political text in the trappings of a sacred scripture. Although Whitman denied the influence of Eastern mysticism, his poetics of spiritual union was probably influenced by Emerson's use of dialectics, fusing the unresolvable tension of opposites into the mandala-like synthesis of the transcendental: "Clear and sweet is my soul . . . and clear and sweet is all that is not my soul. / Lack one lacks both and the unseen is proved by the seen, / Till that becomes unseen and receives proof in its turn."[58] Similar dialectics are repeated throughout *Leaves*, giving the appearance that Whitman had abandoned his earlier rhetoric of binary opposition for a transcendental poetics of inclusion based on the synthesis of opposites: "And these tend inward to me, and I tend outward to them, / And such as it is to be of these more or less I am, / And of these one and all I weave the song of myself."

Whitman is sometimes labeled "the poet of democracy" for the apparently open, all-inclusive synthetic quality of *Leaves*. He often gives the impression of representing the voices of the multitudes on equal terms in his barbaric yawp: "Through me many long dumb voices, / Voices of the interminable generations of slaves, / Voices of the diseased and despairing, and of thieves and dwarfs . . ." etc., all the way down to "beetles rolling balls of dung."[59] Whitman promises a spiritual democracy comparable to the Christian communion ceremony:

> This is the meal pleasantly set . . . this is the meat and drink for natural
>   hunger,
> It is for the wicked just the same as the righteous
> I make appointments with all,
> I will not have a single person slighted or left away,
> The keptwoman and sponger and thief are hereby invited
>   the heavy-lipped slave is invited . . .
>   the venerealee is invited,
> There shall be no difference between them and the rest.[60]

Ideally, the spiritual synthesis of Emersonian Transcendentalism is apolitical, simultaneously incorporating alternative discourses, paradoxically supporting and refuting both sides of an opposition. Yet Whitman's apparently open invitation to equality is deceptive, for he does not relinquish his position at the head of the table: "I do not ask who you are . . . that is not important to me, / You can do nothing and be nothing but what I infold in you."[61] The discourse of the politically powerless is overwhelmed by the dominant, barbaric yawp of the American Bard: "I act as the tongue of you, / It was tied in your mouth . . . in mine it begins to be loosened."[62] Emerson states that "events, actions arise, that must be sung, that will sing themselves."[63] However, with familiar assertiveness, Whitman uses the concept of synthesis to incorporate both the nation and reader within an all-inclusive self: "I CELEBRATE MYSELF, / And what I assume you shall assume . . ."[64] Far from being tolerant of ideological opposition, *Leaves* is a often a monologue rather than a dialogue and, though more subtle, no less authoritarian than Whitman's early editorials: "Long enough have you dream'd contemptible dreams / now I wash the gum from your eyes."[65] Having seduced the reader into assuming his recumbent posture, Whitman displaces his own voice and transfers it to the would-be disciple, vanishing beneath his bootsoles in a kind of Eucharistic self-sacrifice, circumventing argument by disembodying himself in a merger with the reader that is not *really* a synthesis but a transplanting of Whitman's *Leaves,* weed-like, in the ground of all potential opposition. As a poetic system, Whitman's Transcendentalism is essentially a means of securing the primacy of his meaning by reducing the nation and the reader to extensions of himself.

Like Whitman's editorials, *Leaves* appropriates the ideology of the American Revolution along with the authority of a religion. The publication of Whitman's *Leaves* on the Fourth of July, 1855, announces itself as another Declaration of Independence, confirmed by the symbolic blessing of Washington's compatriot Lafayette exactly thirty years before. But *Leaves* was more than a secular manifesto of revolutionary egalitarianism; like the *Book of Mormon* (supposedly revealed to Joseph Smith in New York in the 1830s), *Leaves* emerged from the American soil as the founding document of a utopian community comparable to Nauvoo, New Harmony, New Lebanon, and Brook Farm. *Leaves* was intended as the founding gospel of an evangelical religion: "I am not content now with a mere majority. . . . I must have the love of all men and women. / If there is one left in any country who has no faith in me, I will travel to that country and go to that one."[66] Laboring as a carpenter, Whitman likened himself to Christ before taking up his ministry. *Leaves* later announces Whitman's persona as such: "I, now thirty-seven years old in perfect health begin, / Hoping to cease not till death."[67] In his private notes Whitman describes the enormity of his project: "The Great construction of the New Bible. Not to be diverted from the principal object—the main life work—the three hundred and sixty five.—It ought to be ready in 1859."[68] Whitman not only alludes to religious texts, but borrows the trappings of a sacred work. The organic-looking *Leaves of Grass* (1855) bears the name of no author or publisher as though it were sacred relic—"I guess it is the handkerchief of the Lord / . . . Bearing the owner's name someway in the corners, that we may see and remark, and say *Whose?*"[69] Although the author's name, "Walt Whitman, an American," can be found in the corners of the text, the photographed Whitman taken near the period of the original frontispiece is known as the "Christ likeness." Inclusive as they may claim to be, an intentionally crafted sacred text risks the appearance of authoritarianism, particularly when it is crafted to indoctrinate readers into a cult with the idealized figure of the author at its center. Although *Leaves* may appear more inclusive and inviting than Whitman's earlier journalism, the position that it is based entirely on an inclusive, compromising poetic model is as untenable as the myth that Whitman, with all his experience as a journalist and self-promoter, expected *Leaves* to be an immediate success.

For all of its inclusive rhetoric, *Leaves* rooted itself in the literary marketplace through the careful manipulation of a divided public, orchestrating dispute between rival editors. Whitman knew how to attract attention, mostly through sensation and scandal (believing, as did his contemporary P. T. Barnum, that negative attention was preferable to indifference). As during his newspaper days, Whitman used every available tactic for the promotion of his work, including writing his own favorable reviews. It was certainly plain to Whitman that intelligent readers would make the connection between Whitman's reviews of his own work, which are nearly a verbatim transcriptions of the "1855 Preface," and this would generate more sensation among editors who stepped forward to condemn this violation of ethics. The consensus on the 1855 Whitman was that his poetic form was bizarre, his sexual license scandalous, and his self-promotion shameless. Some critics were alienated by the Biblical proportions of Whitman's egoism. This is apparent in the first notice of *Leaves* by Charles A. Dana which appeared in the New York *Daily Tribune* on July 23, 1855: He [Whitman] vouchsafes, before introducing us to his poetry, to enlighten our benighted minds as to the true function of the American poet." Dana observes that Whitman's "coarse and defiant" tendency to elevate himself above the reader "will justly prevent his volume from free circulation in scrupulous circles."[70]

Of all the negative reviewers, perhaps Rufus Griswold was the most scathing:

> There are too many persons, who imagine they demonstrate their superiority to their fellows, by disregarding all the politeness and decencies of life. . . . Bloated with self-conceit, they strut abroad unabashed by daylight, and expose to the world the festering sores that overlay them like a garment. Unless we admit this exhibition to be beautiful, we are at once set down for non-progressive conservatives, destitute of the "inner light," the far-seeingness which, of course, characterizes those gifted individuals.[71]

Whitman's spiritual democracy did not initially include Griswold, the Irish, Catholics, the humble citizens of Woodbury, or anyone else who failed to be illuminated by the "inner light" of the poet's vision. Yet, as Whitman was undoubtedly aware, such scandals made his book more attractive not only to those in search of salacious gossip, but also to literary conservatives, who wanted reasons for condemning the book, and to liberals who sought to defend free expression from the censorship of the conservatives. When Fowler & Wells agreed to back a second and larger edition of *Leaves* (1856), Whitman provided the following announcement: "The emphatic commendation of America's greatest critic has been ratified by the public."[72] Contrary to the myth of failure created by Whitman and his followers in the 1880s to suit different promotional circumstances (as the next chapter examines in detail), the first edition of Leaves was a noteworthy promotional achievement using direct mail, celebrity endorsements, controversy, hyped events, and unpaid advertising.

During roughly the time of Whitman's hiatus as a carpenter, Lincoln mourned the end of his political career after the events of 1849. As with Whitman, becoming a representative of the people required a transformation of his public voice targeted at the mass of Americans, a resolution of both his internal struggle with class identification and a separation of his private authoritarianism and his public discourse. Lincoln's backcountry origins, his gangly appearance, and his vestigial roughness, made it difficult for him to gain a foothold in the parlors of the wealthy and powerful; despite his increasing detachment from his origins, Lincoln had to derive much of his political power from the collective strength of a popular, even rustic, constituency. Thus, by the mid-1850s, Lincoln's rhetoric began to abandon self-conscious verbal and intellectual showmanship for polished simplicity, self-deprecating humor, and the conventions of religious piety. Once again as a candidate, Lincoln's rhetoric became comparable to the Biblical-Shakespearean cadence and style of Whitman's poetry.[73] Capable of adapting himself to an audience, he even sometimes modified his speeches into a country vernacular. When drafting an autobiographical sketch for his presidential campaign, Lincoln revised the phrase "reading, writing, and arithmetic" to "readin, writin, and cipherin."[74] Although a lifelong freethinker, Lincoln began to make increasingly frequent appeals to God. Edmund Wilson observes that "now he must have deliberately adopted the practice of stating his faith in the Union and the conviction of his own mission in terms that would not be repugnant to the descendants of the New England Puritans and to the evangelism characteristic of his time."[75] Lincoln's conversion, like Whitman's, may not have been a personal one; rather, it is the mode of discourse that has been reborn in an authoritative form that conceals the driving force of personal ambition with deceptive simplicity and the trappings of spiritual devotion. By 1861, for example, in the formulaic "Farewell Address at Springfield, Illinois," Lincoln, in an impromptu moment of strong emotion, alludes to the American Revolution, to his own possible martyrdom in the cause of his political religion, to his own humility, and to his participation in conventional religious sentiments:

> I now leave, not knowing when, or whether ever, I may return, with a task before me greater than that which rested upon Washington. Without the assistance of that Divine Being, who ever attended him, I cannot succeed. With that assistance I cannot fail.[76]

Just as Whitman mollifies the reader's opposition by signifying that he and reader both incarnate a single national identity, so Lincoln uses his self-proclaimed participation in the cultural work of the Revolution to eliminate political disagreement. Whatever opposition an individual may have to Lincoln's political positions is displaced by the linking of his rhetoric to the larger, canonized values of the American Revolution and Christianity.

Wilson writes that Lincoln, like Whitman, "created himself as a poetic figure, and he thus imposed himself on the nation."[77] Lincoln seems to have won the nineteenth presidency not for his political views so much as for his success in creating an acceptable persona and the success of the Republican Party at promoting that image. Just as Walter Whitman, gentleman journalist, transformed himself into the rough, idiomatic "Walt," Abraham Lincoln, upwardly mobile lawyer, became a man of the common people, "a homespun hero brimming with prairie wit and folk wisdom."[78] The 1860 campaign stressed, with Lincoln's tacit approval, the use of Populist symbols like "The Railsplitter" and the log cabin; he was "Honest Abe," who, like the poet of *Leaves of Grass* speaks "at every hazard, / Nature without check with original energy."[79] One campaign biographer called him "a personification of the distinctive genius of our country," and another described him as "a representative of that energetic . . . and progressive people, who have, by their own strong arms and stout hearts, cleared the forests, plowed the prairie, constructed the railroads and carried the churches and schoolhouses into the once wilderness."[80]

Lincoln won the election of 1860 in the North, but he never even appeared on the ballots in the South where he was regarded, despite his temporizing discourse and the party propaganda, as a fanatical "Black Republican," a representative of Northern industry and centralized federal power. Although Lincoln's "First Inaugural Address" alludes to the joint struggle of the Revolution and metaphorically attempts to harmonize the discordant voices of a house divided against itself, it is a chorus directed by Lincoln's own authoritarian interpretation of the Constitution as a statement of federal authority over the rights of states:

> [T]he Union is perpetual, confirmed by the history of the Union itself.[81]

Lincoln denies the legitimacy of the South's grievances (just as he did not recognize the Confederate government during the entire course of the Civil War), and passes the responsibility for compromise and negotiation to a clearly defined opposition: "In your hands, my dissatisfied fellow countrymen, and not in mine, is the momentous issue of civil war. . . . You can have no conflict without yourselves being the aggressors."[82]

Just as Whitman presents his political agenda of spiritual union as a synthesis of all Americans, Lincoln empowers the Union (and himself as the embodiment of that Union) by transforming it from a voluntary association to a mystical entity transcending regional interests, representing the consent of the majority and the sacrifice of the Revolution from which any deviation is an attack against the established laws of government if not Liberty itself. "The crucible provided by the Southern insurrection," writes Anderson, forced Lincoln's rhetoric "to return to its origins, where it discovered not a cerebral agreement on social ends, but a religious absolutism and fanaticism."[83] The 1860 election was a personal triumph for Lincoln, but it precipitated an unprecedented national crisis. Despite the rhetoric of the "First Inaugural," Lincoln offered no tangible compromise to the South—such as abandoning Fort Sumter—and the Civil War was underway within six weeks, leaving him with a task undoubtedly "greater than that which rested upon Washington" with still greater opportunities for becoming the father of the "Second American Revolution."[84]

IV. RECONCILIATION

As the Civil War was drawing to a close, a Union officer who had witnessed the mistreatment of Union prisoners pronounced that Jefferson Davis should be hanged. Lincoln chastised the indignant officer, reiterating the Biblical injunction quoted in his "Second Inaugural Address": "Judge not, that ye be not judged."[85] At a time when many called for retaliation against the leaders of the rebellion, Lincoln's policy of reconciliation seemed to contradict the revolutionary imperative of the "First

Inaugural," the "Gettysburg Address," and much of Lincoln's private correspondence.

The President had paid an enormous personal toll during the Civil War, and it was reflected by a substantial change in his public discourse and persona. Lincoln once told a friend, "If there is a worse place than hell, I am in it"; he was the constant object of merciless criticism, and he often felt responsibility for hundreds of thousands of lives lost, including several members of his wife's family.[86] After four years of uncertainty, tragedy, and personal abuse, Lincoln's visit to Richmond must have seemed the culminating hour of his presidency; it was the transfiguring moment when the "Ranchero Spotty of one term" became "Father Abraham," a semi-divine conqueror, liberator, and dispenser of justice tempered by mercy. Lincoln's transformation from what many—including Chief Justice Roger B. Taney and Secretary of War Edwin Stanton—considered a military dictator into the "'Great Emancipator," the deliverer of "a new birth of freedom," was more than the outcome of postwar euphoria; Lincoln reinvented himself and his political religion in response to the personal trauma of the war and radically changing demands on his role as President.

As the political necessities of sectional conflict became those of restoring national unity, Lincoln altered the rhetorical strategies governing his public discourse. The certainty of the "First Inaugural Address" gave way to the ambiguity of the "Second Inaugural Address," which refuses to pronounce judgment on the South. On his departure from Springfield before the war, and at the height of the war at Gettysburg, Lincoln presented himself in the role of Washington, summoning the spirit of the Revolution with a call for heroic action justified by the "Declaration of Independence." Near the conclusion of the war, Lincoln's "Second Inaugural" expands the temporal scope of the testing ground for these values, teleologically linking the "Second American Revolution" not only with the first Revolution—which the South had ceased to support—but with the exodus of Israel from Egypt and the founding of a New Israel in America, a paradigm for unity transcending the differences accumulated in the eighty-nine years since independence. In addition, the rhetoric of the "Second Inaugural" and much of Lincoln's final public discourse reinforces his move away from the principles of earlier rhetoric by finding a new judicial paradigm in the New Testament: "let us judge not that we be not judged." Having secured a military victory and the liberation of the slaves at great cost, Lincoln expands his role as the preserver of revolutionary values to become a national patriarch using a religious rhetoric common to both North and South rather than a personal—and often self-aggrandizing—ideology rooted in the sectional values of the American Revolution. Having safely quelled any remaining sectional opposition, Lincoln refuses to feign impartial judgment; instead, he becomes the national father-healer, proclaiming "charity for all," refusing to define the boundaries of justice, seeking only "to bind up the nation's wounds."[87]

Returning to Washington from Richmond, Lincoln demonstrated this charity by visiting the Union hospital camps, shaking hands that day with seven thousand wounded soldiers and their caretakers. There Lincoln might have encountered the poet who felt closer to him than to any other man, but Walt Whitman had taken a leave of absence from Armory-Square only two weeks before. Whitman had been in Washington for more than two years by then; he arrived in December 1862, after the papers reported that his brother George had been wounded at the Battle of Fredericksburg. After tending to George, who was not seriously hurt, Whitman was excited by the opportunity to remain in Washington witnessing the armed conflict he had wholeheartedly supported from a distance. After seeing the deplorable hospitals and their "great army of the wounded," however, Whitman volunteered his services as a nurse, dispensing small gifts, writing letters, reading his poetry, and occasionally dressing wounds: "I am faithful, I do not give out, / The fractur'd thigh, the knee, the wound in the abdomen, / These and more I dress with impassive hand."[88] The war exacted a great personal toll on Whitman as well. In June 1864, echoing Ulysses S. Grant's firm resolution, Whitman wrote his mother, "it seems to me if I could only be here two or three days. . . . I should be willing to keep on afterward among these sad scenes for the rest of the summer—but I shall remain here until this Richmond campaign is settled, any how."[89] Whitman's health deteriorated during that year, largely because of the rampant contagion in the hospitals, but possibly also as a result of acute mental suffering; his new comrades often died painfully, and the anticipated success of the well-promoted 1860-61 edition of *Leaves* never materialized. Moreover, the political religion Whitman celebrated in *Leaves* was not only threatened by the destruction of the Union but was increasingly revealed to him as a cause of the suffering he now struggled to heal: "I know my words are weapons full of danger, full of death."[90]

In his study of the relationship between Whitman and Lincoln, William Barton observes that both men "had that adult enlightenment, that time of self-discovery. . . . Lincoln and Whitman were in this sense, and each in his relation to his own life-work, twice-born men."[91] Grossman makes a similar observation, "Both men, together with most of their literary contemporaries, saw the historical moment as one requiring new structures of response."[92] In 1862 Lincoln said, "As our case is new, so we must think anew, and act anew. We must disenthrall ourselves, and then we shall save our country."[93] Echoing Lincoln's attitude toward the process of history, years later Whitman would say, ". . . the free human spirit has its part to perform in giving direction to history."[94] The poetic product of Whitman's war, *Drum-Taps*, like Lincoln's political oratory, traces an evolution in the rhetoric of his poetry, moving from an uncompromising political religion to the uncomfortable tolerance of a nation forced to come to terms with "irreconcilable differences." In *Memoranda During the War* Whitman writes, "I have myself, in my thought, deliberately come to unite the whole conflict, both sides, the South and the North, really into One, and to view it as a struggle going on within One Identity."[95]

At the outbreak of the war, Whitman was a pro-war Unionist opposed to compromise or separation: "War! an arm'd race is advancing! the welcome for battle, no turning away; / War! be it weeks, months or years, an arm'd race is advancing to welcome it."[96] Whitman's private correspondence also confirms this position:

> I believe this Union will conquer in the end. . . . I sometimes feel as if I didn't want to live—life would have no charm for me, if this country should fail after all . . . this country I hope would spend her last drop of blood, and last dollar, rather than submit to such humiliation.[97]

The early poems that became part of *Drum-Taps* reflect Whitman's zealous dedication to the Northern cause; he could not bear to see the agrarian aristocracy of the South impede the expansion of a united empire for liberty to the borders of the North American continent if not beyond. Aroused by the approach of war (and, no doubt, by its commercial opportunities), Whitman intended to publish a pamphlet of mobilization poems coinciding with the release of the 1860-61 edition of *Leaves*. One of the poems, "Song of the Banner at Day-Break," expresses Whitman's frustration with self-interested economic impediments to war through the competing voices of Poet, Child, Banner, and Father. Gazing upon the Banner, the Poet summons the Child to glorious battle while the Father discourages the Child from abandoning practical domestic interests: "Look at these dazzling things in the houses, and see you the money shops opening." Ultimately, the Child heeds the call of the Poet, following the Banner in battle: "I see but you, O warlike pennant! O banner so broad, with stripes, I sing you only, / Flapping up there in the wind."[98]

Much of Whitman's pent-up anger was released by the bloodless firing on Fort Sumter. Along with much of the population, Whitman was caught up in the excitement and optimism; he avoided representing the tragic potential of war, and, far from his usual poetics of merger and embodiment, he demonized the secessionists:

> What can I say of that prompt and splendid wrestling with secession slavery, the arch enemy personified, the instant he unmistakably showed his face? . . . In my judgment it will remain as the grandest and most encouraging spectacle yet vouchsafed in any age, old or new, to political progress and democracy.[99]

Although by this time Whitman's pamphlet of mobilization poems remained incomplete, he attempted to capitalize on popular interest with "Beat! Beat! Drums!", which was published on September 28, 1861, in *Harper's Weekly*, the *New York Leader*, and the *Boston Evening Transcript*. "Beat! Beat! Drums!" was an uncharacteristically conventional poem in which the call to arms silences the old and timid, the women and children who resist the passionate fanaticism of Whitman's war ardor: "Beat! Beat! drums!—blow! bugles! blow! / Make no parley-stop for no expostulation."[100] However, "Beat! Beat! Drums!" and "Song of the Banner at Daybreak" were surely part of an effort to promote Walt Whitman and his other works to a larger audience. The third edition of Leaves was being printed, so Whitman attempted to expand the market for his unconventional work by presenting himself in a more acceptable guise (and "Beat! Beat! Drums!" may be the second most anthologized Whitman poem after "O Captain! My Captain!" in the nineteenth century). Unlike *Leaves*, the collection of poems that eventually became the beginning of *Drum-Taps*—the title poem (later called "First O Songs for a Prelude"), "Beat! Beat! Drums!," "Song of the Banner at Daybreak," and "Eighteen Sixty-One"—each have regular stanza divisions, incremental repetitions, refrains, iambic-anapestic lines, and express rather simplistic sentiments betraying the authoritarianism camouflaged by *Leaves*. These poems represent a move away from the experimentation of *Leaves* toward work that was more conventional, more inclusive, and more commercial; they were a harbinger of Whitman's later concessions to popular sentiments. Yet this is not to say that the private Whitman, despite the apparently inclusive poetics of *Leaves* and "Calamus," did not wholeheartedly believe in the militarism advocated by these poems. Whitman often recited these poems for his friends at Pfaff's Cellar and even instigated a fistfight there with a man who facetiously proposed, "Success to Southern Arms!"[101]

The escalation of the war long past sixty days caused Whitman to transform what began as an expression of political absolutism and a self-promotional tool into a continuation of *Leaves*, appropriately reflecting the changing manifestations of the poet. After linking the present to the Revolution, the poetic self is diminished, as if the successive sketches of military activity were summoned in response to his call to arms. In "Cavalry Crossing a Ford," "Bivouac on a Mountain Side," and "An Army Corps on the March" the political content of the earlier poems is entirely absent; they depict scenes of camp life impressionistically without comment. As *Drum-Taps* continues, the poems increasingly focus on the suffering caused by war rather than reaffirmation of former glories. "Vigil Strange I Kept on the Field One Night" marks a transition from the distant observation of the previous poems; the speaker is forced to confront the death of a beloved comrade: "I rose from the chill ground and folded my soldier well in his blanket, / And buried him where he fell."[102] This shift parallels a change in Whitman's attitude toward the war when its costs began to exceed those of the Revolution and when he was forced to confront it on an individual level in the hospitals of Washington, DC.

At the beginning of the war Whitman observed that the troops leaving New York for Washington "were all provided with pieces of rope, conspicuously tied to their musket-barrels, with which to bring back each a prisoner from the audacious South." After the disaster at Bull Run, he writes, "Where are your vaunts, and the proud boasts with which you went forth? Where are your banners, and your bands of music, and your ropes to bring back your prisoners? . . . there isn't a flag but clings ashamed and lank to its staff."[103] As the war progressed and the losses mounted without perceptible gain, Whitman began to lose his optimism; the war would be far more destructive than he had imagined. Victory began to seem unattainable, and, more significantly, the rhetorical underpinnings of Whitman's political religion became problematic for him. This confusion is reflected by "Quicksand Years," a fragmentary poem from Whitman's notebooks of the time: "Schemes, politics fail— all is shaken—all gives way / Nothing is sure."[104] Near the center of *Drum-Taps*,

"Year That Trembled and Reel'd Beneath Me" likewise reveals how Whitman's war-like disposition had flagged, how former moral certainties had to be questioned: "A thick gloom fell through the sunshine and darken'd me, / Must I change my triumphant songs? said I to myself, / Must I indeed learn to chant the cold dirges of the baffled?"[105] If the Union cause was based on the exchange of human suffering during the American Revolution as proof of the value of its continued existence, then the sacrifices of Civil War, vastly greater than those of the Revolution, began to assume a greater meaning of their own. If more people were willing to die to uphold a view of the Constitution diametrically opposed to his own, then Whitman's polemical conception of the American mission needed rethinking. Whitman's direct confrontation with the moral certainty of his opponents persuaded him to question the possibility of preserving a union by silencing the equally inflexible voice of opposition: "(was one side so brave? the other was equally brave)."[106] Whitman abandons a Constitution backed by the uncompromising certainty of guns and bayonets; they could not long preserve a union characterized by political tension: "(Were you looking to be held together by lawyers? / Or by an agreement on a paper? or by arms? / Nay, nor the world, nor any living thing, will so cohere)."[107] Correspondingly, the rhetoric of *Drum-Taps* moves away from a forced Union deriving its authority from the sacrifice of the Revolution to an uncomfortable pluralism or complementarity, deriving its authority from tolerance for individual convictions, even when these convictions seem to contradict each other.

When his brother George was wounded at Fredericksburg, Whitman was thrust suddenly into personal contact with the tragedy of the war. One of the first sights that greeted him in Washington was "a heap of amputated feet, legs, arms, hands, & c., a full load for a one-horse cart."[108] Moved by the suffering and an opportunity to experience the war directly, Whitman remained in Washington working as a nurse in the hospitals. Several months after his arrival, he writes to his mother expressing a change in his understanding of war:

> I think the killed & wounded there on both sides were as many as eighteen or twenty thousand [in fact, it was 50,000]—in one place, four or five acres, there were a thousand dead, at daybreak on Saturday morning—Mother, one's heart grows sick of war, after all, when you see what it really is—every once in a while I feel so horrified & disgusted—it seems to me like a great slaughter-house & the men mutually butchering each other.[109]

The genuinely transformative experience Whitman relates in his letters is parenthetically explained in the central poem of *Drum-Taps*, "The Wound-Dresser": "(Arous'd and angry, I'd thought to beat the alarum, and urge relentless war, / But soon my fingers fail'd me, my face droop'd, and I resigned myself / To sit by the wounded and soothe them, or silently watch the dead)."[110] Realizing the inadequacy of his poetics to comprehend the enormous tragedy of the war, Whitman recreates himself yet again as a pacifist. Despite his superheated patriotism, Whitman was not a violent man; "I could never think of myself as firing a gun or drawing a sword on another man," he wrote in 1863.[111] As the "Wound-Dresser," commissioned healer of the victims of his former mode of discourse, Whitman could personally and poetically overcome the dissonance between his ideology and experience, cleansing himself and restoring his poetic voice by penitentially nursing the wounds he discursively inflicted: "[I] Cleanse the one with a gnawing and putrid gangrene, so sickening, so offensive."[112]

The poet's healing of the soldier extends symbolically to purging the nation of a greater infection: ". . . it seem'd sometimes as if the whole interest of the land, North and South, was one vast central Hospital."[113] In "Give Me the Splendid Silent Sun," Whitman again parenthetically announces a reversal of his rhetoric: "(O I see what I sought to escape, confronting, reversing my cries, / I see my own soul trampling down what it ask'd for)."[114] Gazing at the vista of a future based on an equal voice for white men and women, former slaves, and immigrants, Whitman realizes that an imposed ideological uniformity could only produce conflict. The irreconcilable differences between Americans required a new rhetoric of tolerance, even self-subordination, in which antithetical perspectives are regarded as equally valid. Whitman abandons the rhetoric of war, the "Spirit Whose Work is Done," and becomes, as Betsy Erkkila calls him, a "fuser and reconciler of the American republic."[115] Linking the nation under a single word, "Beautiful as the sky," which spans North and South, "Reconciliation" acknowledges the spiritual equality of the fallen enemy and unites former foes in a tableau of remorse and forgiveness:

> For my enemy is dead, a man divine as myself is dead,
> I look where he lies white-faced and still in the coffin—I draw near,
> Bend down and touch lightly with my lips the white face in the coffin.[116]

While "Reconciliation" demonstrates regret for the death of another man, the death is not represented as meaningless, for it enables the Union to endure. The deaths of more than 600,000 people makes the manifest destiny of the American future possible again for Whitman, but it will be an expansion based on a recognition of duality: "The Northern ice and rain that began me nourish me to the end, / But the hot sun of the South is to fully ripen my songs."[117]

Horace Traubel once asked Whitman if his inclusive rhetoric was not self-contradictory; Whitman replied, "I shouldn't wonder: in trying to represent both sides, we always run the risk of finishing on the vague line between the two."[118] But neither side possessed a claim to absolute righteousness in the conflict: "The South was technically right and humanely wrong," and, by implication, the North was technically wrong and humanely right. The main lesson of the war, however, was "to stick together," with all the difficulties that implies. [119] Like the poet who chronicled his own transformation, the Civil War enabled the nation to contradict itself.

Whitman was in Washington on 4 March 1865, the day of Lincoln's "Second Inaugural Address," but he could not get close enough actually to hear the President. He watched Lincoln and Tad ride down Pennsylvania Avenue to and from the stairs of the U.S. Capitol, its dome finished after several years of intermittent construction. From his distant vantage point, Whitman wrote, "I like to stand aside and look a long, long while up at the dome. It comforts me somehow." Whitman read the meteorological portents: "As the President came out in the Capital portico, a curious little white cloud, the only one in that part of the sky appear'd like a ho'vering bird, right over him." [120] Like the altered manifestation of the poet in *Drum-Taps*, Lincoln had abandoned the certainty of the "First Inaugural" and had revised the inflexible resolutions of Gettysburg with a governing metaphor that seemed to mirror the "Wound-Dresser's" concept of "Reconciliation":

> With malice toward none; with charity for *all*; with firmness in the right, as God gives us to see the right, let us strive on to finish the work we are in; to bind up the nation's wounds; to care for him who shall have borne the battle, and for his widow, and his orphan—to do all which may achieve and cherish a just, and a lasting peace, among ourselves, and with all nations. [121]

Just as the conciliating inclusiveness of *Drum-Taps* stands at variance with most of Whitman's previous writing, the rhetorical strategies of Lincoln's "Second Inaugural Address" mark a dramatic departure from Lincoln's earlier speeches and writing. In his pivotal campaign speech at the Cooper Institute in New York City on 27 February 1860, Lincoln succinctly delineates the rhetoric that the "Second Inaugural" reverses:

> Let us be diverted by none of those sophistical contrivances wherewith we are so industriously plied and belabored contrivances such as groping for sane middle ground between the right and the wrong . . . reversing the divine rule, and calling, not the sinners, but the righteous to repentance. [122]

There is no uncertainty in Lincoln's appropriation of the intentions of the "founding fathers"; he denies the privilege of Confederates to invoke Washington, "imploring men to unsay what Washington said, and undo what Washington did." Moreover, Lincoln claims to perceive the intentions of the Almighty against their "false accusations against us," and with fire and brimstone pronounces a violent and inflexible secular religion certain to plunge the Union into civil war: "LET US HAVE FAITH THAT RIGHT MAKES MIGHT."

Such rhetoric enabled Lincoln to win the election in the North, but its radical absolutism suggested the insurrectionary fervor of John Brown to the slaveholding South. Predictably, Lincoln was soon the object of constant assassination threats. On his trip to Washington, Lincoln stopped in Philadelphia on 22 February 1861, to give a speech at Independence Hall. Like the Founding Fathers—like John Brown—Lincoln publicly affirmed his resolution to sacrifice his life for the principles of the Declaration: "I would rather be assassinated on this spot than to surrender it." [123] Yet these principles that "all should have an equal chance" were not in the Declaration of Independence but carefully excluded from it in order to create a Union out of military necessity. The right to self-determination and separation from an oppressive government was guaranteed; as a representative of Northern political interests, Lincoln's authority in this case was applied selectively. Even by 1 December 1862, in his "Annual Message to Congress," Lincoln continues to apply the binary rhetoric that precipitated the conflict: "'One section of our country believes slavery is *right*, and ought to be extended, while the other believes it is *wrong*, and ought not to be extended. This is the only substantial dispute."[124]

Just as Whitman turns to the American Revolution and religion for his rhetorical style, Lincoln's rhetoric at the beginning of the war is rooted in a political religion worshipping the heroic Age of Washington as a source of absolute ideological principles. As the casualties of the Civil War began to enormously exceed the costs of the Revolution, the inflexible authority of the revolutionary ideology was transformed by this added sacrifice into a resolution giving birth to a new Constitution passed by the silent consent of 50,000 martyred patriots: [W]e here highly resolve that these dead shall not have-died in vain—that this nation, under God, shall have a new birth of freedom—and that government of the people, by the people, for the people, shall not perish from the earth."[125]

At Gettysburg, Lincoln reconvenes the Revolutionary era of "four score and seven years ago," but he appropriates the meaning of the Founding Fathers, by making the Civil War a "Second American Revolution," rather than a sectional dispute, and, by definition, not "in vain." As Whitman observed of his own poetry, Lincoln's words were weapons, for the "Gettysburg Address" not only reaffirmed the North's resolution to win what had became a war of attrition, but it secured the high ground of moral virtue in a war of slave liberation. While the Declaration did propose that "all men are created equal," it intentionally did not provide for equality in practice. The emancipation of the slaves remains in the subtext of the "Gettysburg Address," not directly confronting the legal principles of the Declaration as Lincoln had during his campaign. At Gettysburg Lincoln single-handedly recreates the national government in a sentence deriving its rhetorical authority from a tenuous link to the American Revolution, making future battles a trial by combat of the moral ascendancy of the Union over the Confederacy.

Lincoln's words at Gettysburg do more than restore and reshape the ideology of the Revolution; they transform a sectional dispute over political power into a crusade for self-evident human rights. By transforming the conflict into a war of slave liberation, Lincoln teleologically expands the temporal scope of the American mission to a Biblical scale and transforms himself from a political leader into a religious patriarch, "Father Abraham." By the 1864 Presidential election, the clean-shaven pioneer, with his uncombed hair, disheveled homespun clothing, backcountry origins, and ubiquitous rails, had become a bearded statesman, the head of a family, a paternal figure fond of reading to his adoring son in the most popular of the Lincoln engravings. But the transformation of Lincoln went beyond a revision of the American temporal and political scope and his own public persona. With the successful conclusion of the war at hand, Lincoln adopted a rhetoric of uncertainty, comparable to *Drum-Taps*, in which political enemies, formerly labeled "sinners," "aggressors," and "destroyers," are welcomed back into the fold.

At the time of the "First Inaugural," Lincoln had inadvertently become President of only a section of the United States; by the "Second Inaugural" he had to be President of all the states whether they wanted him or not. The "Gettysburg Address" implies that the ideological propositions of the North stand in opposition to those of the South, and that the Union should be forced to abide by the principles of the Declaration as Lincoln redefined them. The South was not persuaded of the justice of the Northern ideology; it was defeated by a superior force and could only grudgingly accept Northern determination of their rights. Jefferson Davis stated that "no peace is attainable unless based on the recognition of our indefeasible rights," and Confederate General John Bell Hood pronounced, "We will fight you to the death. Better to die a thousand deaths than submit to live under you . . . and your Negro allies."[126] Rather than submit to Yankee rule, Edmund Ruffin, who fired the first shots on Sumter, now shot himself in the head. Unlike the "First Inaugural" which opened with "Fellow citizens of the United States," Lincoln now includes even the disloyal, beginning the "Second Inaugural" with "Fellow Countrymen."[127] Facing intransigent moral certainty comparable to his own, Lincoln adopts a rhetoric of reconciliation that questions the possibility of acting consciously as a force for justice since one cannot look into the hearts of others: "It may seem strange that any men should dare to ask a just God's assistance in wringing their bread from the sweat of other men's faces; but let us judge not that we be not judged."[128]

This tolerance demonstrates the impact of the war on Lincoln's development as a statesman able to place the needs of the nation above regional interests, for Lincoln never really came to sympathize with the South, even though he began to abstain from passing public judgment on it. Only three months before, Lincoln wrote a piece for Noah Brooks called "The President's Last, Shortest, and Best Speech" which more openly expresses the President's private sentiments:

> I am not much of a judge of religion, but that, in my opinion, the religion that sets men to rebel and fight against their government, because, as they think, that government does not sufficiently help some men to eat their bread on the sweat of other men's faces, is not the sort of religion upon which people can get to heaven![129]

Lincoln's rhetoric once precluded the possibility that both sides of an argument could be simultaneously right and wrong: "God cannot be for and against the same thing at the same time." In 1861 Lincoln said, "If the Almighty Ruler of nations, with his eternal truth and justice, be on your side of the North, or on yours the South, that truth, and that justice, will surely prevail."[130] At the time of the "Second Inaugural" in 1865 Lincoln still claimed to believe in the justice of the Union cause within the temporal scope of American history and moral judgment of worldly politics, but from the perspective of human history—"as was said three thousand years ago"—and the omniscience of God, the actions of both North and South are unjust: "Both read the same Bible, and pray to the same God; and each invokes his aid against the other . . . The prayers of both could not be answered; that of neither has been answered fully. The Almighty has His own purposes."[131] Thus Lincoln promulgates a perspective transcending sectional politics, enabling the North to tolerate the readmission of the South and the South to coexist with "the perfidious, malignant and vile Yankee race."[132] As Glen Thurow observes, "Only by seeing themselves as standing under the judgment of God's will could the intoxication of their own sovereignty be sobered by the awareness of human limits."[133]

During the Civil War Lincoln mobilized the Northern and Southern populations through a rhetoric of binary opposition; after victory seemed inevitable, it was incumbent upon the winners, faced with reconstruction and disorder, to cultivate the sentiments of camaraderie and joint economic interest. Lincoln's evangelical vision of a born-again nation had to become large enough to accommodate diversity; to patch the crack in a house divided, the rhetorical model of exclusion had to be abandoned. Both the North and the South are punished by the scourge of war for their joint complicity in the sin of slavery: "He gives to both North and South, this terrible war, as the woe due to those by whom the offense came." In Lincoln's last public address he said, "We simply must begin with, and mold from, disorganized and discordant elements."[134] By the end of the war, with slavery abolished, Lincoln had passed from a vision of the Union as a uniform continuation of the Age of Washington to a vision of a nation with a position in the Biblical scope of history unified by tolerance for diversity, founded on compromise, contradiction, and irreconcilable differences.[135]

It appears that Lincoln attempts in the "Second Inaugural" to offer the final, definitive statement of the meaning of the Civil War and his Presidency. In a letter to Thurlow Weed written eleven days after the speech, Lincoln writes:

> I expect the latter ["the Second Inaugural"] to wear as well as—perhaps better than—any thing I have produced; but I believe it is not immediately popular. Men are not flattered by being shown that there is a difference of purpose between the Almighty and them. . . . It is a truth which I thought needed to be told; and whatever of humiliation there is in it falls directly on myself.[136]

Whitman had greater hopes for *Drum-Taps*, but he too considered it his definitive expression of the war, a poem that seeks to make a "wound-dresser" of the reader even as *Leaves* sought to make poets. In a letter to William O'Connor on 6 January 1865, Whitman writes, *Drum-Taps* "is in my opinion superior to Leaves of Grass—certainly more perfect as a work of art, being adjusted in all its proportions . . . Drum-Taps has none of the perturbations of Leaves of Grass."[137] Just as the "Second Inaugural" presents a more compromising, universally representative Abraham Lincoln soon to be canonized as America's greatest President, *Drum-Taps* presents a Walt Whitman radically different from the outspoken individualist of *Leaves*: a weary, wise man of experience soon to become "The Good Gray Poet."

"Each of these two men, Abraham Lincoln and Walt Whitman, was given a vision of the ampler frontiers of the American ideal," writes William Barton, comparing their careers; "Each of them discerned something of this wider significance of American freedom."[138] With a mixture of politics, poetics, and self-promotion, Lincoln and Whitman reflected and created a historical revolution away from a divisive political religion towards a rhetoric of reconciliation and reconstruction. In Whitman's case, it was a remarkable transformation from his earlier persona, but it was also a canny strategy for ensuring the survival of that earlier persona by simultaneously detaching himself from it—trying making himself as sacrosanct as the martyred President—while emphasizing how he continued to be persecuted by literary critics who, he claimed, were the enemies of the democratic impulse in American culture.

Chapter Three

"He Not Only Objected to My Book, He Objected to Me"
Walt Whitman, James Russell Lowell, and the Rhetoric of Exclusion

"If the late James Russell Lowell—aristocrat and exquisite gentleman that he was—had been possessed of prophetic as well as of poetic insight, he might have foreseen that some day, not long after his death, that very 'common' person, the author of Leaves of Grass, would be reckoned by John Burroughs, John Addington Symonds, Swinburne, and even by many college professors, as among the real poets of America."

—Letter to *The Boston Globe,* 1912[1]

A S PIERRE BOURDIEU OBSERVES, THERE IS AN INVERSE RELATIONSHIP BETWEEN the symbolic capital accumulated by writers engaged in the restricted production for the cultural avant-garde and the economic capital accumulated by writers engaged in unlimited production for a popular audience. The cultural field, though it is dominated by the fields of power (economics, politics), is nevertheless structured by opposition to the realm of large-scale production. "It is based," Bourdieu writes, "on a generalized game of 'loser wins,' on a systematic inversion of the fundamental principles of all ordinary economies: that of business (it excludes the pursuit of profit and does not guarantee any sort of correspondence between investments and temporal greatness), and even that of institutionalized cultural authority (the absence of any academic training or consecration may be considered a virtue)." Rather than valuing sales or popularity, the cultural field asserts its autonomy from the field of power by "seeing failure as a sign of election and success as a sign of compromise."[2] This model of cultural production partly accounts for the tendency of bourgeois cultural institutions, in the wake of the avant-garde, to consecrate (and commodify) writers who once reached a limited audience, who seemed rejected in their own time, and who were excluded, at first, from the centers of power and authority. Typically under the aegis of egalitarian inclusiveness (particularly in the U.S.), they are incorporated into the official culture at the moment when they cease to threaten existing hegemonic structures, when they are, in fact, refashioned into reflections of it.[3]

Useful as it is, however, Bourdieu's economic model can lead to a reductive interpretation of the range of available positions within and between cultural fields: that there are only two models of cultural production available under capitalism. There is Emily Dickinson, an "autonomous" writer who produces only for herself and remains uncontaminated by the marketplace; and there is P. T. Barnum, a "heteronymous" writer who produces only for the market to sell books and attract customers for the "Greatest Show on Earth." Unknown in her time, Dickinson is now a consecrated artist, a secular saint, canonized in a cultural establishment purged of religious icons; Barnum is remembered as the epitome of a vulgar businessman, a "humbug" or sinner only redeemed, perhaps, by philanthropic munificence, which is typically criticized as counter-revolutionary redistribution to the proletariat in support of capitalist ideological social structures.

American culture seldom produces unalloyed products. In the United States, at least, there has been a creative tension between the autonomous and heteronymous modes of literary production. The vast majority of American authors fall somewhere between these images of Dickinson and Barnum. Moreover, the relationship between the avant-garde and the popular developed unevenly in the United States during the nineteenth century as relatively isolated regional, sectarian, class-based markets gradually converged into a national, secular, middle-class marketplace in which literature became an increasingly autonomous field that sought to distinguish itself from geographic location, commerce, and political and religious discourse. Nevertheless, Bourdieu's dialectic is a useful tool for understanding the redistribution of various forms of capital as a struggle to define the existence and boundaries of the literary field and its relation to other fields. Although the cultural field in the nineteenth-century United States seems to have been more complex than the cultural field as presented in Bourdieu's France—more fragmented, more fluid, with a greater diversity of culture, religion, and geography, and a greater number of contenting authorities and institutions within a trans-Atlantic, post-colonial context.

Narratives of literary history—which is typically an unreflexive form of sociology—often construct pairings in which the consecration of one author is based on the desecration of another author with whom a politicized dialectic can be constructed (e.g. Harriet Beecher Stowe by Nathaniel Hawthorne—and vice versa).[4] These pairings, in retrospect, become useful representations of rivalries between modes of authorship and the available definitions of art competing for legitimacy in a given representational space (as the literary field was and generally continues to be structured). There is a limit to the degree of consecration an author can receive—widespread attention in required and elective curricula, uncontested space in anthologies, vestigial forms of "religious" deference in the spheres of power (primarily business and politics)—without provoking direct challenges to his or her position in the field (characteristic of nationalist, feminist, multiculturalist, and other forms of identity-based criticism), or efforts to fragment it into a diminished set of constitutive influences (typical of New Historicism, deconstruction, and psychoanalytic criticism). Quite often, the pattern suggests the metaphor of a waterwheel in which one author's accumulation of symbolic capital (prestige, public consecration, canonization) eventually causes the elevation of the undercapitalized author who, being relatively empty, can only accumulate water while the filled bucket's contents are spilled away. Consecration breeds iconoclasm, which, in turn, produces new icons. The revolutionary becomes the canonized artist, and the ideological/aesthetic cycle of cultural production continues from generation to generation and among competing interest groups.

Just as critics transfer cultural capital to themselves by reversing an existing critical consensus, one significant means by which undercapitalized authors obtain capital is by juxtaposing themselves to overcapitalized authors, placing themselves in a position to acquire the capital released by their displacement. It is a remarkable paradox that direct challenges to authority cannot be faced directly without ceding legitimacy to the challengers. Typically, the overcapitalized represent an empowered ideology, which becomes vulnerable as its opposite is produced and demands capital for itself invoking what I here call a "rhetoric of exclusion," a claim that prevailing norms unjustly and undemocratically silence an author and the people or ideology he or she represents. It implies that one's work, indeed one's very being, is a threat to the existing power structure and, therefore, a more accurate rendering of the "truth," which the power structure seeks to suppress through the "symbolic violence" of the critic, the censor, or, most egregiously, the state authority itself. The "rhetoric of exclusion" has exerted considerable force in the United States, where the rhetorics of populism and egalitarianism dominate the sphere of power, where Christian typology (particularly the jeremiad and the Christ narrative of suffering and redemption) continues to shape a superficially secularized culture, where the literary field—at least in the nineteenth century—exists in relation to the critical authority of a former colonial power.

In U.S. literary history (by which I mean the narrative constructed by it), one of the most telling examples of the authorial dialectics produced by the "rhetoric of exclusion"—and the corresponding cyclic inversions of the cultural field—is the supposed rivalry between Walt Whitman and James Russell Lowell, two exact contemporaries who published, at first, in semi-autonomous literary sub-fields but whose poetry and personae came to define the extreme boundaries of institutionalized literary production in the United States in the period leading up to literary modernism. This period of the autonomization in the U.S. literary field—the increasing inversion of its values in relation to the field of power—corresponds precisely to the time in which Whitman replaced Lowell as a "representative" and "great" American poet of the nineteenth century.[5] The ascendancy of Whitman represents the separation of the literary field from those fields that supported the initial ascendancy of Lowell: the New England cultural hegemony, institutional authority rooted in a parent country, class deference, and religion-based moral codes—all of which were once called "The Genteel Tradition."

Although it was not of great importance in their lifetime, the subsequent tradition of comparisons of Whitman and Lowell became inevitable as a result of a prosaic coincidence: they were almost exact contemporaries who were born and died within months of each other.[6] This has resulted in frequent juxtaposition of their writings in literary histories, anthologies, and early survey courses.[7] Efforts to commemorate one—as in the years immediately following their deaths and in the centenary of their births—have competed with commemorations of the other in ways that seem absurd to contemporary readers.

In 1892, Harold Frederic, a London correspondent for *The New York Times*, writes that Whitman's death "created twice the amount of comment that Lowell's evoked."[8] In 1919, the journal *Poetry* responded to one Lowell commemoration by wondering "whether Walt Whitman's Manahatta, having paid her tribute to the Bostonian, would also devote two or three days to honoring the greater bard's now so imminent centenary."[9] Lowell was among the first to be commemorated in the Hall of Fame in New York City, but "Whitman was in the Hall of Fame unofficially for a few hours in 1919," reports *The New Republic*. "On his birthday, May 31, some of his admirers smuggled in a bust by the French sculptor Deré, and placed it next to the Lowell memorial. It was quickly ejected by the New York University authorities."[10] The populist tone of such notices implies that Whitman—though a greater literary artist (one recognized by superior European critics) and a more representative American than Lowell—was excluded from an official culture hidebound by class prejudice and Victorian prudery.

By 1919, the centenary of Whitman's and Lowell's births, a critical consensus had emerged that, although pieties were due to Lowell, Whitman was the greater poet. This was largely achieved by the abandonment of the religious and political basis for canonization utilized by the "hot little prophets" who were Whitman's followers. As Paul Elmer More realized, to accept Walt Whitman, we "must begin by forgetting his disciples."[11] The "hot little prophets" needed to be replaced by cool aesthetes. The literary sentiment was being transformed from something rooted in religion (and partly substituting for it) into secular, rationalistic formalism and the celebration of artistic autonomy from all systems of thought external to "literature." Although Whitman had been celebrated by socialism and various offshoot ideologies outside an increasingly self-contained literary field, he eventually gained status over Lowell, not as an inspiration for reformers or as a religious figure, but as a "literary" genius—one who refused to be limited by politics—whose experimentation paved the way for literary modernism and as one who sought the liberation of the artist from "external" standards of taste: not just bourgeois morality but, as we shall examine, the many political movements that attempted to appropriate and determine the meaning of his poetry.

The foundational reason for the increasing status of Whitman has been his usefulness in reinforcing the autonomy of the literary field in relation to political and economic considerations, making his work seem unconnected to its historical context. The critic for *The New Republic* stated dogmatically, "Now, in their common centennial year, we regard the tardy and eccentric Whitman in the light of current developments; but we estimate the timely and centripetal Lowell almost wholly with reference to his own generation."[12] Lowell's poetry, at its most political, reflected a genteel abolitionism, but Whitman's politics of mass democracy and inclusiveness had, it seems, become the apolitical norm for a New York-centered, secularized literary culture that had overcome its traditional deference to a Boston-based Anglophile Protestant elite. By the 1970s, after the onset of a renewal of explicit politicization of the literary field, Lowell had become so obscure that Marjorie Kaufman (writing for Houghton Mifflin) felt the need to plead for him in her anthology of his poetry by applying the rhetoric of exclusion formerly used by Whitman's supporters: "Now, with Whitman's reputation safe . . . we may at last be able to afford a place for the *successes* of Lowell."[13]

My purpose here is not to restore Lowell to some rightful position in the "American literary canon"; rather, it is to examine how the pairing of Whitman and Lowell demonstrates the structural dynamics of what Bourdieu calls "the field of cultural production": the cyclic, intergenerational process under which major shifts in the distribution of cultural capital takes place. I seek to understand how authors who do not seem to possess any of the attributes of power and authority often arrive at or near the center of the "American canon." And, conversely, to understand how one who possesses all of the elements of cultural authority can lose his position as one of the major American poets. In addressing these questions, I attempt to reach some macro-level conclusions about the processes governing the field of literary production over time, as the institutional legitimacy of one generation of producers is inverted by the economics of cultural production in the next.

While there seems to be an inherent cultural tendency to transpose canonical positions, authors themselves exert some force on this process. Authors, over the course of a career, gravitate towards the intersection points of various fields of power. As the development of Whitman and Lincoln away from their early radicalism has shown, tactical absolutism, if it is ever possible, is costly to one's standing with both popular and elite constituencies. Absolute artistic self-referentiality leads to incomprehensibility; absolute market orientation leads to déclassé obviousness. Consecrated artists and popular writers typically gravitate towards either side of the center of the spectrum. Individual acts may belong to one extreme or another, but, in the long run, it is the average that is most significant in the construction of an author. Whitman, though commercial at times, compensated for more blatant acts of self-promotion by well-publicized gestures of artistic integrity and a doctrinaire refusal to behave like a corporate or market professional. Lowell, though an uncompromising artist in some circumstances, tended towards the fields of power (economic and political), particularly late in his career, which tended to place him behind the vanguard of the literary field as it increasingly privileged autonomy. This increasing association with the field of power contributed to Lowell's slow decline and eventual disappearance from the literary field—a common pattern of declension suffered by writers who lack a sufficient diversity of appeal; their literary consecration is compromised or obliterated by the shifting of field boundaries beyond their original constituencies. On the average over the course of their careers, Whitman minimized (or concealed) his acquisition of economic or political power but maximized his symbolic capital; Lowell maximized economic and political capital but, inadvertently, minimized his symbolic capital in the long run. Paradoxically, even as Whitman's seeming struggle for autonomy enhanced his symbolic capital, he courted a popular audience, even, on one notable occasion, attracting the admiration of Lowell at the moment when he was most identified with the field of power.

I. "THE MOST IMPRESSIVE HOUR"

On 14 April 1887, Walt Whitman delivered his annual lecture on the "Death of Abraham Lincoln" in New York City's Madison Square Theater on the twenty-second anniversary of the President's assassination. Whitman's days as a bombastic political orator were long past. Nearly seventy, the "Good, Gray Poet" had grown white, and he was partially paralyzed by a series of strokes. He had difficulty speaking. His voice was high, raspy, barely audible; certainly not the "barbaric yawp" of 1855. But after nearly a decade of pruning before increasingly receptive audiences, Whitman's once roughhewn liturgy was now as carefully shaped as a Victorian topiary garden. As one observer noted, "The Death of Abraham Lincoln" had, by this time, become an annual rite of consecration in which both the martyred President and Whitman, his prophet, were transfigured into icons of "holy democracy."[14]

Beginning in the late-1870s, Whitman's Lincoln lectures facilitated his acceptance among a growing number of wealthy and influential literary critics in the United States, particularly in New York City, increasingly the center of American cultural authority. While Whitman and his supporters presented him as a patriotic lecturer and moderate social progressive (in contrast to his earlier populist, sexualized persona), local patrons of the high cultural scene in New York were shamed by exaggerated English reports of Whitman's poverty and suffering, which were supposedly a result of Americans' (particularly Bostonians') indifference to their national bard.[15] To aid in redressing these presumed wrongs (and to refute the notion of Americans as Philistines), a wealthy jeweler named J. H. Johnston organized a benefit for Whitman with the help of Edmund Clarence Stedman, an influential literary critic and anthologist, and Richard Watson Gilder, the prominent editor of the *Century Magazine*.[16] Using their extensive social and literary contacts—and the services of the flamboyant impresario Major James B. Pond (a promoter of Mark Twain and P. T. Barnum)—they managed to attract a significant crowd to the Madison Square Theater to participate in a fashionable tribute—not to the rough son of Manhattan, but to the "Good, Gray Poet," a grand old man who has served his country in the Civil War (despite the sour protests of Thomas Wentworth Higginson, another Bostonian) and who now dedicated his considerable poetic energies to enshrining Lincoln in the American civil religion.[17]

Although the audience was not very large, many of its members were noteworthy for their associations with Lincoln and their power to shape public opinion.

They included John Hay, Lincoln's personal secretary and biographer; Frank Carpenter, who had painted Lincoln's portrait; Augustus St. Gaudens, who was preparing to unveil a monumental bronze statue of Lincoln; and Edward Eggleston, the author of a novel about Lincoln, *The Graysons: A Story of Illinois* (1887). Also seated were the President of Johns Hopkins, Daniel Coit Gilman, and notable writers Joel Benton, Frances Hodgson Burnett, Moncure Conway, Mary Mapes Dodge, and Frank Stockton. Mark Twain, whom William Dean Howells called "the Lincoln of our literature," made a curiously unremarkable appearance.[18] Andrew Carnegie, who appreciated Whitman's celebration of industry and was ashamed of America's supposed neglect of the poet, donated $350 but did not attend. Also seated among the society figures were some comparatively unknown admirers, suggesting the revolutionary political and religious qualities associated with Whitman in some quarters. Among them were José Martí, a Cuban revolutionary who popularized Whitman's poetry in Latin America, and Stuart Merrill, a student from France who came to hear "the voice of a prophet who moved in advance of his race and beyond his own time."[19]

The most improbable guest in this assembly, however, was James Russell Lowell, whom Whitman by this time regarded as his greatest literary enemy. Gilder had invited him. It was Lowell, Whitman believed, who had exerted his influence to "freeze" him out of the respectable journals and to "burn" him out of the others.[20] Although Whitman told his disciple Horace Traubel, "It is of no importance what Lowell thinks," from the late 1880s to the early 1890s he was obsessively concerned with Lowell's activities; according to Traubel, he "reads about everything he sees about Lowell."[21] Whitman heard and repeated many times that years earlier Lowell had libeled him as "nothing but a low New York rowdy . . . a common street blackguard," and that he had supposedly discouraged an eminent English admirer—probably Moncton Milnes, Lord Houghton—from visiting him in Camden.[22] A Brahmin, a noted practitioner of such traditional genres as the sonnet and the neomedieval romance, a Harvard professor, a politician—Lowell seemed the antithesis of everything Whitman claimed to represent: "'Lowell is one kind: I'm another,'" he said.[23] Whitman described his friends as "manly, generous, noble," but enemies were "venomous, mean, lying, cowardly, dirty, malignant." As for Lowell, Whitman said, "I count him the most malignant of all."[24] A year after the New York benefit Whitman still said, "'Lowell is one of my real enemies: he has never relaxed in his opposition: Lowell never even tolerated me as a man: he not only objected to my book: he objected to me.'"[25]

Perhaps it was only punctilio that prompted Lowell to write back to Gilder, "I can't go gratis to a Benefit," and to pay for prominent box seats for himself and his Harvard colleague, Charles Eliot Norton.[26]

Whitman considered Lowell "the chief of staff in the army of the devil," and here he was, seated in a box to witness "the culminating hour" of Whitman's life.[27] Perhaps Lowell's presence was explained by Norton, who was one of Whitman's earliest admirers. When *Leaves of Grass* was first published Norton unsuccessfully tried to persuade Lowell to review it in the *Atlantic Monthly*. Norton had even written an amusing imitation of Whitman's "barbaric yawp," but Lowell had no stomach for Whitmanism, "No, no, the kind of thing you describe won't do."[28] Norton's taste for Whitman was not atypical among Lowell's associates. Eggleston was one of Lowell's devoted students, and Lowell's Midwestern protégé, William Dean Howells, made one of the earliest gestures to acknowledge Whitman as an important poet in 1860. (Howells is sometimes mistakenly thought to have attended the lecture.[29]) Stedman, who was a friend and admirer of both Lowell and Whitman, had the misfortune to be seated in the box between the elegant Lowell and the rustic John Burroughs, a Whitmanite who also moved among the Boston literati, although, according to one reporter, he looked like a "well-to-do farmer."[30]

Gilder would likely have been aware of the enmity between Lowell and Whitman's disciples when sending invitations. One younger critic, Robert Underwood Johnson, was present at a meeting attended by both Lowell and Gilder. Someone mentioned Whitman's poetry, and "Lowell broke out, 'It isn't poetry at all,' and in his *ex cathedra* way he went on to discuss it with Gilder." Johnson "ventured to suggest whether the body of Whitman's writing was not something between prose and poetry," and Lowell said, 'There isn't anything between prose and poetry.'"[31] As a leading New York critic, Gilder held mixed professional allegiances, as well as a general disdain for the Camden enthusiasts and their religious devotion to the "Good, Gray Poet." As he later wrote to Whitman's biographer—and Harvard professor—Bliss Perry, "Disciples we were not, but great admirers of his poetry we assuredly were."[32]

Gilder and Whitman had been friends since 1877, when they were introduced by Johnston. Years after Whitman's death Gilder wrote, "my memory of the old man is of a lovely, affectionate, clean character. The good in him was more powerful than the bad."[33] Perhaps Gilder hoped to change Lowell's opinion of Whitman's character. Lowell's attitudes toward Whitman had been formed before the Civil War, before *Drum-Taps* or the Lincoln Lectures, and this event offered the possibility of a re-evaluation from one of American's foremost critics. Gilder would have also recognized Lowell as an authority on Lincoln, one who was associated with memories of the President and the Civil War, and thus, as appropriate a guest as Carpenter, Eggleston, Hay, or himself.[34]

Shortly before the benefit, Lowell had written to Gilder regarding the editor's effort to compile a reminiscence of Lincoln:

> You tell me you were going to say something about my article on Lincoln (in 1864). Are you still of that mind? I ask because one of our Boston papers said the other day that Emerson first did him justice, but after his murder. In this case, I am inclined to be jealous of my thunder like the late John Dennis.[35]

Lowell had, in fact, written two essays about Lincoln in 1864: "McClellan or Lincoln?," which supported Lincoln's re-election, and "Abraham Lincoln," which praised the re-elected Lincoln in distinctly Whitmanian terms: "Mr. Lincoln's perilous task has been to carry a rather shaky raft through the rapids, making fast the unrulier logs as he could snatch opportunity."[36] Most importantly, Lowell had delivered the "Commemoration Ode" at the dedication of Harvard's Memorial Hall on 21 July 1865. Rivaled in popularity only by Whitman's "O Captain, My Captain!," the "Commemoration Ode" was regarded by many critics as the greatest poetic tribute to Lincoln, whom Lowell called "our Martyr-Chief":

> Great Captains, with their guns and drums,
> > Disturb our judgment for the hour,
> > But at last silence comes;
> These all are gone, and, standing like a tower,
> Our children shall behold his fame,
> > The kindly-earnest, brave, foreseeing man,
> Sagacious, patient, dreading praise, not blame,
> > New birth of our new soil, the first American.[37]

If Lowell's ode did not create some of the mythic categories by which Americans came to remember Lincoln, then it helped to enshrine them in the American civil religion. Despite his frequent claim that he did not read Lowell, Whitman seems to have been unable to avoid alluding (whether consciously or not) to the "Commemoration Ode."[38]

The stage at the Madison Square Theater that night was set to resemble a well-appointed Victorian drawing-room; in its center stood a blue plush reading stand and a large armchair. On the left hung a laurel wreath decorated with streamers of red, white, and blue, one of which was lettered "So long! Walt Whitman!," a curious salutation alluding to one of Whitman's poems. It was just past four in the afternoon, and above the whispers of the audience one could probably hear the Manhattan traffic. When anticipation had reached a carefully calculated pitch, Whitman emerged, supported by a shepherd's crook and Billy Duckett, a working-class boy from Camden whose youth highlighted Whitman's apparently great age. Whitman's appearance was as contradictory as his poetry: rosy-cheeked, luxuriant-bearded, delicate, yet robust, wearing a stylish black velvet sack coat, a gray waistcoat and trousers, and an open-collared linen shirt with elaborate lace ruffles. At once an Old-Testament prophet, a rakish boulevardier, and a rough workingman, the aged Whitman "contained multitudes." The whole event seemed carefully planned to stir the religious underpinnings of the high literary culture and sentimental nationalism. As one observer whispered to his companion, tellingly, "He looks like a god."[39]

Whitman settled into the throne-like armchair, put on his eyeglasses, leaned an elbow on the reading stand, and fumbled nervously with his tumbling white hair and beard, waiting for the applause to subside. He then began to improvise an introduction from nearly illegible notes:

> My subject to you, my friends, this evening for the next forty or fifty minutes
> talk is 'the Death of Abraham Lincoln.' I am not going to tell you anything new
> and it is mainly because I wish to reverently commemorate the Day and
> Martyrdom and name, I meet here with you.[40]

Gaining his composure, Whitman spoke in a steady, reverent tone, using none of his
once grandiloquent gestures or theatrical modulations of voice. At times, he was
barely audible, and he occasionally lost his place and improvised, sometimes errati-
cally, and sometimes eloquently alluding to his poetry:

> I remember where I was stopping at the time, the season being advanced, there
> were many lilacs in full bloom. By one of the caprices that enter and give tinge
> to events without being at all a part of them, I find myself always reminded of
> the great tragedy of that day by the sight and odor of these blossoms. It never
> fails.[41]

Then Whitman related the circumstances of the terrible night at Ford's Theater with
understated drama as it had been told to him by his onetime lover Peter Doyle.
Merrill was transfixed; "I was there, the very thing happened to me," he writes.[42]
Whitman continued, suggesting the ritual that customarily followed his lecture,
and, surprisingly, reached a crescendo by alluding, perhaps at second hand, to the
"Martyr Chief" of Lowell's "Commemoration Ode":

> Dear to the Muse—thrice dear to Nationality—to the whole human race—pre-
> cious to this Union—precious to Democracy—unspeakably and forever pre-
> cious—their first great Martyr Chief.[43]

As the applause subsided, a little girl presented the "Good Gray Poet" with a
basket of lilac blossoms and said gravely, "I've brought you some lilacs that in our
door yard bloomed."[44] Aware of the conventionalized sanctifying power of the admiration of children (partly derived from Matthew 19:14), lovable old Walt caught the
child up in his arms and blessed her with repeated kisses. The audience erupted in
a warm-hearted ovation, which some, like Merrill, considered irreverent at this
moment of catharsis: "I was in the presence of the sublime, and I could only
weep."[45] At least one audience member, William Sloane Kennedy, felt some ironic
detachment, describing the whole affair acerbically as "a sort of coronation."[46]

As always, Whitman concluded with "O Captain!"; it rendered some admirers
speechless: "I was gripped by some strange power and I couldn't find my tongue,"
said poet James Lane Pennypacker in response to it at another performance.[47]
Stedman had praised Whitman's poem, "When Lilacs Last in the Dooryard
Bloom'd," as comparable to Lowell's "Commemoration Ode," and the performance
seems to have been arranged to allow Whitman to recite "Lilacs."[48] Despite
Stedman's carefully choreographed lilac symbolism and Whitman's allusions, someone in the audience called for Whitman to recite "O Captain!," and the old poet

obligingly sobbed his way through what is probably the most conventional poem he ever produced:

> O Captain! my Captain! our fearful trip is done,
> The ship has weather'd every rack, the prize we sought is won,
> The port is near, the bells I hear, the people all exulting,
> While follow eyes the steady keel, the vessel grim and daring;
> But O heart! heart! heart!
> O the bleeding drops of red,
> Where on the deck my Captain lies,
> Fallen cold and dead.[49]

Although "Lilacs" had been praised by many critics, it was never so well known as "O Captain!," which was likely known by heart by many members of the audience, who mouthed the words with Whitman in a kind of communal ritual. Perhaps the lecture did not conclude as Stedman had planned, but this moment must have seemed the fulfillment of a prophesy he had made at another benefit a few years before: "I felt that here, indeed, was a minstrel of whom it would be said, if he could reach the ears of the multitude and stand in their presence, that not only the cultured, but 'the common people hear him gladly.'"[50] Few of the "common people" were there that night, but it seemed that Whitman had at last found the message and the medium required to gain the approval of both of the cultured and the common. It seemed inevitable that "Good, Gray Poet," who rose to fame as a self-sacrificing martyr to censorship and bureaucratic persecution, would receive the adulation that was due to him.[51]

Astonishingly, at the end of Whitman's performance, the reserved, skeptical James Russell Lowell is said by Johnston to have wiped tears from his eyes saying, "This has been one of the most impressive hours of my life."[52] Burroughs did not hear this; he quickly left Lowell to congratulate Whitman with the other disciples, reporters, and socialites who called on the poet immediately after the lecture and at a reception held at the Westminster Hotel. Lowell did not introduce himself to Whitman or attend the reception. When asked whether he "Had he seen Lowell at the reception, '87?," Whitman said, "'I did not see him, but I was told he was there.'"[53] Perhaps Lowell was not invited to attend the reception or could not be sure of his welcome. Burroughs later said that "It was the dress circle that was on trial, and not Walt Whitman."[54] "The last thing I did for Lowell," Burroughs recalled, "was to hand him his hat."[55]

One must certainly question the accuracy of Johnston's account of Lowell's admiration; it is not corroborated by Norton, Stedman, or Burroughs. (Lowell himself apparently never wrote anything about the lecture.) Johnston wrote his account many years after the event, and other aspects of his description—such as the size of the audience—seem exaggerated. Even if Lowell did say nearly those words, one must question his precise meaning. Was Lowell impressed by Whitman, by the story of Lincoln's death, by this gathering of people associated with that time, or by something else about the event? Was he acting for the benefit of Norton or Burroughs? This case—one of the few instances of Lowell's possible admiration for Whitman— is fraught with ambiguity. Nevertheless, Whitman's supporters among the New York's cultural elite seem to have quickly publicized a revolution in Lowell's opinion. A few months after the lecture, the following statement was published in *The Critic*, written by Jeanette Gilder, who almost certainly knew better:

> 'WHITMANIA' is a word coined by Mr. Swinburne to describe the mental state of persons who admire the genius of Walt Whitman. One of these persons was Mr. Emerson; another is Mr. Lowell.[56]

Four years later, in 1891, Whitman still asserted that Lowell "was every way, bitterly, set against me." But he continues, "I have been told of late years that Lowell markedly toned down his criticism—came round a good deal. I have it from Trowbridge, who thought it was a revolution."[57] Indeed, Trowbridge describes Lowell as coming around to Whitman, when his writings became "less prophetical, and more consciously literary in their aim." By the late 1880s, "Lowell and the others of his class began to see something besides oddity in Whitman, and his popularity widened."[58] Reports came in that "Lowell admitted that Walt Whitman had more to him than had in earlier days seemed the case."[59] Lowell even appears to have sent "his 'felicitations and good wishes' on Whitman's birthday in 1891, although, significantly, Traubel did not read them at the birthday celebration.[60] William Sloane Kennedy—one of the more judicious of Whitman's later disciples—did not place Lowell on his list of Whitman's "Bitter and Relentless Foes and Villifiers" in 1926, even after many years of exaggerated reports of Lowell's enmity by the more extreme disciples, who tended to be socialists who hated all wealthy writers.[61] Ultimately, "Lowell recognized some of the elements in Whitman's greatness," as William Roscoe Thayer summarized judiciously, "but I think that on the whole he did not place him among the masters."[62]

Surely the evidence suggesting that Lowell suddenly became a great admirer of Whitman is questionable; however, the evidence of Lowell's antipathy for Whitman is also quite ambiguous and was subject to even greater exaggeration by Whitman, his supporters, and later opponents of the so-called "Genteel Tradition." In general, it can be said that Lowell's opinion of Whitman reflected the critical consensus, both before and after 1887. He thought Whitman's early work in *Leaves of Grass* (1855–61) was vulgar, formless, unoriginal, and probably immoral, but he appears to have appreciated the spirit—if not the form—of Whitman's later efforts, post-*Drum-Taps* (1865), as a patriotic, occasional poet and lecturer much like himself. One can only speculate on Lowell's precise meaning at the 1887 lecture, and one may even reasonably doubt that he said those words at all. More to the point, however, is why Lowell's enmity was so important to Whitman and his disciples when more established supporters in New York (Stedman, the Gilders, Johnston) were eager to publicize Lowell's admiration and to craft a more popular Whitman. More broadly, why were Whitman and Lowell, two poets with seemingly so little in common, so frequently juxtaposed from the 1880s through the 1920s? And why has the negative view of Lowell as an intolerant persecutor—rather than the reality of Lowell's complex relationship with Whitman—persisted for more than a century and succeeded in transforming Lowell into a villainous dramatic foil for the "Good, Gray Poet?"

The fierceness of more reasonable Whitman advocates such as Burroughs (who moved in broader circles than disciples such as Traubel and Bucke), his determination to cast Lowell as an enemy, suggests that there was a good deal more at stake than a few hundred dollars at the Madison Square Theater benefit. The stakes were, perhaps, larger than the players themselves could realize. The process by which Whitman eclipsed Lowell in the twentieth century as one of the preeminent American poets of the nineteenth century included the refashioning and promotion of Whitman for various constituencies of readers in the post-bellum period, but these efforts were also enmeshed in a larger network of interrelated shifts in the structure of the literary field itself and its relationship to the field of power. Unlike the more hierarchical, consolidated culture of a relatively small, homogeneous nation with an uncontested metropolitan center such as France, the cultural field of the United States, through much of the nineteenth century, was composed of a number of semiautonomous literary cultures gathered in metropolitan areas in the Northeast (and later in the near West). Status hierarchies were not only complicated by the developing relations between these cities (primarily Boston, Hartford, New York, Philadelphia, Cincinnati, and Baltimore) as their relative capital shifted, but also by the condition of postcoloniality, which caused literary practitioners in each subculture to negotiate a position with respect to the literary cultures of England (and, in a few other diasporic subcultures, to other parent countries). Partly as a result of the dominance of transatlantic shipping routes (providing for both closer cultural ties to England and more surplus economic capital producing higher levels of education and leisure for literary production), Boston came to dominate the antebellum literary culture, but, between 1855 and 1919, with the expansion of canal and rail networks, the rapid growth of domestic population and internal trade resulted the greater accumulation of publishing capital in New York, which emerged by the 1880s as the dominant arbiter of literary taste in the United States. As a national culture emerged, it helped to break down the postcolonial triangulation of literary judgment through England and Boston that dominated the U.S. literary field until the postbellum economic expansion. After a period in which several metropoles competed for preeminence, the growing dominance of New York served to benefit writers with well-established networks of influence in that city and its satellites while the symbolic capital of writers enmeshed in other urban networks declined unless they managed to transplant themselves into the new cultural center (as Howells did when he left *The Atlantic* in Boston for *The Century* in New York in 1881).

Before this shift occurred, Lowell was deemed one of America's poet laureates. In 1866 a reviewer for the *Nation* writes, for example, "Without a doubt, the four living poets who fill the highest places are Emerson, Bryant, Longfellow, and Lowell," and, he continues, "of all these writers he [Lowell] may be rated, all things considered, as the first."[63] After a brief bohemian period as a romantic poet, Lowell became an editor for the *North American Review* and *The Atlantic Monthly*, a Harvard professor, and the Ambassador to the Court of Saint James (positions which carried considerable authority in a era characterized by a greater overlap between literature and institutional, economic, and political power, as well as a lingering sense of American cultural inferiority to England). Lowell lived in a mansion on Cambridge's "Tory Row" called "Elmwood," and, from the early 1850s through the early 1880s, his patronage could seriously affect a literary career. (His protégé Howells, for example, as well as many of Lowell's students at Harvard became prominent writers and critics who continued to pay him tribute well into the early twentieth century).

Although Lowell was still an important cultural authority in 1887 and would remain so for another generation, it was already evident (demonstrated, perhaps, by his coming to New York at all) that he was slowly losing his consecrated status even as Whitman was becoming acceptable to the literary mainstream as well as in a variety of subcultures that tended to appropriate Whitman for extra-literary purposes (Traubel combined Whitman and socialism; Bucke combined Whitman and spiritualism). Perhaps, what was most impressive for Lowell about Whitman's 1887 Lincoln lecture was that it was one event among many that signified the ceding of Boston's cultural hegemony to New York. Although economic and political power were slowly losing authority over an autonomizing cultural field, it was evident by this time that the accumulation of surplus capital in New York was surpassing Boston so rapidly that the declining cultural authority of the field of power was delayed in some areas by the vast imbalances in the distribution of capital. This association of the field of power with Whitman in New York (e.g., the support of Andrew Carnegie) might have compromised his status, just as Lowell was harmed by his inextricable association with the field of power in Boston. No matter how thoroughly Whitman subordinated himself to business and political interests, Lowell, by contrast, remained an easy target for anger in a period that privileged artistic autonomy. Between 1855 and 1919, Whitman's symbolic capital seems to have increased in direct proportion to the decrease in Lowell's. The year of the Madison Square Theater performance, 1887, aside from being a moment of personal intersection, may well represent the crossing of their trajectories as the reputation of one ascended and the other descended. It appears as if the gradual separation of the overlapping fields of literature, politics, economics slowly stripped Lowell of his accumulated symbolic capital and rendered it to Whitman. By 1919 there would be no question that Lowell was bound for obscurity and Whitman for Parnassus.

II. "LOWELL—WHITMAN: A CONTRAST"

Whitman and Lowell had much more in common than is ordinarily realized. In fact, Lowell's criticisms of Whitman were often re-articulations of criticisms that had been made of him: egotism, technical infelicity, lack of clarity, and subordination of grace to didacticism. Both were literary nationalists who, at one point, desired to become national poets, producing an American epic comparable to Joel Barlow's *The Columbiad* (1807). Both were interested in the cultivation of an innovative, American language; Whitman compiled, but never published *An American Primer*, a dictionary of American English; and Lowell's *Biglow Papers* was the most notable rendering of Yankee dialect in verse.[64] Like Whitman under the influence of Transcendentalism, Lowell sought to cultivate an original relation to the universe: "Surely the highest office of a great poet," he writes, "is to show us how much variety, freshness, and opportunity abides in the world about him."[65] Both regretted the loss of the antebellum agrarian democracy and the commercial vulgarity of America in the Gilded Age. And, as noted earlier, both became perceived as poet laureates of the Civil War, particularly as celebrators of Lincoln; Lowell's "Commemoration Ode" was frequently compared with "O Captain, My Captain!" and sometimes with "When Lilacs Last in the Dooryard Bloom'd." Although they were self-consciously "American," the success of both in the United States was largely based on their foreign reception; both courted an English readership and sought critical approval from abroad, correctly believing that it would sway American critics in their favor. And both eventually drifted from youthful bohemianism into Victorian respectability, though Lowell reached it sooner, on a grander scale, and with considerably less ambivalence than Whitman, whose consecrated status is partly attributable to the image he maintained of economic disinterestedness and artistic integrity.

On the other hand, the differences between Lowell and Whitman have been exaggerated, largely as a means of enhancing Whitman's status as a poet. Whitman was never a radical socialist; nor was Lowell a reactionary Tory. Whitman was not always an artisanal producer; nor was Lowell an entirely "establishment" writer. The author of "O Captain, My Captain!" was not always experimental and indifferent to criticism; nor was the author of the *Biglow Papers* always traditional and formal. Whitman was not entirely shunned by his country; nor was Lowell always celebrated by it. Lowell's opinions, along with those of a good many other critics, may have thwarted the advancement of Whitman's reputation as a poet at first, but Whitman and his allies retaliated by constructing a pervasive myth of Lowell's active hatred for the "Good, Gray Poet," Lowell's centrality in an organized conspiracy to thwart, not only Whitman, but the democratic, progressive impulse in American literature. In fact, the written record of Whitman's statements against Lowell is much more extensive than Lowell's attacks on Whitman. And, ultimately, it was Lowell who served as Whitman's foil and partly enabled his canonization as a visionary martyr in the creation of an alternative, oppositional American literature. Although he was just one character in a larger narrative of persecution, Lowell became the principal antagonist in the narrative of Whitman's exclusion from the literary field. Even in recent critical literature, one is likely to find inaccurate depictions of Lowell by admirers of Whitman. In his biography of Whitman, Paul Zweig states that Lowell, upon reading the 1855 edition of *Leaves*, "threw his book into the fire."[66] Zweig is confusing Lowell with an identical account of John Greenleaf Whittier's famous first encounter with *Leaves*.[67]

Although they had similar goals and found themselves moving in overlapping literary cultures for extended periods, the tension between Whitman and Lowell can be accounted for partly by the professional trajectories determined by their respective class positions. As a consequence of their economic origins, Whitman and Lowell entered the antebellum literary field (though it is, perhaps, a misnomer to call it a distinct "field" at this time) from entirely different careers. As Lawrence Buell observes, there were two paths into the literary profession in the mid-nineteenth century: a lateral move from law or divinity, or a slow ascent through printing and journalism.[68]

For the more affluent classes—those with incomes to sustain them through unprofitable periods and the inevitable early phase of reputation-building—the surest route to literature, for males at least, was divinity or law. These lawyers and ministers, after abandoning their initial calling, usually entered the literary profession as staff writers for newspapers and magazines or sometimes began as editors. Family ties and social connections often played a significant role in the placement of these would-be writers, many of whom had parents who were already published authors or leading public figures. This, of course, did not guarantee that any scion of the educated classes could become a notable author, but it frequently provided the economic capital necessary to sustain an early career and the social capital necessary ensure a judicious critical hearing. One could, under these conditions, begin as a self-conscious aesthete, a bohemian in pursuit of the eternal verities and unconcerned with the marketplace. Many would-be authors in the United States in the early nineteenth century modeled themselves on the leading figures of aristocratic English romanticism.

Such was the case with Lowell, who was born in Cambridge, Massachusetts, the intellectual and literary center of the United States in 1819. The Lowells were among the first families of New England; though not directly involved, their name would soon become synonymous with the factories that absorbed many of the workers displaced by the industrial revolution. Lowell's father was a graduate of Harvard Divinity School and an eminent Boston minister. As the son of a reasonably secure and established family, Lowell was not initially attracted by the empowered professions; he was a rebellious undergraduate at Harvard, where his teachers "rusticated" him from the campus as a discipline problem. Although he was encouraged and supported by his family to practice law, Lowell continued to resist the culture of commerce and politics. Like his father, he was convinced that he possessed a sacred calling, akin to a religious vocation: "I know that God has given me powers such as are not given to all, and I will not 'hide my talent in mean clay.'"[69] He abandoned law by degrees and considered writing a novel: "I have the plot nearly filled out. I think—I know it will be good. It will be psycho-historical . . . Goethe wrote his 'Sorrows of Young Werther,' and I will mine."[70] The novel, however, never advanced beyond the first chapter. But Lowell had been writing romantic poetry since his early teens, and images of him from the early 1840s suggest that he was emulating the personal style of English romantics such as Byron. Despite the aristocratic associations of the English romantic style, Lowell adopted a pose of exclusion from power, presenting himself as poor while preserving the semblance of a genteel taste superior to those engaged in practical concerns. Near this period Lowell writes, "Let men who are born with silver spoons in their mouths quarrel. They who are born with pens in their hands have *nobler* work to do."[71] Lowell once complained of an allegory of literature on the cover of a magazine: "how any man in his senses could set forth such a fat, comfortable looking fellow as the *vera effigies* of what is the hungriest, leanest, empty-pursiest, and without-a-centist on earth I am at a loss to say."[72] Every claim of voluntary poverty enhanced Lowell's claims on the production of avant-garde literature while preserving his distinction from those who were merely poor as a result of a lack of ambition or "loafing."

Then as now, consecrated literary forms such as poetry tend to be acceptable only to those who possess sufficient alternative means of securing their class position such as inherited wealth or a family business (to which one will revert after a period of adolescent rebellion). This is an economically logical position, since success in the consecrated fields of art are typically best facilitated by elite social connections. Despite his rebellious pose, Lowell was not abandoned by his family or his social network; unable to extricate himself from the moralistic elements of his religious upbringing (and his dependency on inherited capital still controlled by his family), he never achieved the radical cachet of a Byron. But, largely as a result of religious and institutional social ties, in 1841 the Boston firm Little, Brown published Lowell's *A Year's Life*, a 182–page compilation of his poetry, which was financed by Lowell's father. As Lowell later acknowledged, it was an immature book, full of easy rhymes, conventional images, faux-aristocratic allusiveness, and narcissism: "My veins are fired with ecstasy," and so on. But, for an unknown writer, Lowell fared well in the reviews, most of which were from the Boston-Cambridge area.[73] Predictably, the favorable reception to *A Year's Life* was partially the result of preexisting social connections. His old classmates William Wetmore Story and C. S. Wheeler gave him flattering puffs, Orestes Brownson favored him, and Charles Peterson of *Graham's* proclaimed that Lowell had refuted the sneers of European critics of American literature. Margaret Fuller of the *Dial* compared Lowell with the young Byron and Coleridge.[74] Even those who dismissed Lowell's poetry—Charles Gordon Green of the Boston *Morning Post* and G. S. Hillard of the *North American Review*—found his moral virtue impeccable at a time when this was an important value in literature.

Despite Lowell's connections, *A Year's Life* probably sold fewer than 300 copies. This, however, was not unusual for a book of poetry. With few exceptions (such as Longfellow during his best years), authors of poetry seldom produce bestsellers.

Poetry was generally, as William Charvat observes, "inflicted on friends and libraries" as a means of signifying one's possession of cultural or moral capital.[75] In 1821 William Cullen Bryant, for example, took the entire risk for a volume of his poetry; bookstores accepted it on consignment. Of an edition 750 copies, only 270 were "disposed of" (meaning given away as well as sold). In this context, *A Year's Life* is typical for the period and the genre.

As Lowell aged he inevitably took his place in the Brahmin establishment, and he shed his rebellious, romantic pose, which he increasingly regarded with ironic detachment as if it had been a foreign affectation. Nevertheless, Lowell (unlike contemporaries such as Oliver Wendell Holmes) remained committed to literature as an elevated, intellectual calling, and in 1843 he and his friend Robert Carter founded *The Pioneer*. It was largely a provincial periodical; it published the Boston-area writers known personally by the editors: Longfellow, Hawthorne, Emerson, and Jones Very. "The object," the *Pioneer's* prospectus announced, "is to furnish the intelligent and reflecting portion of the Reading Public with a rational substitute for the enormous quantity of thrice-diluted trash, in the shape of namby-pamby love tales and sketches, which is monthly poured out to them by many of our popular Magazines."[76] Partly as a result of its too exclusive commitment to the avant-garde of literary tastes of New England, the *Pioneer* was bankrupt after only three issues, and Lowell was left in debt. His father and brother loaned him the money to recover himself, but it seemed that Lowell's career as an independent publisher was over in 1843.

The apparent failures of *A Year's Life* and *The Pioneer* may have only enhanced Lowell's pretensions to art in later years, but Lowell was increasingly gravitating to those parts of the literary field which overlapped with the fields of power. The move towards "respectability" in bourgeois culture often comes, as Bourdieu observes, immediately before marriage, and it accelerates afterwards with the arrival of children, when the social pressure to provide for one's family outweighs the symbolic capital derived from the bohemian artistic style, even when assumed voluntarily. Lowell's marriage to Maria White in 1844 may have improved his financial security and expanded his circle of literary contacts, but, as their four children arrived, it also marked his transition from bohemia into positions of official cultural authority. His thoughts turned increasingly to the profitability of his work, writing to a friend at this time, "I have quite a reasonable prospect of getting into a lucrative literary employment next year." He continues, with his eye squarely on the bottom line:

> I think I may safely reckon on earning four hundred dollars by my pen the next year, which will support me. Between this and June 1843, I think I shall have freed myself from debt and become an independent man. I am to have fifteen dollars a poem from the Miscellany, ten dollars from Graham, and I have made an arrangement with the editor of the Democratic Review, by which I shall probably get ten or fifteen dollars more.[77]

The acquisition of wealth and the need for family respectability served to break down Lowell's earlier romantic style, and he gradually adopted a new set of literary values that utilized his expanding social, institutional, and political capital to greatest advantage in the short term, though in the long term these moves compromised his status as an artist.

Over the next decade, Lowell's poetry became increasingly political, and he became well known as an abolitionist (thanks, in part, to the influence of his wife, Maria White). Association with political movements enhanced the base of power supporting his literary output on multiple grounds. Much of his non-political writing took on an academic, philological quality, and his growing knowledge of romance languages, combined with his social connections, enabled him to replace Longfellow as the Smith Professor of Modern Languages at Harvard in 1855, coincidentally, the year that marks Whitman's descent from his early literary professionalism to the kind of bohemian career Lowell had abandoned. Many years later Lowell described his transformation in verse, "We sailed for the moon, but, in sad disillusion, / Snug under Point Comfort are glad to make fast . . . the man whose boy-promise was likened to Pascal's / Is thankful at forty they don't call him bore!"[78] Like most middle-class writers who marry, sire children, and own property, Lowell was drawn away from the inverted economy of avant-garde literature and into those areas of literary production that overlapped with the field of power at that time: politics, education, critical institutions, and religion, enabling him to lead a comfortable, secure life but gradually diminishing his status as an elite artist, a goal which normally carried risks too great for conventionally married men who aspired to middle-class stature.

While a wealthy writer such as Lowell might cultivate the appearance of romantic poverty in support of his poetic credentials, most writers from lower-class origins identify up the social spectrum in their initial literary aspirations. Although literature was just emerging in the antebellum United States as a specialized vocation, it remained only marginally acceptable, and largely only possible, for members of the educated elite residing in more developed urban areas to pursue consecrated subfields of literature such as "Poetry" as a career—and then only temporarily in youth or as a sideline to another profession with a steady income. As Charvat writes, "poetry is and always has been primarily an avocation—an amateur activity rather than a professional one."[79] Among the laboring to the lower middle classes, even in Boston, anything beyond street balladry and popular political verse was considered effeminate, impractical, and suggestive of unrealizable aspirations above one's social origins. As Benjamin Franklin's father rightly warned, "Verse-makers are generally beggars."

For those without independent wealth, access to higher education, and the social opportunities these presented, the primary means into a literary career was through a print shop. One often began in adolescence as an unskilled apprentice printer, a "printer's devil." In a few years one might become a printer or a compositor, and, while still performing these duties, one might also serve as a staff writer, and eventually as an editor. This experience might lead to freelancing for magazines or writing books, usually of a cheap, popular nature involving explicit violence and sex (another reason that lower class writers historically have had difficulty launching themselves into more consecrated genres). An ambitious journalist with some financial backing might venture out on his own to found a new periodical, which usually failed after a few issues, or after the political party it represented lost its cohesiveness. It was a rare individual who emerged from poverty and obscurity to become a prosperous publisher or a "literary" figure who would be recognized by the elite culture inhabited by Lowell from the outset of his career. There were few familial or educational connections to facilitate advancement, although writers and editors often developed powerful networks within the local political parties, trade unions, churches, and social clubs. Imaginative printers from this background might assume literary aspirations, but they were not often Byronic heroes tainted by feudalism, nor did they adopt the naive rusticity of a Coleridge or the sham dishabille of literary bohemia; instead, they were often Young American *flaneurs* in the mode of Dickens: nationalistic, upwardly mobile, sharply dressed boulevardiers with an eye for the main chance.

If Lowell's beginnings are the embodiment of the affluent, educated classes' route to the literary profession in the 1840s, then Whitman equally represents the literary career path of the lower classes, for a print shop was his Harvard. He began his literary career in 1831, age twelve, as a printer's apprentice for the Long Island *Patriot*. By 1835 he was a typesetter in New York, but a disastrous fire soon sent him home to Long Island, where he found short term jobs as a country schoolteacher and soon attempted to publish his own weekly newspaper, the *Long Islander*. Meanwhile, Whitman became increasingly involved with New York politics, making contacts in Tammany Hall and sending short stories out for publication in political magazines that were organs of the Young America movement. By 1842 eight of Whitman's stories—patriotic and sensational efforts such as "Last of the Sacred Army"—had been published in New York's *Democratic Review*. As Lowell would later do, Whitman was making a name for himself as a partisan writer. His politics were becoming increasingly populist, but he retained aspirations to become more than a writer of propaganda; his model was Dickens, the most successful—and most pirated—popular writer of the time: "I love and esteem him for what he has taught me through his writings."[80] Like the vast majority of journalists with literary aspirations, Whitman initially aspired to leave the pressroom to become not a poet but a novelist.

While Lowell could regard poetry as a sacred calling, the romantic endeavor of a genteel amateur, Whitman began his career in an environment of economic opportunism as a market professional. "After continued personal ambition," Whitman later said, he "determined "to enter with the rest into competition for the usual rewards, business, political, literary, &c."[81] While Lowell was exposed to foreign languages and Classical literature, Whitman received a better commercial and practical education. Then as now, the surest route to a quick profit as a writer was not the well-turned phrase, the subtle chord, or moral scrupulousness; it was lascivious and bloodthirsty sensationalism, celebrity gossip, the political and popular bandwagon, and the legal loophole. Whitman's employers at the *New World* in 1841, Park Benjamin and Rufus Griswold, were masters of the trade. By printing magazines like *Brother Jonathan* in a newspaper format—sometimes pirating whole novels—they beat the high postal rates that hindered their competitors. Besides pirating English fiction, it was also profitable to hire an American hack to write a sensationalistic novel catching the latest fad: temperance, male purity, vegetarianism, phrenology—all of which became interests of Whitman at one time or another during the 1840s.

Whitman had few illusions when Griswold and Benjamin commissioned him to write his first novel, *Franklin Evans*, a temperance thriller advertised as the work of "one of the best Novelists of this country." With true professional hubris, Whitman later claimed to have written *Franklin Evans*, which sold at least 20,000 copies, while drunk on a variety of hard liquors.[82] Supplementing this effort, Whitman also wrote temperance poetry such as "The Young Grimes," and sensational fiction like "The Child and the Profligate" and "Reuben's Last Wish." During this time he was also working on another novel, *The Madman*, but he never completed it. Within a year Whitman had advanced from the *New World* to become a freelance writer and eventually editor of the New York *Aurora*.

As the previous chapter describes, at the *Aurora* Whitman became actively embroiled in political controversies: capital punishment, slavery, Catholic-bashing, and other forms of nativism, which often led to friction between Whitman and his employers. But Whitman was pursuing a logical strategy for attracting attention when one is an undercapitalized young writer. As a consequence of his Young Turk stance, subscriptions to the *Aurora* during this period were increasing, but its politically independent owners tried without success to "tone" Whitman's editorial voice. (While notoriety helped Whitman, it harmed the already established editors who, being empowered, were better served by a conservative stance.) During the next eight years Whitman worked in a similar manner for at least ten more papers in New York, Brooklyn, and New Orleans before his steady journalistic career came to an end in 1849. Until the last decade of his life, Whitman would seldom have a successful long-term relationship with a publisher, but he would use these repeated "rejections" to mythologize his artistic integrity and commercial innocence.

Just as Lowell drifted away from a bohemian phase and began to achieve success in the late 1840s as a critic and with the *Biglow Papers* and the *Vision of Sir Launfall*, Whitman underwent a substantial revision of his authorial persona and field of generic practice by the end of the decade. Whitman was the product of a family of skilled craftsmen who were declining in the social scale during the industrial revolution, and it seems clear that he aspired to become a manager in the new industrial order, to make his way as what Raymond Williams calls a "market" or "corporate professional" in the New York metropolitan area, and briefly in New Orleans.[83] The rather dandified image Whitman presents in daguerreotypes from the early 1840s seems to prove that he identified up the social spectrum; his writing during this period also suggests that Whitman had high literary pretensions; when he was a teacher in Woodbury, Long Island, his letters suggest that he was urbanized and alienated from the populist persona with which he would later associate himself:

> If Chesterfield were forced to live here ten hours he would fret himself to death: I have heard the words 'thank you,' but once since my sojourn in this earthly purgatory.—Now is the season for what they call "huckleberry frolicks."—I had the inestimable ecstasy of being invited to one of these refined amusements."[84]

This is a shocking departure from the Whitman known to American literary history. Nevertheless, it is a common pattern for working-class writers to make initial attempts to rise several rungs in the social ladder, identifying, in particular, with the elite, managerial culture of the metropolis. But, for the vast majority of these émigrés, insurmountable social and economic obstacles drive them into working-class chauvinism as they make a virtue of their failure to rise very far. As Bourdieu observes, working-class and provincial writers are often attracted to the leading figures of the metropolis at first, and, when they find that when they cannot enter this world, they "return to their own particular idiom . . . they mark themselves positively with what is stigmatized—their provincial accent, dialect, 'proletarian' style, etc.—but the more strongly, the less successful their initial attempts at *assimilation* have been."[85] Through the 1840s Whitman increasingly found himself forced into subordinate positions (one cause of his tendency to insult editors, noted in the previous chapter), denied access to real economic and political capital, and denied status as an literary artist to boot. By the end of the 1840s, after a period of increasing friction between Whitman and his managers, he returned to outmoded "artisanal" or "post-artisanal" modes of production—both as a carpenter in his family business and as a cottage-industry poet, both of which comported well with the pre-industrial culture he basically longed to restore and the aristocratic model of disinterested production he sought to emulate.

Although Whitman and Lowell had not yet come into personal collision, the name "Lowell" itself was calculated to stir mixed feelings in Whitman. In 1846, one New Englander describes how a "'slaver,'" one of many employed by the Lowell mills, founded by James's uncle, "makes trips to the north of the state [Massachusetts] cruising around Vermont and New Hampshire who is paid one dollar a head for all he brings to market."[86] On the one hand, the name "Lowell" aroused stirrings of working-class solidarity; it suggested New England factory towns, a combination of moral priggishness yoked to economic exploitation that Whitman loathed. On the other hand, James Russell Lowell was associated with the American equivalent of an aristocratic, Anglophile culture, and the highest levels of literary cultivation and institutional authority. For Whitman, this Lowell would have been a man to be both resented *and* cultivated.

Whitman and Lowell actually met near the beginning of their careers. Largely as a result of early economic and educational advantages, Boston was still the intellectual center of the United States in the 1840s, New York, thanks to the Erie Canal (1825), was becoming dominant in the actual printing and distribution of reading material to the growing Western market. Lowell, like many New England writers, increasingly traveled to New York to arrange for the printing of his books. In 1843 Lowell visited the office of the appropriately named *Plebeian*, where Whitman was an editorial assistant. Whitman described the meeting to Traubel almost fifty years later:

> 'I met Lowell, once, many, many, many years ago—perhaps 50 years or on to that—in New York. . . . I was about 22 then. One day, evening, Lowell and [William Wetmore] Story . . . took them to the Park Theatre, which was the crack theatre those days—spent the evening with them. Lowell—oh! he was very handsome, at that time, very. Such a complexion! . . . He was one of those fellows (do they call them *nil admira?*—or something that way) admired nothing, expressed no surprises, all-hell-knowing, going everywhere, regarding everything, impassively, like an Injun, as if to say; that's no news, there'll need worse than that to be news!'[87]

This encounter is not corroborated by Lowell or Story in any document I have been able to uncover; perhaps it never happened. Twelve years later, Lowell could only recollect, "Whitman—I remember him; he used to write for the *Democratic Review*. He used to do stories then, a la Hawthorne."[88] Certainly Whitman would have wanted Lowell's patronage, would have regarded him as a fellow literary aspirant, and it seems likely that Whitman would try to impress Lowell—and probably fail. It also seems likely that Lowell would not have been interested in the companionship of Whitman, given the social gulf between them. There are grounds here for risky speculation about the reasons for subsequent tensions between them, particularly Lowell's careful avoidance of direct contact with Whitman for over forty years. Did Whitman make a sexual pass at Lowell, whom he claims to have found physically attractive? Did something that evening reveal Whitman as a sexual libertine, if not a "homosexual," in a manner offensive to a Yankee minister's son about to embark on a respectable bourgeois marriage? Lowell seems to have put on the air of a world-weary decadent, but was he actually offended by the Park Theater, which was probably a cruising ground for prostitutes and homosexuals, to say nothing of the lingering moral disdain for the theater that lasted longer in Boston than in New York?[89]

Without more evidence it is safer to interrogate what Whitman's narrative implies about his initial impressions of Lowell mediated by fifty years of increasing tension between them. For Whitman, Lowell was not a romantic bohemian; he was a jaded critic. If he did not view them with moral disdain, Lowell probably looked down on the New York entertainments enjoyed with such earnestness and booster enthusiasm by Whitman. While Whitman could write, "The orchestra whirls me wider than Uranus flies," Lowell would always maintain critical reserve, partly as a defense against the whims of short-term fashion, partly as a personal style, the patrician reserve of Brahmin culture.[90]

Although it was not so in the early 1840s, Whitman's poetic persona was characterized by universal empathy and enthusiasm; he could share the most serious emotions of opera, the cosmic drama of everyday life: "A morning-glory at my window satisfies me more than the metaphysics of books."[91] Whether or not the evening at the theater actually happened, Whitman's description of Lowell summarizes the crucial difference he later perceived as existing between them, the reasons Lowell could not appreciate Whitman: he was already more of an austere critic, a man of books, rather than a lover of Nature at first-hand; he could only deflate the grandiose presumptions of the Park Theater as he would later do with the earnestly theatrical and empathetic *Leaves of Grass*.[92] Despite this subsequent critical dialectic, it seems likely that the future tension between Whitman and Lowell was precipitated in part by the attraction/repulsion complex this account suggests: Whitman believed he was creating a new literary form that defied existing hierarchies, but he needed the critical authority and social éclat of Lowell to gain a judicious hearing for his work from the centers of the elite literary culture.

A major source of Whitman's ongoing fascination for us must surely be his ambiguous relation to the fields of restricted and large-scale production, to the elite salons and mass market. As Charles Eliot Norton remarked, Whitman was a mixture of a "Yankee Transcendentalist and a New York fireman."[93] Whitman presents the paradox of a supporter of the common folk who was mostly read by an elite literary establishment which he actively courted. Whitman's shift away from popular journalism and fiction to poetry in the early 1850s, albeit of an unconventional sort, was simultaneously an expression of his desire to work in an elite medium without abandoning ideological loyalties to his social origins. It is clear that *Leaves of Grass* (1855) was not aimed at laborers but rather at the arbiters of the high literary culture such as Ralph Waldo Emerson, John Greenleaf Whittier, and James Russell Lowell—it sought and sometimes obtained their notice. This was, no doubt, a vestige of the pre-capitalist patronage system, as evidenced by Whitman's referring to Emerson as "master." Although the frontispiece of 1855 (Fig. 1) presents Whitman as a surly workman, the first edition of *Leaves* was published in the aristocratic tradition of anonymous authorship without a publisher and without a professional marketing apparatus. The format of the first *Leaves*—in contrast to the second edition—also suggests that Whitman was producing a premium product for the high-end market; as Charvat observes, "the upper classes associated 'good' literature with expensive format; concomitantly, a cheap format was the natural dress of cheap content."[94] With few exceptions (such as the 1856 edition), Whitman always published *Leaves* in moderate to expensive formats that were beyond the means of many ordinary readers, who were almost always a secondary consideration when Whitman determined the mode of presentation.

By 1855 it was clear that the careers of Whitman and Lowell were diverging. Lowell was increasingly moving into the fields of power, while Whitman was moving away from them. At the same time that Whitman was emerging as a radical new poet in the mid-1850s, Lowell was drifting away from his early Byronic phase into the respectability of a Harvard professorship and corporate professionalism. On October 12, 1855, Lowell had already taken up the Smith Chair of Modern Languages at Harvard when his colleague Charles Eliot Norton wrote him about a strange new book called *Leaves of Grass.* "I have got a copy for you," he writes to Lowell, "for there are things in it that you will admire." But Lowell could not find anything to admire in the work of his old acquaintance; once again, he seemed to say, "nothing new here": "When a man aims at originality he acknowledges himself consciously unoriginal," he writes to Norton; "The great fellows have always let the stream of their activity flow quietly—if one splashes in it he may make a sparkle, but he muddies it too, and the good folk below (I mean posterity) will have none of it."[95]

As Bourdieu observes, those who emerge "from more comfortable social backgrounds", and who are "endowed with substantial educational capital, are opposed to . . . the sons of craftsmen," who are "devoid of educational capital." They are as "the *salon*" is to "the *café*."[96] The entry of writers from outside the tightly controlled circle of the literary-intellectual elite threatened to compromise their monopoly of taste as an expression of the values of the Boston mercantile hegemony. According to Bourdieu, "the fundamental stake in literary struggles is the monopoly of literary legitimacy, i.e., *inter alia*, the monopoly of the power to say with authority who are authorized to call themselves writers; or, to put it another way, it is the monopoly of the power to consecrate producers or products."[97] While Whitman was experimenting with a literary form that supported the increasing autonomy of the field—that expanded the boundaries of what literature could be and who could produce it— Lowell—following his own interests in the preservation of his own symbolic capital—gradually became part of a rear guard who struggled to maintain old standards, the subordination of literature to economic and political power, specifically located in the Brahmin elite of Boston or under its influence.

Before the divergence of the field of culture and the field of power, poets in nineteenth-century America were not, as yet, defined as subversive of the dominant order. They were often decorative elements in public rituals; their task was to celebrate the exalted and exceptional, the holders of economic and political capital rather than themselves or the people en masse. Poetry was essentially a feudal institution; in the nation-state the poet might also be sustained as a propagandist, or as a proponent of a political or philosophical movement such as nationalism or abolitionism. Prior to "Memories of President Lincoln" in 1865, Whitman was not writing odes to great personages—warriors, religious figures, or aristocrats. Far from placing himself in a subordinate role, his poetry "celebrated" himself and the culture that produced him. It was a form that threatened to expand the topical boundaries of poetry as well as who was entitled to write it and read it. As Bourdieu observes, as the most consecrated form of literature, poetry has "protective barriers characteristic of the genre which, like a club, the closed network of critics and consecrated authors deploys to frustrate pretentious *parvenus*."[98] Whitman's lack of form as much as his vulgar content was offensive; free verse represented a threat to the restricted guild of craftsmen produced by accumulated ancestral cultural capital, developed by European travel, and training in elite schools. Although Whitman identified up the class spectrum, he threatened to democratize the most consecrated field of literary production. Lowell, along with many of his students at Harvard (Barrett Wendell, for example), sought to preserve and transmit a literary culture, and Whitman and his allies threatened to expand its boundaries, to make it less formal, less Anglophile, more open to Americans of different backgrounds.

As a consecrated poet, and a critic with the power to consecrate, Lowell held several positions from which he could deny the authority of Whitman. He could perpetrate considerable symbolic violence on him; he could deny him access to the field of power that still controlled much of the literary culture. Lowell was in a position to write an influential negative review of Whitman, but he did not do this. Perhaps Whitman was beneath his notice, or perhaps Lowell recognized the problem that "adversaries whom one would prefer to destroy by ignoring them cannot be combated without consecrating them."[99] Lowell's policy, which he maintained with few exceptions, was to say and write nothing directly about Whitman in public; his strategy was to cut him from the society that controlled avant-garde literary production. Whitman described this silence as "freezing" him out.[100]

One example of the private means Lowell used to suppress Whitman occurred in 1863, when Lowell was specifically asked by Rev. W. L. Gage to remove a copy of *Leaves* from the Harvard College Library, where it might corrupt the morals and tastes of students. Lowell wrote back to Gage, *Leaves* "is a book I never looked into farther than to satisfy myself that it was a solemn humbug," continuing, "As for the evil influence of this particular book, I doubt if so much harm is done by downright *animality* as by a more refined sensuousness. . . . For my own part I should like to see a bonfire made of a good deal of ancient and modern literature—but 'tis out of the question." He did promise Gage, however, that he would "take care to keep it out of the way of students," and *Leaves* was placed in a locked case with anatomical texts, where it remained for many years, before being transferred to the rare book collections of the Houghton Library after Whitman's critical ascent as a kind of sacred relic.[101]

This copy of the Thayer and Eldridge edition of *Leaves* (1860) is still in collections of the Houghton Library.[102] It has numerous passages underscored and marginalia that appear to be in Lowell's handwriting. For example, in the margin beside Whitman's line "The earth does not exhibit itself, nor refuse to exhibit itself," is the comment "*Nor should man!*" Also the line "I shall demand perfect men and women out of my love-spendings" is heavily underscored as if to indicate the obscene quality of the work.[103] It seems clear that the writer, whether or not it was Lowell, associated Whitman with the pornographic depiction of the body and bodily functions, which the writer regarded as unsuitable subject matter for a poet.

Although evidence suggests that Lowell continued to disapprove privately of Whitman in 1860, he never expressed any public opposition, and, as Martin Duberman observes, "in his capacity as editor, Lowell made an effort to overcome his personal distaste, recognizing that if men like Emerson found unusual value in Whitman's poetry, some place should be found in the new magazine."[104] A contemporary writer, E. H. House, describes how Whitman came to be published in the *Atlantic,* which Lowell edited from 1857–1861.

Lowell was describing to House how "every man who wrote with an earnest purpose was entitled to a hearing."

> 'Do you mean a hearing in the *Atlantic*?'
> 'I do. I should be sorry to deny any one his fair chance, if it can possibly be given.'
> 'And does that apply to persons against whom there may be a popular prejudice?'
> 'Why not? Unless the prejudice is founded on circumstances that would make exclusion necessary. Are you thinking of anybody in particular?'
> 'I was thinking of Whitman. It would be a great satisfaction to him if he could see his work in your magazine.'
> 'Has he spoke about it?'
> 'Not to me . . . But I am certain that nothing would please him more.'
> 'Well,' said Mr. Lowell, after reflecting a moment, 'you may tell him that the *Atlantic* is open to him. He has a clear right to be heard; there can be no question of that . . . I shall probably print whatever he sends, whether I like it or not. But I should very much prefer to like it.'[105]

As House describes this conversation, Lowell had to be maneuvered into a position in which his editorial principles of free expression and egalitarianism overrode his sense of literary standards and exclusivity. At the further instigation of Emerson—and possibly in anticipation of the forthcoming Thayer and Eldridge edition of *Leaves* about to be published in Boston—Lowell finally published an edited, unsigned version of Whitman's "Bardic Symbols" in the *Atlantic* in 1860. Although it was a rather conventional poem for Whitman, House claims, "Mr Lowell was rather sharply criticised" nonetheless for the poem's graphic description of a corpse.[106] The poem's subject, the author's inability to achieve his poetic mission, and its overall tone of self-subordination, might also have contributed to Lowell's appreciation of it:

> O baffled, lost,
> Bent to the very earth, here preceding what follows,
> Terrified with myself that I have dared to open my mouth,
> Aware now, that, amid all that blab whose echoes recoil upon me, I have not
> once had the least idea who or what I am.[107]

"Bardic Symbols" was a strange admission from a poet on the verge of publishing a major new edition of his works (in which it would appear as the opening poem of the "Leaves of Grass" section), but it marks the first of a series of transitions in Whitman's persona that would bridge the gap between his initial aspirations and the demands of the literary marketplace.

Although Lowell's publication of "Bardic Symbols" and Whitman's growing celebrity should have facilitated their renewed acquaintance, it was during the production of the 1860–61 edition of *Leaves* that the open antagonism between Whitman and Lowell unquestionably began. When Whitman came to Boston to work with Thayer and Eldridge, Emerson acted as his patron and secured reading privileges for him at the Boston Athenaeum; he even tried to take Whitman as a guest to the Saturday Club, a leading member of which was James Russell Lowell. Lowell, along with Longfellow and Oliver Wendell Holmes (both more influential at this time than Lowell), vetoed the proposed visit. The exact reasons were never placed on paper. Years later Whitman said, Emerson "was wrestled with, fought with, argued with, by the whole claque of them—the Boston second, third, raters."[108] Apparently, some of the "Fireside Poets" did not want to mingle socially with Whitman. Surely, there were rumors about the poet who was not yet good or gray. Some, like Norton, were doubtless intrigued by Whitman as an American primitive. Others, perhaps the majority, had strong reservations about Whitman's reputed character. Aside from the radical implications of his poetry, Whitman's self-proclaimed looseness in sexual matters (whatever the reality), placed his morals in question. He was also known to drink and consort with rough types, using obscene language.[109] It was not known whether Whitman possessed a sense of contextual decorum or whether he might precipitate some grotesque scene. Those who knew Whitman personally, like Emerson, found that he could be a soft-spoken, sensitive man; the protagonist of "Song of Myself" was an idealized American persona. But Emerson's opinion could not sway the prejudices of the other members formed by Whitman's descriptions of himself in his poetry: "I had pictured him proud, alert, grandiose, defiant of the usages of society; and I found him the quietest of men."[110] They may also have reacted defensively to Whitman's well-known abuse of Emerson's confidence. Four years earlier, he had published a line from Emerson's private letter, "I greet you at the beginning of a great career," on the spine of the 1856 edition of *Leaves*, after publishing the entire letter in the New York *Tribune*. Whitman was clearly an opportunist; he had no scruples about violating confidentiality for the sake of self-promotion. Who could be sure that their private remarks and personal gossip would be safe from the New York tabloids or the next appendix of *Leaves?* Although Lowell was one among several justified opponents of Whitman's social acceptance in Boston, he would later be held fully responsible for Whitman's exclusion from the Saturday Club.

Despite Whitman's populist pretensions, it seems clear that the rejection from the Saturday Club was a crushing blow that redoubled Whitman's working-class chauvinism. However, it is not clear that Whitman immediately attributed his exclusion to Lowell. Once again, in October 1861, Whitman submitted several poems to Lowell at the *Atlantic*, where Lowell was no longer the editor (either Whitman was not informed or expected Lowell to act on his behalf). Appropriately, Lowell passed them to James T. Fields, who was now editor, and who made the final decision not to publish them. Whitman probably assumed the rejection was from Lowell, even though it was signed, "The Editors." It must have seemed to Whitman that this rejection was related to his exclusion from the Saturday Club, but the rejection of the opening poems of what became *Drum-Taps* (1865) seems perfectly reasonable, given that the pro-war position of these poems would have been out of date by the time of publication (or so Fields thought). It was the last time of which I am aware that Whitman would seek Lowell's aid. Rejected by the Saturday Club, seemingly excluded from the *Atlantic*, the Boston edition of *Leaves* having failed to attract as large an audience as he had hoped (largely due to the onset of the Civil War), Whitman began to assemble a club of his own, with its own publications, and with himself as the object of the members' adulation, all the while claiming that he had been unfairly shunned by the literary establishment.

Lowell's foremost protégé, William Dean Howells, was the first person make a written comparison of Lowell and Whitman in 1860—the same year that the Saturday Club had declined to admit the author of *Leaves* but had opened its doors to the young Ohio poet. Howells had just published *Poems of Two Friends*, but he was better known as the campaign biographer of Abraham Lincoln. Making a tour of New York, Howells found Whitman at Pfaff's Cellar, the rowdy, subterranean center of New York's literary bohemia. Whitman described it as populated "by workmen and drivers," full of "the noises of coming and going, of drinking and oath and smutty jest."[111] Howell's describes his recollections of Pfaff's in *Literary Friends and Acquaintance*, "I remember that as I sat at that table under the pavement, in Pfaff's beer-cellar, I thought of the dinner with Lowell, the breakfast with Fields, the supper at the Autocrat's [Holmes], and felt that I had fallen very far."[112] Although he was recently from the Midwest, the ambitious Howells no more considered himself a provincial rustic than Whitman did when he taught at the Woodbury school; he presents his encounter with Whitman as slumming and, for many years, Howells would criticize Whitman in public, possibly acting as a mouthpiece for the private opinions of the leading Brahmin poets (who generally stayed above the fray), until he abandoned the setting for the rising sun, leaving Boston for New York in 1881.

Howells did not publish this account of his first encounter with Whitman until 1895 in *Harper's*, along with a telling illustration, which seems to have little relation to the rough tavern described by Whitman (Figure 6). Though the illustrator does depict the actual consumption of beer, and some rather slouchy postures indicative of boozy informality, the crowd seems decidedly middle-class, certainly not drivers or workmen. Although Whitman is dressed informally, without a necktie, his collar splayed open, he and the crowd around him appear considerably more refined and fashionably dressed than the patrons of Pfaff's would have appeared. In fact, the clothing is characteristic of the 1890s rather than the 1860s, particularly Whitman's

Figure 6. "The Meeting with Whitman." From W. D. Howells's *Literary Friends and Acquaintance* (New York, 1902).

square-toed boots and the bowler and straw-boater hats. Whitman appears jovial, possibly intoxicated, he doesn't make eye contact with the formal yet amiable Howells, who is more properly and fashionably dressed, almost an evocation of the surviving daguerreotypes of the younger Whitman. Whitman receives Howells, who bows and removes his hat; the hatless Whitman does not rise, but he shakes hands with Howells in a democratic fashion. He seems about to gesture Howells into the empty chair in the far right, to join him and his companions at a round table. Although Whitman is presented as informal and egalitarian, the overall quality of the image suggests the refined interiors of the Charles Dana Gibson's Gilded Age rather than the New York's antebellum bohemia. If this was a descent, then the illustrator for *Harper's* chose not to represent it as very precipitous. The sanitized Whitman of 1895 appeared without any suggestion of grosser immoralities for which he was known in 1860; instead, he is a Rabelaisian figure, a Gilded Age Bacchus as affable as Father Christmas and as harmless.

Although it was published many years after the event, Howells's encounter is significant not only because it is probably the earliest coupling of Whitman and Lowell in print but because it represents the ideological basis upon which Whitman's literary reputation would be catapulted skyward by the counterbalancing weight of

Lowell's status as a patrician enemy. During the next century in the development of American literature the comparison of Whitman and Lowell attained the persuasive force of a Biblical parable, and advocates of Whitman—who increased more rapidly than advocates of Lowell—used these comparisons to transfer symbolic capital from the Boston cultural hegemony, which they regarded as corrupted by political and economic influences, to Whitman, who seemed from his relatively powerless, impoverished position to contribute to the construction of a literary field that operated under an inversion of the structure of the field of power and thus enhanced its own autonomy.

III. "THE PROOF OF A POET"

Whitman presents the paradox of a reasonably popular local writer who largely abandoned journalism and fiction to write in the more highly consecrated, exclusive genre of poetry, all the while claiming that he wanted to reach a national audience. In the "Preface" to the first edition of *Leaves,* Whitman writes, "The proof of a poet is that his country absorbs him as affectionately as he has absorbed it."[113] From the beginning, Whitman expressed a desire to attain a national readership, to democratize the culture through his writings, particularly the American West, which he rightly regarded as less contaminated by the anti-democratic, elitist impulses of the Eastern literary establishment and as a rapidly expanding market for new forms of characteristically "American" literature (such as the popular works produced by writers such Mark Twain, Petroleum Nasby, and Bret Harte). Nevertheless, he continued to seek the approval and acceptance of the Eastern literary establishment, initially in Boston, when it was the arbiter of literary taste, and later in New York when it became the literary center. Throughout his long career, Whitman struggled to achieve a double success (both popularity and consecration) that was nearly impossible in the ante-bellum period and only became possible in a mitigated form with the rapid growth of an educated middle class of readers in the post-bellum period leading up to literary modernism. As the "Schoolroom Poets"—Longfellow, Whittier, Holmes, and Lowell—successfully marketed by Houghton Mifflin in the 1890s demonstrated, it eventually became possible to be both popular *and* consecrated—to seek an equilibrium point—among the growing middle classes that transformed the market from the clearly defined high/low, refined/vulgar categories of the early nineteenth century.

Partly as a result of writing poetry at a moment when the relationship between the field of literature and the field of power were in flux, critical readers of the early editions of *Leaves* perceived a dissonance in the typical mode of its production (small scale, artisanal) and the means of its promotion (market professional), between the actual audience for Whitman's poetry (small, intellectual, and usually affluent) and the audience he claimed to seek (large, uneducated, and working-class). Indeed, over the course of Whitman's career, the categories increasingly lost their meaning, as the public culture merged into a single, more-or-less homogeneous middle class culture. The resolution of this tension—between alternative modes of literary production and their corresponding modes of self-presentation—promoted, in part, Whitman's continual revision of *Leaves,* the personae, and the public relations campaigns constructed to support it between 1855 and 1892 as he adapted to the changing structure of the literary field, which was itself a reflection of the changing class structure. These tensions between competing versions of "Whitman"—as abandoned identities continued to exist alongside new ones—are also at the root of the ongoing struggle (both inside and outside of academic culture) to construct a stable, usable "Walt Whitman" out of ill-matched biographical fragments in order to appropriate his growing symbolic capital for varying ideological constituencies (Marxists, socialists, feminists, nationalists, gay rights advocates, and so on). The critical interpreters of Whitman often have chosen between the competing versions of the poet—artist or charlatan—without regard to the balanced, productive duality that enabled Whitman to achieve moderate popularity and some level of consecration without sacrificing one or the other entirely. On the whole, however, it was the persona of a mild subversive, the enemy of the older, established tradition of poetry, that gave Whitman an air of youth and rejuvenation to the modernists, who established their own power by elevating the rejected poets of their parents' generation.

It is remarkable that Whitman did not initially perceive an inherent contradiction between popularity and poetry. He appears to have believed that mass-market strategies, which successfully sold partisan newspapers and more than twenty thousand copies of his novel *Franklin Evans* in 1842, might also work when applied to *Leaves of Grass,* a self-published book of poetry, in 1855. This attitude is apparent in the reviews he wrote of his own work: "An American bard at last . . .We shall cease shamming and be what we really are."[114] Whitman's *obvious* self-reviews were probably not the result of ignorance or vanity; rather they were at least partly a form of ante-bellum, working-class humor, akin to the tall-tale. Cultivated readers, who valued humility and missed the comic wink, called Whitman a "humbug." Mass-market hype (that is, the aggressive marketing of an essentially worthless product) typically works against claims for serious stature in the cultural field (at least prior to the emergence of Pop Art in the 1950s, and perhaps never in the genre of poetry). Years later, William Sloane Kennedy rightly satirized the marketing of Whitman in Barnumian terms: "'Gentlemen, walk up and view the greatest poet on earth. We've captured him here in Philadelphia. We'll give you his dimensions in inches, cut him open and show his anatomy; and we've got a phonographic report of his talk. We show the whole animal, gentlemen.'"[115]

Had Whitman's chosen genre not depended on the reception of the cultural elite, the popular market might have appreciated the ironic, self-mocking undertone of Whitman's flyting and braggadocio as a species of the carnivalesque, a strategic inversion of conventional social hierarchies. Elite writers such as Lowell, who took the removal of poetry from marketplace considerations with the utmost seriousness, could not help but be offended by the manner of Whitman's self-promotion, which not only violated the bourgeois values of humility and honesty for the sake of popularity, but also threatened to complicate the generic hierarchy which placed poets like Lowell above mere journalists and writers of mass-market fiction. The typical response of such critics, including Lowell in particular, was to deny that *Leaves* was poetry at all and to refuse Whitman membership in their coteries without confronting him directly, pretending that he was beneath their notice.

Other qualities and habits derived from Whitman's experience as a popular journalist did not transfer well into his poetic career in the short-run, however they may have served him in the long-run: exaggerated personal attacks, the lack of scrupulosity in reprinting other people's private messages, the temptation to catch the latest political bandwagon, sensationalism in every form, looseness in appearance, language, modesty, sexual behavior, and immoderation in food and drink. All of these characteristics, much of which was associated with the freewheeling quality of working-class culture (Whitman as Falstaff), served to block his acceptance by the elite poets who lived by a middle-class code of restraint and self-discipline. Yet, until the 1880s, the elite audience constituted almost all Whitman's readership. As the reviewer for the *Critic* later said, "while he is an aggressive champion of democracy and the working-man, his admirers have been almost exclusively of a class the farthest possible removed from that which labors for daily bread by manual work. Whitman has always been truly caviare to the multitude."[116]

Although Whitman would increasingly capitalize on the inverse relation between artistic consecration and popular success, his initial strategy of self-presentation with *Leaves* in 1855 prevented him from attaining the symbolic capital he desired: the status of an "American bard," simultaneously popular *and* consecrated. He achieved neither aim to any great extent, but Whitman's self-promotion did provoke some discussion and controversy among elite readers such as Emerson, Lowell, Norton, Whittier, Alcott, and Thoreau, who regarded Whitman either as an authentic American primitive or a fraud, one of "sham-shaggy," as Lowell put it, who embarrassed the culture before foreign critics who wanted to imagine Americans as charming savages. In this respect, the first *Leaves* was a success: an unknown, socially unconnected writer attracted the attention (and some cases the support) of the restricted circles of elite literary production. Whereas a more modest attempt at poetry from a literary outsider (Dickinson, for example) might have simply been ignored, the radical implications of *Leaves* (whether sexual, formal, or promotional) contributed significantly towards Whitman's visibility as a poet; he demonstrated that, for an outsider to the cultural establishment, greater symbolic capital could be obtained as a Young Turk than as a shrinking violet. If he was not acknowledged as a poet as Lowell was from his first flowering, it was impossible for the literary establishment to ignore him, even if the general public was indifferent to Whitman's violations of literary decorum. Whitman's experience in journalism and politics revealed to him that, for those without much symbolic capital to lose, there is no such thing as bad publicity; unknown writers cannot be attacked without consecrating them. Whatever his ultimate aim, Whitman's use of the mass-market strategies secured his admission into the literary field.

Despite the many negative reviews the first edition of *Leaves* received, Whitman did not employ a rhetoric of exclusion at all in his publicity for the next edition in 1856. He did not deviate from his initial mass-market tactics, in fact, he intensified and redoubled them. He claimed that the first edition "readily sold," and he announced that after a "few years, and the average annual call for my Poems is ten or twenty thousand copes—more, quite likely."[117] In another review—calculated to refute claims that he was a sham working-class writer—Whitman describes himself as "a person singularly beloved and welcomed, especially by young men and mechanics."[118] Whitman fantasized that his next edition would be a success of the proportions of *Uncle Tom's Cabin* and that he would be in demand as a lecturer like Emerson, spreading the message of his "Great New Bible" all over the country.

When Fowler and Wells, America's leading phrenological publishers in New York, agreed to back Whitman for a second edition of *Leaves* in 1856, Whitman provided the following announcement:

> Walt Whitman's poems, the now famous 'Leaves of Grass,' would scarcely have been thought likely to become speedily popular. They came before the public unheralded, anonymous, and without the imprint of a publisher. Yet 'Leaves of Grass' found purchasers, appreciators, and admirers. . . . The emphatic commendation of America's greatest critic has been ratified by the public.[119]

Here, again, Whitman expresses a desire for both critical and commercial success: "the commendation of America's greatest critic" and "the public." Contrary to the myth of failure created by Whitman and his followers after the Civil War, the first edition of *Leaves* was not represented as a failure but a notable success.[120] Just as Barnum sold the Feejee Mermaid as an amazing fraud, readers were asked to wonder what they were missing and judge for themselves by buying a copy.

In the year after the first edition, Whitman was already attempting to strike a balance between the high and low markets in the material production of *Leaves,* telling Fowler and Wells, "I want a beautiful book, too, but I want that beautiful book cheap: that is, I want it to be within reach of the average buyer."[121] In format and size, the 1856 edition imitated closely the form of a popular edition of Longfellow's *Song of Hiawatha,* which was a bestseller at the time.[122] Whitman also insisted that *Leaves* was decidedly a book of poems not prose or "proems"; he numbered them and placed the word "Poem" in the title of each piece, and he made it clear that there was enough thematic variety to satisfy the tastes of almost every reader: "Poem of Faith," "Poem of Procreation," "Poem of Women," "Poem of You, Whoever You Are."

The 1856 edition, priced at a dollar, did not sell as many copies as Whitman hoped; it was often placed "under the counter" with pornography rather than on the shelves with Longfellow where the readers of poetry would typically browse. Most of the advertising for the book appeared in the phrenological journal published by Fowler and Wells, and there were almost no reviews of this edition, except for those written by Whitman himself. In the 1856 "Preface" he rightly revised his prospects, "the proof of the poet shall be sternly deferr'd till his country absorbs him as affectionately as he has absorbed it."[123]

Whitman's publicly avowed devotion to Emerson in the second edition was another sign of the ambivalence of his approach to popular and elite audiences. Indeed, the signs were strongest that he increasingly intended to reach, however unprofitably, an elite readership. In 1856 Bronson Alcott, Thoreau, and Sarah Tyndale all came to Brooklyn to pay their respects. Although the cheaper edition of *Leaves* did not find a popular audience after 1856, by 1860 Whitman seems to have increasingly thought of himself as a potential peer of the literary elites of Boston, which was affirmed by the friendship of Emerson, the publication of the third edition of *Leaves* in Boston, and the acceptance of "Bardic Symbols" by the *Atlantic Monthly*. Of course, this dream would be partly shattered by Whitman's exclusion from the Saturday Club at he moment when he was most ripe for such acceptance.

Although Emerson could not persuade him to tone down the sexual content of his poems, Whitman's replacement of the bold, almost arrogant engraving of himself in the 1855 and 1856 editions with a more genteel image (Figure 7) that resembles Lowell or, perhaps, Longfellow, suggests how close Whitman was to identifying himself with the high literary culture he was struggling to join in Boston. The 1860–61 version of Whitman, with its Byronic pose, curly hair, and fashionable cravat, seems so antithetical to the 1855 engraving (Figure 1) that seems like an embarrassing attempt to represent himself as part of the elite culture. Despite the introduction of still more populist celebrations of "comradeship" (perhaps in response to increasing sectional tensions), the 1860–61 edition was described by Whitman in yet another self-review not as a work for the masses but as a work of "sumptuous elegance . . . one of the richest specimens of taste and skill in book-making, that has ever been afforded to the public by either an English or an American publisher."[124]

Again, while he sought this elite audience in Boston in terms of the choice of publisher, the frontispiece, and the quality of the production, Whitman was still motivated by the potential for popularity and economic gain: "The market needs today to be supplied—the great West especially— with *copious thousands* of copies."[125] And Thayer and Eldridge offered him just that: "we can and will sell a large number of copies. . . . We can do you good—pecuniarily."[126] In the midst of this effort, Whitman told his brother Jeff that the new *Leaves* would be "a valuable investment, increasing by months and years, not going off in a rocket way, (like 'Uncle Tom's Cabin')."[127] He had, apparently, scaled down his ambitions for raw sales as he courted, once again, a more elite readership.

The Fowler and Wells edition was Whitman's greatest success up to that time in terms of press coverage, although he would vanish utterly from the public eye in the following year with the onset of the Civil War. By 1861–62, with the initial promise of third edition proving a complete failure, his brusque rejection from the Saturday Club, and the rejection of "Beat Beat Drums!" from the *Atlantic Monthly*, Whitman would permanently abandon his efforts to cultivate the Boston elite by

Figure 7. Walt Whitman, c. 1860.
From *Leaves of Grass* (Boston:
Thayer and Eldridge, 1860–61).

direct appeal. It is significant that he would never again reprint the 1860–61 engraving, but it is also significant that he would not reprint the 1855 frontispiece again until 1880–81—not as the frontispiece, but rather as part of "Song of Myself," a sign of strategic distancing from his earlier self. Increasingly Whitman would emphasize his protean qualities through the motif of the butterfly, which appeared at the end of the 1860–61 edition and reappeared in a literal form (and Whitman always claimed it was a *real* butterfly that landed on his finger) in a promotional *carte-de-visite* for the 1880–81 edition. After 1860–61, Whitman would resist the depiction of himself as either a workman or an elevated poet; he would, instead, increasingly present himself as in a state of becoming or duality. In so doing, he continued to strive for an equilibrium point between the literary consecration of the avant-garde and the popularity and economic benefits of an expanded readership.

Contrary to the early myth of success (which he knew was a false front), Whitman began to accumulate symbolic capital by presenting himself as one who has fallen from position, who has sacrificed everything—particularly wealth and popularity—for the purity of his art: "From 1845 to 1855," he writes in an anonymous self-review published in 1876, "Whitman bade fair to be a good business man, and to make his mark and fortune in the usual way—owned several houses, was worth some money and 'doing well.' But, about the latter date, he suddenly abandoned all, and commenced writing poems."[128] It was the reverse of the American self-made man narrative, but it was an exact parallel to the Christian narrative of redemptive self-sacrifice. And the postbellum cult of Lincoln, whom Whitman regarded as so akin to himself, was one means by which Whitman found a wider audience. Even while presenting himself as a failure, rejected by the bourgeoisie, he would increasingly represent himself as a harmless storyteller and patriot, a kind of Civil War veteran on tour. He made it appear that he was persecuted by elites such as James Russell Lowell (who had not served in the war), even as his work changed to become acceptable to a middlebrow audience who scarcely remembered the earlier persona panned by the elite critics. It made the enmity of Lowell (which Whitman constantly proclaimed to anyone who would listen) seem like a sacrilege against the sacred cause of the Union, embodied by Lincoln, which dominated the public discourse of the postbellum period.

IV. "O CAPTAIN! MY CAPTAIN!"

The "Death of Abraham Lincoln," particularly Whitman's practice of concluding the performance with "O Captain! My Captain!," is usually considered a regrettable rejection of Whitman's earlier pose as the defiant workman-poet of *Leaves* (1855). In his discussion of the Lincoln lectures, for example, Kerry Larson laments, "nothing could more severely point up the decline into mental and creative lethargy overtaking Whitman's later years than such hackneyed sentiments," all of which seem "a weak and distant echo of ambitions embraced and articulated far more energetically at the outset of his career."[129] At the end of his career, the poet who presented himself in *Leaves* as the ideal American, the equal of any President, came to present himself as Lincoln's avuncular eulogizer. But Whitman's final act of subordination to the demands of the expanding literary marketplace was a logical outgrowth and intertwining of his life-long political beliefs and his skill as a self-promoter. Whitman presented Lincoln as the redeemer of the promise of American democracy, which had been threatened with the outbreak of the Civil War and compromised by the widening class disparities of the Gilded Age. Although these performances threatened to desecrate Whitman's image, particularly among the modernists, they initially served the opposite function: to purify Whitman's image by appropriating the consecrated status of Lincoln. Ultimately, it was Whitman's celebration of Lincoln instead of himself that facilitated his ascent from the depths of notoriety to the heights of fame.

After the Civil War, Whitman refashioned himself as an interpreter of Lincoln partly to secure a wider readership for *Leaves of Grass*, but his lecture, "The Death of Abraham Lincoln," and his poem, "O Captain! My Captain!," were not simply a crass capitulation to Victorian sentimentalism and American nationalism; rather, they were the complex outgrowth of Whitman's life-long democratic idealism and his personal admiration for Lincoln which emerged during the years in which Whitman probably lost much of his hope for *Leaves of Grass* as a prophetic text. Initially, *Drum-Taps*, the collection that contains the Lincoln poems, was conceived as new direction in Whitman's career, even though it was eventually absorbed by the *Leaves* project.

On leave from his clerkship in Washington, DC, Walt Whitman was visiting his mother in Brooklyn when Lincoln was assassinated on Good Friday, April 14, 1865. They heard the news early on Saturday morning:

> Mother prepared breakfast—and other meals afterwards—as usual; but not a mouthful was eaten all day by either of us. We each drank half a cup of coffee; that was all. Little was said. We got every newspaper morning and evening, and the frequent extras of that period, and passed them silently to each other.[130]

It rained all that day. Late in the afternoon Whitman crossed the East River by ferry and walked up Broadway. Many of the windows were draped with black bunting, flags hung at half-mast, and people sheltered in doorways avoiding occasional downpours. Recalling that day in his notebook, Whitman writes, "Lincoln's death—black, black, black—as you look toward the sky—long broad black serpents slowly undulating in every direction."[131] All the stores were closed, and the streets were nearly empty—a striking contrast to what the poet had seen four years earlier, at the time of Lincoln's inauguration. Then the streets had been bustling, "crowded with solid masses of people, many thousands."[132] As he walked up Broadway, Whitman passed the Astor House where he had first seen the now martyred President.

One of Lincoln's many stops on the twelve-day trip from Springfield, Illinois, to the White House was on 19 February 1861, in New York City, then a nest of hostile "Copperheads" who violently opposed Lincoln's pro-Union militancy. Whitman was there that day, observing the President-elect from the top of an omnibus stuck in the gridlocked traffic; "I had, I say, a capital view of it all, and especially of Mr. Lincoln." After Lincoln's assassination, Whitman recalled, "I have no doubt, (so frenzied were the ferments of the time,) many an assassin's knife and pistol lurked in hip or breast-pocket there, ready, soon as break and riot came." This first encounter with Lincoln, an apparently defenseless but defiant man as endangered as the Union he represented, made a lasting impression on Whitman: "this scene, and him in it, are indelibly stamped upon my recollection," he writes.[133]

Whitman's memories of Lincoln gathered specific but widely resonant images and associations, which led quite directly to his memorial poems. The day after Whitman first saw the President-elect, he heard him respond to an angry challenge posed by New York Mayor Fernando Wood, who thought the South should be permitted to secede. Lincoln responded:

> I understand a ship to be made for the carrying and preservation of the cargo, and so long as the ship can be saved, with the cargo it should never be abandoned. This Union should likewise never be abandoned unless it fails and the probability of its preservation shall cease to exist without throwing the passengers and cargo overboard.[134]

Lincoln's speech was printed in the *New York Herald* and the *Tribune* on 21 February, both of which were read regularly by Whitman. Over the next four years,

Whitman began to visualize Lincoln as a mariner, as the weather-beaten captain of the "Ship of State":

> Perhaps the reader has seen physiognomies (often of old farmers, *sea captains*, and such) that, behind their homeliness, or even ugliness, held superior points so subtle, yet so palpable, making the real life of their faces almost as impossible to depict . . . such was Lincoln's face [my emphasis].[135]

Whitman would later say of Lincoln, "He reminds me most often of a captain—a great captain—chosen for a tempestuous voyage—everything against him—wind, tide, current, terrible odds—untried seas—balking courses: yet a man equal to all emergencies."[136]

In 1865, when the poet's thoughts turned to the assassinated President, this image of Lincoln as "Captain," first launched in 1861, was almost certainly reinforced in Whitman's mind by published stories about Lincoln's dreams prior to his assassination. Secretary of the Navy, Gideon Welles, wrote that Lincoln had a recurring dream in which he saw himself commanding "some singular, indescribable vessel, moving with great rapidity towards an indefinite shore."[137] Now, after more than four years in which the Union seemed lost, Lincoln had guided the ship of state into port, only to fall victim to the hidden pistol Whitman had anticipated long before. By the time of his assassination, Lincoln had not only built the political foundation for his canonization in the American civil religion, but he had even suggested the poetic metaphors by which he would be commemorated. Before long, Whitman, newly refashioned as the "Good, Gray Poet," would develop this latent image of Lincoln in the most popular poem ever written on the Union's fallen helmsman: "O Captain! my Captain!"

By Monday morning, April 17, Whitman was back in Washington, but his office at the Department of the Interior was closed. On Tuesday, Lincoln lay in state in the East Room of the White House, his coffin banked with lilacs, which were just coming into bloom. Although he did not attend the funeral on Wednesday, Whitman watched the vast procession passing through Washington while composing a new poem, "Hushed Be the Camps To-day." As the funeral train bore Lincoln back to Springfield, reversing the route taken to the Capital in 1861, Whitman, along with hundreds of other poets, writers, journalists, and clergymen, was fast at work on a series of poems that would soon form the "Sequel to *Drum-Taps.*"

Poems commemorating the martyrdom of Lincoln quickly became a popular sub-genre. There were scores of them in the newspapers by Sunday; soon afterwards there were hundreds. Perhaps no event in American history produced so great an outpouring of verse.[138] "Never had the nation mourned so over a fallen leader," writes Stephen Oates, "Not only Lincoln's friends, but his legion of critics—those who denounced him in life, castigated him as a dictator, ridiculed him as a baboon, damned him as stupid and incompetent—now lamented his death and grieved for this country."[139] Artist D. T. Wiest even replaced the head of Washington with

Lincoln's head in John James Barralet's famous engraving, *Apotheosis of George Washington*, changing the title to *In Memory of Abraham Lincoln: The Reward of the Just*. In homes and schoolhouses across the nation, Lincoln's portrait gradually took its place beside Washington, now second in the hearts of his countrymen. Chatting with a wounded solider on 28 May 1865, Whitman was surprised to find that even some Confederates had revised their opinion: "Take him altogether, he was the best man this country ever produced. It was quite awhile I thought very different; but some time before the murder, that's the way I have seen it."[140]

Whitman apparently felt a genuine admiration and affection for this President who seemed so akin to his own idealized self-representations: a common but heroic man who incarnates his nation and articulates its most deeply held beliefs. The poet immediately knew that *Drum-Taps*, his account of the Civil War, would be incomplete without some mention of his "Captain." Moreover, there were burgeoning opportunities in the sale of remembrances of Lincoln: poems, prints, essays, biographies, monuments, and lectures. In the coming decades, political careers would be built on Lincoln and his rhetoric, for everything and everyone connected with him became sacrosanct. As Daniel Aaron observes, "To quarrel with Lincoln was to quarrel with America."[141] After Lincoln's death, Whitman surely saw an opportunity both to honor the man with whom he felt a strong kinship and a means to capitalize on the greatest outpouring of public grief and fascination in his lifetime, and, in the process, to revise further his formerly unsuccessful public persona. Initially, Whitman may have only expected to improve his standing as a poet by capitulating to mainstream political and poetic values, but, after the success of "O Captain!" and the ongoing relative failure of *Leaves*, Whitman attempted in the years after 1866 to position himself as a friend of Lincoln, a comparable type, and his foremost interpreter.

Although Whitman began to cast himself as a commercial failure by the end of the Civil War period, he remained concerned with material and popular success. After 1861 Whitman had difficulty finding work as an editor or journalist; he had given up all hope of joining the lyceum circuit, and the literary acclaim he desired continued to elude him. A sinecure had been obtained for him (through Emerson's endorsement) as a petty bureaucrat in Washington, DC, after he relocated there in search of his brother, whom he thought was wounded at the Battle of Fredericksburg. Whitman found solace as a volunteer nurse in Washington's hospitals during the Civil War and in the hope that the poems inspired by these experiences would prove more successful than *Leaves*, which he once expected, "to be a valuable investment." That success never materialized, but in 1863 Whitman had another plan; he wrote publisher James Redpath, "My Idea is a book of the time—something considerably beyond mere hospital sketches—a book for sale in a larger American market."[142] As *Drum-Taps* began to take shape in 1864, Whitman wrote his mother, "I think it may be a success pecuniarily."[143] He told Nelly O'Connor, "I want it to have a large sale."[144] And, by 1865 Whitman was determined to make his forthcoming book bring him the wealth he needed and acclaim he deserved, even if that meant submitting to more conventional tastes in form and subject matter.

By 1 April 1865, Whitman made arrangements to print 500 copies of *Drum-Taps*, but he halted production on 17 April, two days after Lincoln's death, to insert the short poem "Hush'd Be the Camps Today." By 1 May, he stopped printing *Drum-Taps* altogether in order to complete a more extensive tribute to Lincoln. During the summer Whitman labored over his Lincoln poems, and by October 1865, *Drum-Taps* had a twenty-four page addendum, "Sequel to *Drum-Taps*." The "Sequel" contained four poems about Lincoln, one of which would be regarded by many as Whitman's greatest poem, another as his most popular.

The first and longest poem in the "Sequel," "When Lilacs Last in the Dooryard Bloom'd," is, in part, a recapitulation of the resignation expressed near the end of *Drum-Taps*, particularly in "Reconciliation." "Lilacs" attempts to reconstruct the voice of the poet, embodied by the thrush, whose song has become inadequate in the face of seemingly meaningless tragedy, the death of Lincoln symbolized by the "powerful western fallen star."[145] The poetic response is the regenerative symbol of the lilac, "With every leaf a miracle," which the poet places on Lincoln's coffin, itself a symbol of universal death: "With loaded arms I come, pouring for you, / For you and the coffins all of you O death."[146] Ultimately, the poet regains his voice through an intertwining with other voices, a mystical union that parallels the rebirth of the nation. "Lilac and star and bird," he writes, "twined with the chant of my soul."[147] The dialectical struggle between death and rebirth is resolved through the poet's grief, just as the divided Union is restored by the redemptive sacrifice of Lincoln and hundreds of thousands of soldiers. As Whitman would observe later in his lecture on Lincoln, "Strange, (is it not?) that battles, martyrs, agonies, blood, even assassination, should so condense—perhaps only really, lastingly condense—a Nationality."[148]

"Lilacs" was central to the reconstruction of Whitman's persona as a poet in the post-bellum period. It theorizes the reconstruction his poetic voice, and it presents the poet as the "perennial" mourner of the nation's "first great Martyr Chief":

> When lilacs last in the dooryard bloom'd
> And the great star early droop'd in the western sky in the night,
> I mourned, and yet shall mourn with ever returning spring.[149]

Although it was postponed by sickness and other personal inconveniences for over a decade after the publication of *Drum-Taps*, Whitman would eventually follow through on this pledge to "morn with ever returning spring" in his lecture on "The Death of Abraham Lincoln."

As Justin Kaplan observes, with *Drum-Taps* Whitman "became a more biddable poet, more accommodating in his pursuit of acceptance, willing to risk less."[150] Despite its relatively recent canonization, there was nothing sacred about "Lilacs" to its author. On 22 November 1867, Whitman wrote his English publisher William

Michael Rossetti about the production of an expurgated edition of *Leaves* and said, "When I have my next edition brought out here, I shall change the title of the piece 'When lilacs last in the dooryard bloom'd,' to *President Lincoln's Funeral Hymn*."[151] That year the comparatively successful *Drum-Taps* and the "Sequel"—now advertising its contents with the title "President Lincoln's Burial Hymn"—were annexed to *Leaves*; by 1872 they were incorporated as part of a transformed package that included their author.

Viewed in this promotional context, the poem that follows "Lilacs" in the "Sequel" is not so inexplicable, although the lurid imagery of "O Captain! My Captain," with its "bleeding drops of red," certainly provides a dramatic contrast to the more understated response to tragedy in "Lilacs." The conventional form of "O Captain!" also violates everything for which Whitman seemed to stand as a poet who resisted the strictures of regular meter, rhyme, and stanza pattern. Moreover, in "O Captain!" Whitman places himself in a subordinate position to another man, which seems to mark a change in the egocentric persona of "Song of Myself" in which the poet asks, "Have you outstript the rest? are you the President? / It is a trifle."[152]

While the poet of "Lilacs" and "O Captain!" seems inconsistent with the "American Bard" of 1855, they reflect Whitman's awareness of the demands of the literary marketplace ten years later. Just as Whitman arranges for the mass publication of cheap, expurgated editions of *Leaves* in 1867, so he constructs a bridge to more conservative readers by submitting to their limitations. If critics could be persuaded to accept "O Captain!," which is almost a parody of the kind of poetry appreciated by Whitman's critics, then, perhaps, they could be coaxed into revising their opinion of the immoral author of *Leaves of Grass*.

Paradoxically, while Whitman appears to subordinate himself in "O Captain!," the title of the entire collection of poems, *Walt Whitman's Drum-Taps*, suggests something else: from this point forward the name of the author, unlike the anonymous *Leaves* of 1855, takes precedence to the title of the book itself. *Leaves* was no longer the poem of "an American," it was the work of a specific, differentiated individual who seemed less willing to assume the role of spokesman for an America so radically different from the nation that had produced him. Although "O Captain" was a song of subordination in the context of a sequence of poems that suggested the limitations of the poet's vision in relation to the larger forces of cultural development, the packaging of the larger project increasingly asserted Whitman's claims on the status of America's poet laureate.

When Whitman finally published *Drum-Taps*, his work was received with cautious approval. The Lincoln poems, if not the others, were reviewed indulgently, particularly "O Captain!" William Dean Howells published one of the first reviews on 11 November 1865:

> The time to denounce or to ridicule Mr. Whitman for his first book is past
> . . . . There were reasons in the preponderant beastliness of that book why a

decent public should reject it; but now the poet has cleansed the old channels of their filth, and pours through them a stream of blameless purity, and the public has again to decide, and this time more directly, on the question of his poethood.[153]

Following Howells's lead, on 15 October 1866, Moncure D. Conway of the *Fortnightly Review,* praised *Drum-Taps:* "This volume is entirely free from the peculiar deductions to which the other is liable . . . There is in this volume a very touching dirge for Abraham Lincoln,—who was his warm friend and admirer."[154] (Whitman never corrected Conway's and others' belief that he had a personal relationship with Lincoln.) Many critics offered cautious approval of "Lilacs"; nearly all praised "O Captain!," and the relative enthusiasm for Whitman's Lincoln poems led to grudging acceptance by some of the more unconventional poems of *Drum-Taps.* Undoubtedly, Whitman believed that the incorporation of *Drum-Taps* in the hastily produced 1867 *Leaves* would improve the standing of the earlier poems as well.

V. "THEY ARE ALL AGAINST ME!"

As he was preparing *Drum-*Taps, Whitman's career as a petty bureaucrat came to an abrupt but artistically advantageous end. In a general housecleaning at the Department of the Interior, James Harlan fired Whitman from his clerkship, along with at least eighty other employees on 30 June 1865. When pressed for a reason, Harlan justified the dismissal on the grounds of Whitman's "moral character" as the author of an obscene book, *Leaves of Grass.*[155] There was nothing unusually malicious about Whitman's dismissal, but now the poet had dedicated supporters who rallied to his defense, proclaiming him an incorruptible artist and prophet struggling against official censorship.

Under Whitman's direction, William D. O'Connor spearheaded a grass-roots promotional campaign by publishing a small book, *The Good Gray Poet: A Vindication,* in 1866. As Kaplan observes, for disciples like O'Connor, Whitman's dismissal "involved a messianic pattern of gospel, persecution and passion"; the termination represented an attack on the very liberties preserved at unprecedented cost by the triumph of the Union.[156] O'Connor, a staunch early Progressive, encouraged Whitman to represent *Leaves* as a work in collision with the most obvious representative of the field of power: the federal government. Whitman was now an enemy of the state, while, at the same time, he was the friend and embodiment of the common people; like Lincoln, with whom he claimed to have so much in common, he was the victim of elitist conspiracies.[157]

For all his populist rhetoric, O'Connor may be viewed as one of the agents of the increasing separation of high literature from the economic or popular sphere (O'Connor was also an outspoken supporter of Edgar Allan Poe, whose status as a literary genius was also rising as the myth of his victimization and neglect gained currency).[158] Emphasizing the cultural intersection between the fields of charismatic religion and literature, Carpenter likened Whitman to Christ and made persecution the basis for Whitman's future consecration. The firing of Whitman (like the assassination of Lincoln on Good Friday) was literally compared with the crucifixion: "God grant that not in vain upon this outrage do I invoke the judgment of the mighty spirit of literature."[159] O'Connor's "Good Gray Poet" also began the myth of Whitman's noble poverty: "Walt Whitman is poor;—he is poor, and has a right to be proud of his poverty, for it is the sacred, the ancient, the immemorial poverty of goodness and genius."[160]

The Good, Gray Poet surely contributed to the heightening of Whitman's public profile in 1866. Whether it sold more copies of *Leaves* is unclear from surviving records; likely it did and set a precedent for the promotion of *Leaves* in 1876 and 1881. This event marks a transformation of the persona and promotional pattern Whitman would follow until the end of his life and his followers would sustain afterwards. Over the next decade claims of Whitman's persecution became increasingly shrill and insistent. Robert Buchanan, for example, published a supportive essay in the *Broadway Magazine* in 1867: "The grossest abuse on the part of the majority, and the wildest panegyric on the part of a minority, have for many years been heaped on the shoulders of the man who rests his claim for judgment on [*Leaves*]."[161] Oddly, such claims were being made at the moment when Whitman was beginning to be celebrated as a patriot for his Lincoln poems.

Coordinated with the poetry of the "Sequel," *The Good Gray Poet* simultaneously promoted *Drum-Taps* while proclaiming Whitman the foremost poetic interpreter of Lincoln:

> There is a single poem ['Lilacs'] in the late volume, which, if the author had never written another line, would be sufficient to place him among the chief poets of the world. . . . Emperors might well elect to die, could their memories be surrounded with such a requiem, which, next to the grief and love of the people, is the grandest and *the only grand funeral music* poured around Lincoln's bier.[162]

Several years later, when Lowell was proclaimed by many critics to have written the greatest poetic summation of the Civil War and tribute to Lincoln in his "Commemoration Ode," Whitman would claim: "Lincoln is particularly my man—particularly belongs to me."[163]

Lowell, however, was not converted by the new, and improved, Lincolnized Whitman, and, as a result, he played right into the hands of the Whitmanites, who were looking for villains against whom they could juxtapose their hero. In an 1866 review of Howell's *Venetian Life*, Lowell praised the book as a "natural product, as perfectly natural as the deliberate attempt of 'Walt Whitman' to answer the demand of native and foreign misconception was perfectly artificial."[164] Two years after this attack, in a review of the *Poems of John J. Piatt*, Lowell did not mention Whitman directly but derided the notion of the primitive American poet Whitman tried to represent: "Shaggy he was to be, brown-fisted, careless of proprieties, unhampered by tradition, his Pegasus of the half-horse, half-alligator breed." Lowell continues,

"Of the sham-shaggy . . . we have had quite enough, and may safely doubt whether this satyr of masquerade is to be our representative singer."[165] Surely, Lowell was thinking of Whitman in these remarks (though he is careful not to mention him), and they enraged Whitman's followers. O'Connor wrote to Fields on 24 November 1868, "after reading Mr. Lowell's review of Piatt's poems in the last *North American*, in which Mr. Whitman is elaborately insulted through two pages and pointedly referred to as 'a sham hero' and 'a satyr in masquerade' I really haven't the face to approach him on the subject, and shall not."[166] Although the relationship between Whitman and Lowell had been a subject of speculation for at least five years, these two reviews provoked Whitman's supporters into creating a myth of Lowell as "the chief of staff in the army of the devil," as Whitman put it.[167] Lowell was Lucifer to Whitman's Jesus. Several additional circumstances began to facilitate comparisons with Lowell, in particular, Lowell's rising status as the poet laureate of the Civil War.

While Whitman's war poetry was lightly praised, in 1869 a critic for *The Nation* said that Lowell's "[Commemoration Ode] by itself it ought to silence those grumblers in America who think their country has no poet."[168] In 1891 C. T. Winchester would write, Lowell's "Commemoration Ode is the one great classic poem produced by our Civil War."[169] On the other hand, Whitman's status as a Civil War poet gained steadily after beginning the Lincoln Lectures in the late 1870s. Brander Matthews writes, "No one of the many tributes to Lincoln, not even Lowell's noble eulogy, is more deeply charged with exalted feeling than Whitman's 'O Captain, My Captain.'"[170] Bliss Perry, an editor of the *Atlantic,* declared that Whitman's "Lilacs" "remains, with Lowell's *Commemoration Ode*, as the finest imaginative product of the Civil War period."[171] And, according to John Macy, "The best of all his [Lowell's] verse, except that in dialect, is the passage about Lincoln in the 'Commemoration Ode'; it is so good that it ought to be great, but the light fades from it when it is put beside Whitman's elegies."[172] Many of these printed comparisons appeared after Whitman's death, but, as his allusion to Lowell's "Ode" in his Lincoln Lectures suggests, Whitman was aware that his Civil War poetry was being compared favorably with Lowell's. Whitman said, perhaps disingenuously, "I too, have often known them put together: but could never see the reason why—except, perhaps, as being upon the same subject."[173] He also complained, "Stedman thinks I should be happy to have my Lincoln poem classed Lowell's ode. I am happy, of course—am bound to be happy—but not for the reason Stedman cites, I can assure you: and yet I do not consider the Lincoln poem the best of them."[174] By 1912 Truman H. Bartlett would try to deny Lowell's status as a Civil War poet and interpreter of Lincoln: "Lowell was the only man," he writes, "who apologized for Lincoln's homeliness, in his odes, and especially in his Birmingham address."[175] This rivalry between Lowell's "Ode" and Whitman's "O Captain!" would continue until both were swept away by modernist revisionism—most notably summarized in Edmund Wilson's *Patriotic Gore* (1962)—and "Lilacs" became *the* major poem of the American Civil War.

As Whitman's productive association with Lincoln increased in the early 1870s, he made plans to write a book about him, but a stroke in 1873 forced him to settle for *Memoranda During the War* (1875), a quickly assembled collection of excerpts from his diaries. Once again, Whitman intended the book "for sale perhaps in a larger American market," hopefully becoming "a lion in the way—$."[176] Probably the most memorable part of *Memoranda* is "The Death of Abraham Lincoln," which is presented as if Whitman had actually been present at Ford's Theater. Although very few copies of *Memoranda* were actually printed, Whitman included the text in *Two Rivulets* the following year and succeeded in getting the *New York Sun* to publish "The Death of Lincoln" as a separate piece on 12 February 1876, where it attracted considerable attention, particularly when Whitman succeeded in launching a press war between England and United States over the abuse he had supposedly suffered at the hands of the American public in general and Lowell in particular.

Whitman's increasingly ill health, which he represented as the outcome of Civil War service, contributed to the claim that he was also a neglected war hero deserving a pension. Whitman tried to sustain the image in *Harper's New Monthly Magazine* (probably the most popular middle-class magazine in the United States at that time) in March 1874, in "Prayer of Columbus," an obviously autobiographical poem in which he describes himself as "A batter'd, wreck'd old man, / Thrown on this savage shore, far, far from home." Again he presents himself as a Jeremiah or a Christ figure, a prophet rejected in his own country. He thought of writing an autobiography called, *Idle Days & Nights of a Half-Paralytic*.[177] And, on 26 January 1876, Whitman published an anonymous article in the *West Jersey Press*: "Walt Whitman's Actual American Position." The article claimed Whitman's poems "have been met, and are met today, with the determined denial, disgust and scorn of orthodox American authors, publishers and editors, and, in a pecuniary and worldly sense, have certainly *wrecked* [my emphasis] the life of their author."[178] Whatever the faults of *Leaves of Grass,* Whitman, it seems, was more sinned against than sinning.

The article provoked little attention, but Whitman sent a copy of it to William Rossetti (publisher of an expurgated English edition of *Leaves* in 1868), encouraging him to publish it. It appeared in the London *Athenaeum* on March 11, coordinated with another letter from Buchanan in the London *Daily News* on March 13 exposing how Whitman had been abused by American publishers, and now, paralyzed and prematurely aged from his Civil War services, he lived in poverty in Camden, presumably perishing in the streets. A pastiche of exaggerations, the article was reprinted several times and provoked a response from the United States that included at least twenty-five articles. With the aid of Rossetti and Buchanan, Whitman had capitalized on Americans' ongoing sense of cultural inferiority to England and on the English desire to assert their superiority over American Philistines. They also tapped into the growing trans-Atlantic progressive impulse that overlapped significantly with the literary avant garde in demanding free expression as well state subsidy for authors, the elderly, the infirm, and veterans, all of which Whitman claimed to represent.

While most American critics denied that Whitman was persecuted, English critics such as Buchanan appropriated the religious tone of O'Connor's defense of Whitman: "As Christ had His crown of thorns, and as Socrates had his hemlock cup. So Walt Whitman has his final glory and doom even though it come miserably in the shape of literary outlawry and official persecution."[179] As donations and reporters poured into Camden from England and America, Whitman was forced to retract his claims of abject poverty.[180] He published a letter in the *New York Tribune* on April 22, stating, "the admitted facts are these: He is old, even less with years than noble service; his labors and emotions in the hospitals of the war have left him paralyzed; and he lives, wholly without personal means, in a humble dwelling of a relative."[181] It was all true, in other words, except that he did have a comfortable place to live. In this letter, however, Whitman implicates Lowell in his suffering:

> You think it mere 'recklessness' in him [Buchanan] to charge that the literary class of America persecute our poet . . . but we can show Mr. Buchanan a Cambridge dinner party, uniting with the very distinguished American author, their host, to persuade an English gentleman not to present the letter of introduction he bore from an eminent English nobleman, by representing that Mr. Whitman, to whom it was addressed, was 'nothing but a low New-York rowdy'—'A common street blackguard.' Is it not 'persecution' to insolently meddle with one's private letters, to intercept foreign visitors, and to give a man of 'fine humanity and integrity' such a character as the epithets and adjectives I have cited convey?[182]

Buchanan was more direct, writing "could someone tell me how much sympathy either Mr. Lowell or Mr. Longfellow, or any other wealthy and influential singer, has shown for the great Poet and Martyr who now lies neglected, insulted, 'old and paralysed,' at Camden dedicating his completed work, as another great poet and martyr did before him, 'To Time.'"[183]

The rumor that Lowell had turned away a distinguished English visitor reached Whitman in a comparatively mild form as early as 1865 when he was told by John Townsend Trowbridge, described by Whitman as "one who was present—was friendly—did not share Lowell's feeling."[184] But, just as Harlan's routine dismissal of Whitman had become magnified over the years, by 1876 this account had increased in detail and intensity. By 1888 the story had expanded to grotesque proportions in Whitman's memory:

> He [Whitman] repeated the story of the nobleman whom Lowell turned back. 'He came over here with a letter of introduction from some man of high standing in England—Rosetti, William Rosetti, I guess. . . . There was the Cambridge dinner: there were many of the swell fellows present: the man I speak of was the principal guest. In the course of their dinner he mentioned his letter to me. Lowell, who had a couple of glasses of wine—was flushed—called out: "What! a letter for Walt Whitman! For God Almighty's sake don't deliver it! Walt Whitman! Do you know who Walt Whitman is? Why—Walt Whitman

is a rowdy, a New York tough, a loafer, a frequenter of low places—friend of cab drivers!"—and all that.'[185]

Although it is the most widely reprinted account of Lowell's persecution of Whitman, I have found no reliable evidence to prove that it is even partially true. The English visitor, who was actually Monckton Milnes (afterward Lord Houghton) was impressed by Swinburne's admiration for Whitman in his biography of William Blake. Milnes did not actually visit the United States but sent Whitman a letter of greeting through an emissary who dined first with the Cambridge literati. Trowbridge was not at this dinner, but Emerson told him that the emissary had been dissuaded from calling on Whitman to deliver the letter because, as Emerson said, "Whitman had not used me well in the matter of letters, he did not deliver it."[186] Whitman's abuse of Emerson in 1856 had come back to haunt him a decade later; again, how could the emissary be sure that his patron's private letter would not appear in the *New York Tribune*? Though Lowell was known to disparage Whitman at some of these Cambridge dinners, it is not clear that Lowell was the one who dissuaded the emissary (though the dinner may have taken place at his house), anymore than it is clear who blackballed Whitman from the Saturday Club in 1860. It seems just as probable, based on other second-hand evidence, that Oliver Wendell Holmes offered the admonition.

Nevertheless, from 1876 forward, other interested parties also embellished upon this story of Lowell's deliberate malice. In 1906, for example, in a *New York Times Book Review* article, Katherine Hillard changed the story dramatically, making Lowell into a Dickensian villain denying Whitman access to his noble inheritance, that is, recognition by the European aristocracy:

> When Dickens was here last he wanted to call upon Walt Whitman, but Lowell, who was always a bit of a Philistine, persuaded him not to do so. Shortly afterward Lowell went to England, where Rossetti and Swinburne and many lesser lights were eager to talk about 'W. W.'—would hear of nothing else, in fact. Lowell took a short trip in Ireland, only to be confronted by a still more eager band, headed by Dowden, who were all clamoring for news about 'W. W.' In despair—or, rather, disgust—Lowell went to Paris. Here he found that one of the leading French critics had just published a long article on "W. W." in the Revue des Deux Mondes, and all Paris was talking of "the greatest American poet." And when Lowell had fled to Germany, he found Freiligrath busy with translations of Whitman's poems into German and all Berlin talking of nothing else![187]

In defiance of his general indifference to Whitman, after 1876 Lowell was lumped with the "Suppression of Vice" crowd who later insisted that Whitman expurgate the 1880–81 edition of *Leaves* or face being banned in Boston.

As J. G. Holland of *Scribner's* complained, "[Whitman] plays the role of the suffering literary genius—the great unappreciated—and he has so far seemed to find his account in it."[188] More was written about Whitman in 1876 than had been in 1860, and his English sales suddenly reached a level that they had never previously attained in the United States. Whitman became embarrassed by the gifts that flowed in, but the press war created significant publicity for the Centennial Edition of *Leaves*, and it sold well. Just as O'Connor had done for him in 1866, Whitman now successfully used the rhetoric of exclusion to make himself an international celebrity. It was a radical departure from his former rhetoric of success; ironically, the claims of exclusion were considerably more successful in establishing him as a legitimate poet. Whitman began to get the attention of the high literary culture, who were increasingly working in New York rather than in Boston. In 1876 Whitman first made contact with John H. Johnston, a wealthy New York jeweler, who introduced him to Richard Watson Gilder and Edmund Clarence Stedman. In March 1877, Whitman visited New York with Johnston, and the Camden *Daily Post* announced "High tone Society now takes him to its bosom."[189] As narrated earlier, it was Gilder who came up with the Lincoln Lectures as a means of promoting Whitman among a general readership and gaining for him a steady income.

On 3 February 1878, John Burroughs wrote to Whitman, "Gilder suggests a 'benefit' be got up for you in N.Y. and that you be asked to lecture on Lincoln. He thinks it would go with a rush under proper management that lots of money $$$ might be made . . . I think in fact we might have a big time and make it pay. $ Write me how you feel about it."[190] Whitman wrote back on 24 February, "I am agreeable to the Lecture project—if it can be put through—about the middle of April (the anniversary of the eve or night of Lincoln's murder)."[191] Burroughs immediately worked out an arrangement with Gilder and Stedman for a lecture in New York on April 15, but Whitman soon begged off because of poor health.

One year after the proposed date, however, Whitman delivered "The Death of Abraham Lincoln" for the first time at Steck Hall in New York City on 14 April 1879. Gilder and Stedman were successful in using their contacts to attract sixty or seventy influential figures in literature and journalism. (Tellingly, most accounts of the lecture dwell on the audience rather than on Whitman.) Whitman presented the same account of the assassination given in *Memoranda* with a new introduction and conclusion, but he also began a tradition that became the main attraction of his annual performance: a melodramatic reading of "O Captain! My Captain!"

Whitman considered this first performance a great success. It roused his forgotten desire to become a national lecturer; he wrote afterwards, "I intend to go up and down the land, (in moderation) seeking whom I may devour, with lectures, and reading of my own poems."[192] He published an anonymous account of the lecture in the *New York Tribune* the following day, April 15: "The poet Walt Whitman made his beginning as a lecturer last night . . . He desires engagements as a reader of his own poems and as a lecturer." Whitman received no offers, but he lectured again on 15 April 1880, in Philadelphia's Association Hall, sending advance notice to papers in several cities. A few papers printed Whitman's own favorable reviews of the event, including the *Philadelphia Press* and the *Camden Daily Times*, and he soon received an invitation to lecture at St. Botolph's Club, perhaps as important a cultural gathering place in Boston then as the Saturday Club had once been.

Whitman's lecture at St. Botoph's on 15 April 1881, seems to have made the long-anticipated public relations breakthrough in Boston; it almost entirely erased the impression his earlier persona had made on figures like Lowell. Sylvester Baxter described the lecture in the *Boston Herald* on April 16: "He is a grand old fellow" is everybody's verdict. Walt Whitman has in time past been, perhaps, more ignorantly than willfully misunderstood, but time brings about its revenges, and his present position goes to prove that, let a man be true to himself, however he defies the world, the world will come at last to respect him for his loyalty."[193] This "grand old fellow" version of Whitman is quite apparent in the photographs taken of him in Boston, one of which Whitman called the "pompous photo" (Figure 3).[194] It was radically different from other images of Whitman in circulation—with the exception of the 1860–61 frontispiece (Figure 7)—and it served to present him as acceptable to the literary and social elites who had rejected him the last time he appeared in Boston; it made the Saturday Club look hopelessly prejudiced and straight-laced. Within a few months, Whitman had a contract with James Osgood (the successor firm of Boston's famous literary publishers, Ticknor and Fields) to publish a complete edition of *Leaves*.

Whitman warned Osgood on 8 May 1881, that "the old pieces, the *sexuality* ones, about which the original row was started & kept up so long, are all retained, & must go in the same as ever."[195] And Osgood agreed to let Whitman "retain all the *beastliness* of the earlier editions," and the seventh edition of *Leaves,* significantly revised by Whitman, was published in November at a moderate price of two dollars a copy.[196] Although Whitman had removed some of the sexual content of *Leaves,* on 1 March 1882, the Boston district attorney, Oliver Stevens, acting under the influence of the New England Society for the Suppression of Vice, classified *Leaves* as obscene literature. Stevens ordered Osgood to remove several offending poems and passages or cease publication altogether.

Whitman was willing to make some changes. He had, after all, allowed the publication of an expurgated edition of *Leaves* in 1868. "I am not afraid of the District Attorney's threat," he wrote on 7 March, "[but] under the circumstances I am willing to make a revision & cancellation in the page alluded to—wouldn't be more than half a dozen anyhow—perhaps indeed about ten lines to be left out, & half a dozen words or phrases." It seems Whitman was trying to force a court case, which Osgood was unwilling to do: "we do not wish to go into court in connection with this case."[197] Osgood was not willing to risk any further action by the District Attorney, and he reached a settlement with Whitman on 17 May 1882: he paid Whitman one hundred dollars in cash and gave him 225 copies of the book along with the stereotype plates.

Whitman suggested that there were others besides the Attorney General behind the suppression, including Lowell: "of course there are others behind it all," but Whitman continued, "they will only burn their own fingers, & very badly."[198] The "suppression" of the Osgood edition of *Leaves* in Boston confirmed the belief among some Philadelphians and New Yorkers that Whitman was indeed the victim of prudery and comstockery, perhaps even an organized conspiracy involving Lowell. Using the plates of the Osgood edition, Rees Welsh and Company of Philadelphia risked prosecution by publishing *Leaves of Grass* and a companion volume, *Specimen Days*, in 1882. It became a point of progressive pride to purchase (though not necessarily to read) *Leaves,* for most purchasers knew Whitman mostly for "O Captain!" rather than "The Children of Adam" or "Calamus." Some members of the American social elite, like their English counterparts, began to patronize Whitman after 1881 as a statement of what Tom Wolfe might call "radical chic."[199]

As a literary artist, Whitman was more successful as an enemy of the state than he ever was as the embodiment of the average American. "The Leaves have had several set-tos with the state," Whitman told Traubel, "all of them serving to advance the book—Harlan's, to begin with, then Stevens's, in Massachusetts, then that fool postmaster Tobey's."[200] One enemy complained, "the book has been advertised more widely than ever by the attempt to suppress it."[201] Advertising copy proclaimed that this edition "Contains every page, every line, every word attempted to be officially suppressed by Messrs. Marston, Attorney-General of Massachusetts—Stevens, Boston District-Attorney—Tobey, U.S. Post Master at Boston, and others."[202] Other contemporaneous advertising for *Leaves* referred to it as "The Suppressed Book."[203] As a result of the publicity of the Boston "banning," Rees Welsh sold about 6,000 copies of *Leaves*.[204] Whitman was beginning to reach a broader audience, and the royalties enabled him to buy a modest rowhouse on Mickle Street in Camden, New Jersey.

There was, of course, some truth in Whitman's portrayal of himself as an excluded artist, but it is also true that Whitman deliberately rejected an opportunity to win the approval of the educated mainstream—the same audience he cultivated with the Lincoln Lectures—with an expurgated Osgood edition. Instead, Whitman sabotaged the publication at the last minute by refusing to submit to minor changes in his work, which he willingly accepted under other conditions such as the 1868 Rossetti edition; *Leaves of Grass: The Poems of Walt Whitman* (1886), edited by Ernest Rhys; *Gems from Walt Whitman* (1889), edited by Elizabeth Porter Gould; and Arthur Stedman's *Selected Poems of Walt Whitman* (1892). Whitman even considered an edition of his own called *Leaves of Grass, Junior.* It is clear that Whitman was not above commodifying his image for the sake of popularity; he even permitted his face and name to be used as a logo for cigars, wine, and canned vegetables. Why, then, would he stand so firmly against modifying his poetry and image for Osgood?

Traubel once asked, "Walt, don't you sometimes put that American neglect business a bit too strong?"[205] Even after Whitman had achieved international celebrity, it was essential for him to be represented as poor and neglected. When money was raised to buy him a cottage in the country to escape the summer heat of Camden, Whitman used the money instead to construct an elaborate tomb for himself in Camden's Harleigh Cemetery, much to the anger of the contributors. It seems clear that a comfortable, prosperous image would have undermined Whitman's appearance of artistic autonomy. Material success, particularly with the Boston literary establishment behind him, would have undermined his rhetoric of exclusion and make him suspect to the artists, socialists, and other progressives who, in the long run, sustained his claims on artistic legitimacy, on not having "sold out." No matter how celebrated he became, Whitman continued to proclaim his economic failure to the end of his life. In 1888 in "A Backward Glance O'er Travel'd Roads," Whitman writes:

> [F]rom a worldly and business point of view 'Leaves of Grass' has been worse than a failure—that public criticism on the book and myself as author of it yet shows mark'd anger and contempt more than anything else—('I find a solid line of enemies to you everywhere,'—letter from W. S. K., Boston, May 28, 1884)—And that solely for publishing it I have been the object of two or three pretty serious special official buffetings—is all probably no more than I ought to have expected. I had my choice when I commenc'd. I bid neither for soft eulogies, big money returns, nor the approbation of existing schools and conventions. . . . I have had my say entirely my own way, and put it unerringly on record—the value thereof to be decided by time.[206]

Although Lowell had never been a serious enemy, Whitman's attacks on him became more frequent and arbitrary with time. Whitman published derogatory remarks about Lowell in the *North American Review* in February 1881: "Mr. Lowell can overflow with American humor when politics inspire his muse; but in the realm of pure poetry he is no more American than a Newdigate prizeman."[207] In 1888, one guest at Mickle Street referred to "something Lowell had written about Thoreau." Whitman replied, "I have never read it: I do not seem to care much about Lowell's work.'"[208] In subsequent years, Whitman would denounce Lowell to his disciples without much provocation. In one such exchange, Traubel asked, "'But what's that got to do with Lowell.' Whitman answered: 'Nothing: but I thought it was about time to drop Lowell.'" Traubel replied, "'You always think it's about time to drop Lowell.'"[209]

Paradoxically, after the *succès de scandal* of the 1880–81 edition, most readers thought of him as the author of the most anthologized tribute to Lincoln, "O Captain! My Captain!" School children were forced to memorize it, and, despite the fame it gave him, Whitman grew to despise it. When Horace Traubel requested the original draft of "O Captain!" Whitman said, "I ought to have destroyed it, but your face always hovers around to rebuke me when I think of destruction so I laid it aside for you. After our talk about the poem the other day I feel nasty enough to do anything with it. But if you will promise not to bring the manuscript back I will promise to let you take it away."[210] Nevertheless, Whitman continued to read "O Captain!" at public lectures even when favorable circumstances, along with growing personal stature, would have permitted him to read a poem that seems more appropriate to the occasion, one which he liked more than "O Captain!," namely, "When Lilacs Last in the Dooryard Bloom'd."

For the next two generations, it was the Whitman of the Lincoln lectures to whom most Americans were first exposed: the patriotic poet of democracy who first appeared in the anthologies and the classrooms. Gilder and Stedman sanitized Whitman by encouraging him to publish his poems, particularly the patriotic poems like "O Captain!" in expurgated anthologies and to promote his work through public appearances at which Whitman never read his more experimental poetry.[211] Whitman the shrewd self-promoter was undoubtedly aware of the contingencies of the literary marketplace, and, by the end of his career, he capitalized on these personae with increasing effectiveness. Although Whitman is now remembered for the formal and thematic radicalism of *Leaves*, by this time his poetry was often as formally conventional and occasional as Lowell's.[212]

Although it was Whitman's refusal to accept certain opportunities for large-scale production that limited his monetary returns, Whitman and his disciples crafted an image of powerlessness and poverty, a history of victimization, that would enhance the poet's claim to be the genuine article: an incorruptible literary artist. Whitman, in general, was more concerned with the accumulation of symbolic capital which he slowly accrued from over a period of almost forty years of steadfastly republishing a book of poems so closely identified with their author. The more the literary field became autonomous from the fields of power, the more Whitman was viewed as a "greater" poet than Lowell. The more Whitman became accepted by the younger generation of critics (and many of the older ones), the more Lowell, who had not yet relented in his distaste for Whitman, would feel pressured to make some public gesture lest he become tainted with the image of being an intolerant persecutor. In this context, Lowell's appearance at the 1887 Lincoln Lecture seems perfectly explicable, but his tears seem to have more to do with the decline of the literary culture that produced him.

The Madison Square Theater lecture was, perhaps, the most telling incident in the metamorphosis of Whitman from the avant garde to a mainstream commodity, for it was the culminating coup in a long career of self-promotion as a journalist, poet, lecturer, and self-conscious literary celebrity. Although Whitman was being packaged for the masses by Gilder and associates, the New York lecture was, in a way, revolutionary, for it represented the final shift of power in publishing from Boston to New York City and the emergence of a vast, middlebrow audience that sustained it. As we have seen, in earlier years Whitman had unsuccessfully canvassed Boston for supporters of *Leaves*, but by 1887 Whitman told Traubel, New York "is a good market for the harvest."[213] Whitman netted at least $600 from his lecture there, but, more importantly, he made an investment toward more lasting fame. Johnston told an unnamed reporter from the *Evening Sun*, the evening was a literary as well as a financial success.[214] As Ed Folsom observes, "while tortured by the paradoxes, Whitman finally acted out of the belief that inclusion and provisional acceptance—even in a safely gemiferous form—were preferable to exclusion and rejection."[215]

When Whitman died in 1892 his obituary in the *New York Herald* stated, "To the mass of people Whitman's poetry will always remain as a sealed book, but there are few who are not able to appreciate the beauty of 'O Captain! My Captain!'"[216] A decade later, even the *Atlantic* expressed admiration at Whitman's transformation from the barbarian of 1855 into the "Good Gray Poet" of the 1880s: "how many of your readers have read his Drum Taps, or indeed how many ever think of him as the author of anything except Leaves of Grass, which have acquired a very unsavory odor. . . . The world is all too prone to assume that men must remain as it first finds them."[217] It is undeniable that Whitman capitalized on his positive relationship with Lincoln to cultivate a mainstream audience and his negative relationship with Lowell to cultivate the appreciation of the literary *avant garde*. The avuncular lecturer was a remarkable transformation from his earlier persona, but it was also a canny a strategy for ensuring the survival of that earlier persona by simultaneously detaching himself from it—making himself as sacrosanct as Lincoln—while emphasizing how he continued to be persecuted by literary critics who, he claimed, were the enemies of the progressive impulse in American culture.

Although the lectures were often before elite audiences, the intended audience was the rising middle-class who increasingly were the consumers of culture. Whitman's success did not owe as much to the literary value of "The Death of Abraham Lincoln" as to Gilder and his associates' success at getting favorable, if not indulgent, reports in at least a dozen newspapers and magazines in the New York area. Among the guests at the Westminster Hotel that night were also at least nine other prominent editors and reporters besides the Gilders.[218] The reception that followed the lecture was, for lack of a contemporaneous term, a press conference assembled by a combination of advertising and networking by the sponsors among their connections in the press and among New York society, which, by the 1880s, far outstripped Boston in size, population, publishing capital, and intellectual influence. The strategic showcasing of local celebrities attending the lecture was calculated to transform a hitherto neglected performance into a manufactured event of social significance. Yet the benefit was not organized for the literati and assorted dignitaries among the audience; rather, it was for the schoolteachers, clergymen, journalists, and government officials who would read about Whitman in 1887 and revise their opinions about the indecent author of *Leaves of Grass*. For representatives of the Genteel Tradition such as Lowell, this coronation of Whitman in New York must have signified the passing of the New England literary culture and, perhaps, a personal rejection as well.

The other group on the fringes—bearded, slouchy, angry, plotting revolutions—also saw Whitman as a counter-cultural figure, but for them Whitman was set in opposition to the bourgeoisie. As the next chapter examines, Whitman's English admirers in particular constructed a socialist hero-redeemer to set up a kingdom of "comradeship" on earth. Their Whitman appeared in anthologies like Edward Carpenter's *Chants of Labour* in which the poet was set to music singing of the "Love of Comrades."[219] These supporters of Whitman—Carpenter, Symonds,

Wilde, Traubel, Bucke, Burroughs, and a parade of lesser figures—reduced the confused and contradictory history of Whitman's life and poetry into a simplified dialectical struggle with the old order of "Fireside Poets": Emerson, Longfellow, Bryant, Whittier, and Lowell. Although Emerson's Brahmin status was pardoned by his early endorsement of Whitman, the radicals considered the remaining four poets to be commercial, hopelessly embedded in the marketplace values of rhyme, sentimentality, clarity, and general conformity. Such poets were part of an elitist network whose institutions supported their preeminence: "Without doubt, the four living American poets who fill the highest places are Emerson, Bryant, Longfellow, and Lowell," said the editors of the *Nation* on 15 November 1866.[220]Although the twentieth century came to regard Whitman as the "Great American Poet," Lowell had a stronger claim to the dubious title in the nineteenth. "As for Lowell," observed the *Nation*, "of all these writers he may be rated, all things considered, as the first." Whitman, on the other hand, had been reviewed by Henry James in the *Nation* in 1865 as "aggressively careless, inelegant, and ignorant . . . preoccupied with [himself] . . . rude, lugubrious, and grim."[221]

Lowell's questionable status as a top-ranking establishment poet made him a conspicuous target of revolutionary anger. More than any of the Fireside Poets, James Russell Lowell—Brahmin, professor, politician—became Whitman's foil in a drama that revived the American archetypes of Royall Tyler's *The Contrast*: "Lowell—Whitman: A Contrast" by Horace Traubel cast Lowell as Billy Dimple, the wealthy Anglophile, and Walt Whitman as Colonel Manly, the sturdy revolutionary.[222] Discussing this contrast, Whitman said, "I think I could easily state the difference myself: Lowell an elegant mansion, equipped with all that is luxurious, rich—not to be despised, after its own kind and degree; Walt Whitman, emulous of the seashore, the forest, even the prairie—or the surging manifold streets of the cities."[223] Lowell imitated nature; Whitman *was* Nature.

Even as Whitman gained popularity, he became increasingly convinced of his own failure and of injustices done to him. In 1888, Whitman told Traubel, "You know, Horace, there are some who in the natural order couldn't accept Walt Whitman—couldn't appreciate the inmost purpose of his art. Lowell, with his almost steel-like beauty, and Higginson, with his strict, straight, notions of literary propriety—I could call them enemies, creatures natively antipathetic."[224] Whatever their critical differences, which were many, Whitman's final articulation of his relationship with Lowell appears to calculated effort to construct himself as the leader of an alternative literary tradition: "Take Lowell, Whipple, Ripley, such men, in this country: they have no use for me: they are all against me."[225] As Bliss Perry oberves: "As his own strength failed, he seem to have grown increasingly suspicious of some cabal against him. . . . That was sheer pathological mania of persecution."[226] Even a casual examination of the biographical facts of the lives of these two men reveals that Lowell's enmity was an exaggeration by the Whitmanites, but it proves the power of ideology to revise the historical facts.

Any diachronic examination of a complete literary career demonstrates that authors frequently migrate from hack to artist, and vice versa, sometimes several times in a career, sometimes seeming to occupy both positions simultaneously, depending on the perspective from which one views them. It seems, however, that writers generally gravitate towards what they perceive to be the equilibrium point where symbolic and economic capital intersect in the specific field of production occupied by the author. Such an interpretation explains the tendency for authors to accumulate symbolic and economic capital simultaneously. Whitman's poetry sold better when he refused to expurgate his work in 1881. Lowell's personal wealth and power did not initially displace him from the literary canon; on the contrary, his political position only drew greater attention to his work. However, it seems that there is some threshold of wealth and power the crossing of which begins to devalue one's art. Apparent contradictions and hypocrisies begin to make the appearance of artistic autonomy untenable. Whitman always tried to conceal his wealth and his powerful friends and to present himself as suffering in poverty. And Lowell was eventually displaced, in part, because the advantages of supporting him in his lifetime undermined the disinterestedness of his supporters when he ceased to exercise real power. It is clear that the appearance of poverty and powerlessness enhance the appearance of artistic integrity, but artists must also find an audience and receive support for their endeavors. As Lowell demonstrates, wealth and power may enable literary success, but they are not sufficient to sustain it, particularly when the enabling social network breaks down. Thus, the most advantageous position for an author—either consciously sought or unconsciously attained—is typically a sustainable equilibrium point between economic and symbolic power, which, nevertheless, is fraught with complexity. This search for balance is complicated because it must take place under rapidly changing marketplace conditions and in relation to the activities of a large number of other authors, critics, publications, and institutions whose collective circulation of symbolic and economic capital constitute that marketplace. An equilibrium position is more often reached by accident than by conscious decision.

It may be that Whitman's long-term success was partly the result of his ability to elude precise definition; to seem to appeal to all groups (the *avant-garde* and the middlebrow, the elitist and the populist, the nationalist and the cosmopolitan, the heterosexual and the homosexual). It is this protean quality—the capacity for admirers of Whitman to refashion him in their own image and themselves in his image—which has kept him the object of interest and speculation for more than a century and half.

Chapter Four

"What Is a Man Anyhow?"
Whitmanites, Wildeans, and
Working-Class "Comradeship"

I. A SPIRITUAL PILGRIMAGE

O N 2 MAY 1877, A HANDSOME ENGLISHMAN OF THIRTY-TWO ARRIVED AT
431 Stevens Street in Camden, New Jersey. It was the residence of Walt
Whitman, notorious among many in the United States as the immoral
author of *Leaves of Grass.* The three-story row house he occupied suggested the genteel aspirations of the poet's brother and sister-in-law with whom he lived. But to
Edward Carpenter industrial Camden must have seemed like the North of England,
ideal for a political poet who shunned the collegiality of middle-class literati such as
Lowell and Longfellow for the "comradeship" of uneducated working men like Peter
Doyle and Harry Stafford. A self-identified homosexual and socialist, Carpenter felt
"cut off from the understanding of others," but Whitman's writings had given him
"a ground for the love of men" that was sexual, political, and religious. For
Carpenter, an ex-minister for whom literature had become a substitute for religion,
this long-delayed journey was tantamount to a spiritual pilgrimage.[1]

Carpenter seems to have had fairly clear expectations about Whitman's appearance and surroundings. The frequently reproduced frontispiece to the 1855 edition
of *Leaves* (Figure 1) presented Whitman as a surly workman, "one of the roughs,"
and Carpenter expected the poet to be "eccentric, unbalanced, violent."[2] By 1877,
however, the actual Whitman appeared to have little in common with his vigorous
image, and the house in which he lived seemed incongruous with proletarian simplicity. "Walt" was upstairs when Carpenter arrived; he lived on the third floor, and
it took him some time to descend, as his left foot was paralyzed by a recent stroke.
Carpenter waited in the sitting-room, noting the accoutrements of middle-class
respectability with some disdain: "one or two ornamental tables," "photograph
books," and "things under glass shades, & c." The young Carpenter was surprised at
Whitman's appearance; he was "an old man with long grey, almost white, beard, and
shaggy head and neck." As they exchanged pleasantries, Carpenter found, contrary
to his expectations, that Whitman was "considerate" and "courteous," with a "large

benign effluence and inclusiveness" combined with a "sense of remoteness and inaccessibility." Although Carpenter still detected "a certain untamed 'wild hawk' look" in Whitman, the sexually assertive, politically radical poet of *Leaves* was now, as John Burroughs describes him, "not an athlete, or a rough, but a great tender mother-man."[3]

Whitman could not live up to his vigorous physical image, but Carpenter was pleased to learn that the poet's preferred setting was not this bourgeois interior but the open-air life of the street and country. Whitman suggested that they go out, walk to the Delaware River, and take the ferry across to Philadelphia. Along the way Whitman hailed his unreserved working-class comrades: "The men on the ferry steamer were evidently old friends," Carpenter notes, as were "the tramway conductor" and "the loafers on the pavement." As Carpenter observes, to Whitman "The life of the streets and of the people was so near, so dear." In Philadelphia the once reserved Englishman even seems to have witnessed something like a re-enactment of Whitman's relationship with Peter Doyle: Whitman met "an old Broadway 'stager,'" who "'had not seen Walt for three or four years'; and tears were in his eyes as he held his hand."[4] In Camden and Philadelphia, all working men, it seems, were the comrades of Walt Whitman.

In contrast with this urban scene, Carpenter also presents Whitman in a tableau of pastoral comradeship at a small farm in the New Jersey countryside that belonged to the parents of Harry Stafford, a young printer's assistant who was a "favourite of Walt's." Carpenter describes the other Stafford children as flocking to Whitman, "the little boy would lie coiled, on his knees, half-asleep, half-awake, Walt's hand covering and compressing his entire face." When he wasn't communing with nature, Whitman would hold forth on his poetry in the midst of Stafford's large, picturesque family: "my original idea was that if I could bring men together by putting before them the heart of man, it would be a great thing." He continues, apparently for Carpenter's benefit, "I have had America chiefly in view, but this appreciation of me in England makes me think I might perhaps do the same for the old world also." In spite of his initial impressions, Carpenter finally claimed that "Whitman seemed to fill out 'Leaves of Grass,'" adding that "all Whitman had written there was a matter of absolute personal experience."[5]

Undoubtedly, Whitman both affirmed and denied Carpenter's preconceptions about him, and the allegory of Carpenter's first visit to Camden highlights the visual and textual complexities of Whitman's significance in the discourses of nineteenth-century American and English masculinities. Carpenter describes Whitman's face as being formally structured, "like a Greek temple."[6] He also drew a sketch of Whitman, noting that "the likeness to Christ is quite marked." But as Gay Wilson Allen observes, "the drawing looks nothing like Whitman . . . except possibly the frontispiece of the 1855 edition of *Leaves of Grass*."[7] Just as Carpenter's visual images of Whitman are caught in a tension between the Hellenic and the Christian models of masculine relations, Carpenter's narrative presents a series of images which transform the masculine roles of their relationship. The child in Whitman's lap, whose face is conveniently covered, seems an infantilized stand-in for Carpenter himself, whose initial expectations of a "comradely" relationship with the rough-trade Whitman of 1855 were now transformed into that of the kindly, ursine father of 1877, the "Good, Gray Poet."[8]

Carpenter had used the textual Whitman to construct a masculine identity, and his account of Whitman attempts to demonstrate a continuity between text and reality that accommodates the transformation of masculine roles over time. He returned to England apparently more convinced than ever that Whitman's masculinities, as transitory as they may have seemed, were models on which to base his own development. Carpenter, though once a refined member of the clergy, continued to seek a more masculine, economically independent existence as a poet, lecturer, writer, farmer, and craftsman in the countryside near industrial Sheffield, where, like Whitman, he could be close to both nature and the life of the urban street. And, like Whitman, Carpenter began a series of semi-public domestic and sexual relationships with working-class men. He continued to be subject to the emerging negative discourses of the effeminate or perverted "homosexual," but this visit to America enabled him to construct a new identity for himself, paradoxically, as the "English Whitman."

II. "WHAT IS A MAN ANYHOW?"

The question of what constitutes a "man" and what makes him so "manly" is central to the identity Whitman constructs and reconstructs in *Leaves of Grass* from 1855 to 1892. In the first preface to *Leaves*, Whitman explained that these poems are the incarnation of the man, who, in sum, incarnates his nation.[9] Whitman said, "This is no book. He who touches this book touches the man himself."[10] In later years Whitman cherished an apocryphal story of Lincoln observing him and saying, "Well *he* looks like a MAN!" And one passage that never changed through the many successive editions of *Leaves* asks pointedly, "What is a man anyhow?"[11] Yet, this question provoked an uncertain answer laden with culturally contested and rapidly changing constructions of "manhood." In 1860, for example, *Vanity Fair* parodied Whitman with, "I am the Counter-jumper, weak and effeminate / I love to loaf and lie about the dry-goods . . . For I am the creature of weak depravities."[12] But in 1880 an English reviewer describes *Leaves* as "the Incarnate Word in which [Whitman] manifests the fullness of his manhood. Here is not merely the poet—here is the Man, through and through, from top to toe."[13] Yet in the American *Woman's Journal* in 1882, Thomas Wentworth Higginson could still denounce Whitman's pose—together with Oscar Wilde's—as "Unmanly Manhood."[14] The ambiguity of American masculinity in the nineteenth century is thrown into sharp relief when contrasted with contemporaneous constructions of English masculinity, particularly regarding the relationship between manhood, class, and what is now called "sexual orientation."

The meaning of manhood as it relates to Whitman was contested notably by two communities of English homosexual men near the end of the nineteenth century. One group, which will emerge as the "Whitmanites," based their identity in part on Whitman's poetic persona, adopting an intermediate view of manhood as a totality, incorporating selected attributes of the male and the female without being brutish or effeminate.[15] The Whitmanites, who eventually included Edward Carpenter and the members of the "Bolton Whitman Fellowship," were primarily middle class, and they adopted Whitman's simplicity and egalitarianism, often becoming advocates of socialism as well as sexual liberation. The other group, the "Wildeans," represented an aristocratic construction of homoerotic masculinity that opposed the rusticity and egalitarianism of the Whitmanites. The Wildeans, who included Oscar Wilde, Aubrey Beardsley, and other followers of the Aesthetic movement in literature and art, signified their sexuality by adopting behaviors culturally designated as "feminine" and the refined style of aristocratic connoisseurship. It was the Wildeans who helped to create the stereotype of the homosexual as "unmanly," and Wilde's imprisonment for sodomy in 1895 helped to end the successful alliance between socialism and sex reform that the Whitmanites struggled to create. These different communities of English homosexual men used different readings of Whitman's poetry and persona to construct their masculinities, but Whitman, who emerged under a specifically nineteenth-century American form of sex-identity construction, often resisted appropriation by these communities, which sometimes used Whitman and his poetry to justify activities and relationships he did not sanction.[16]

From its beginning in 1855 to the "Deathbed Edition" in 1892, *Leaves of Grass* was notorious for its sexual content, though criticism was almost universally aimed at Whitman's representations of heterosexual activity. In the *New York Tribune* in 1855 Charles Dana commented that Whitman's "words might have passed between Adam and Eve in Paradise before the want of fig leaves brought no shame."[17] One English reader wrote to Henry David Thoreau in 1857, "The man appears to me not to know how to behave himself."[18] Only Rufus Griswold, also of the *New York Tribune*, seems to have recognized the homoerotic significance of the first *Leaves*, describing its subject matter as "Peccatum illud horrible, inter Christianos non nominandum."[19]

In the first two editions of *Leaves*, Whitman concealed much of the homosexual content by using subcultural signifiers; most American readers overlooked the full meaning of many passages, seeing them as celebrations of comradely affection, which they partly were. Perhaps unaware of the emerging homosexual culture in their midst, most would interpret poems such as the "Calamus" cluster of *Leaves* as poeticized male friendship or as a response to sexual prudery of all types. In her review in the *Ledger* in 1856, Fanny Fern writes, "I confess that I extract no poison from these 'Leaves'—to me they have brought only healing. Let him who can do so shroud the eyes of the nursing babe lest it should see its mother's breast."[20] While such arguments could be made for "Song of Myself," it was far more difficult for critics to sanctify *Leaves* after the 1860–61 edition, which included a new cluster of poems called "Calamus."[21] Even to those uninitiated in homosexual argot it was all too clear this time what Whitman meant by "the manly love of comrades."[22]

The term "homosexual" was not coined until 1869 by Carl Westphal, and it did not become current in English until the beginning of the twentieth century.[23] There were, however, other words that substituted for the clinical terminology that emerged with the rise of the legal, medical, and psychiatric professions. Thanks in part to the vocabulary of Whitman's poetry, in 1895 Carpenter writes, "Of all the many forms that Love delights to take, perhaps none is more interesting than that special attachment which is sometimes denoted by the word Comradeship."[24] "Comradeship" meaning homosexuality, along with "amatativess" and "perturbation" were only a few among a large subcultural lexicon of words, symbols, gestures, tokens, and poses fixed by Whitman, whose presentation of them in print facilitated the creation of the invisible "fellowship" described in the "Calamus" poems:

> Among the men and women of the multitude,
> I perceive one picking me out by secret and divine signs,
> Acknowledging none else, not parent, wife, husband,
> brother, child, any nearer than I am,
> Some are baffled, but that one is not—that one knows me.[25]

Although not clinical, other poems in "Calamus" reveal that Whitman is not writing of male friendship, but of homosexual eroticism. In "Earth My Likeness," for example, Whitman writes, "an athlete is enamour'd of me, and I of him, / But toward him there is something fierce and terrible in me eligible to burst forth, / I dare not tell it in words, not even in these songs."[26] More or less open invitations and admissions such as these, scattered throughout *Leaves* and concentrated in "Calamus," encouraged some readers to respond on a personal level that Whitman was sometimes unwilling to meet, particularly when they conflicted with the image of himself as the "Good, Gray Poet."

From the 1870s to the early 1890s, as *Leaves* gradually became known in England, Whitman regularly received letters—one biographer calls them "semi-love letters"—from young English homosexual men, who found in Whitman's poetry a language that enabled many of them to construct a trans-national group identity, an imagined community.[27] Whatever Whitman's actual intention (which was surely complicated by notions of democratic solidarity and bodily expressiveness), for these readers Whitman was a celebrator of homoeroticism who convinced them that their sexual orientations were not anomalous or perverted. This was especially true in England, where the earlier growth of major cities and an urban proletariat facilitated the growth of sexual subcultures—and sex legislation—earlier than in the United States.

In one of his earliest letters John Addington Symonds writes that *Leaves* permitted him "to believe that the Comradeship, which I conceived as on a par with Sexual feeling in depth & strength & purity & capability of all good, was real." Contrary to everything he had learned, homosexuality was "not a delusion of distorted passions, a dream of the Past, a scholar's fancy—but a strong and vital bond of man to man." It was Whitman, Symonds writes, who enabled him to escape the moral strictures of Victorian England: "how hard I found it—educated at an aristocratic School (Harrow) and an over refined University (Oxford)—to winnow from my own emotions and from my conception of the ideal friend, all husks of affectations and aberrations."[28]

Symonds was isolated at Oxford but not alone in his experience of Whitman's poetry. Nearly a decade before Carpenter's visit to Camden in 1877, he was a student at Cambridge University struggling to reconcile his own forbidden same-sex desires with the emerging medical and legal categorization of the "homosexual" as an invert or a pervert. In the summer of 1868 or 1869 one of the Fellows of Trinity Hall gave him a blue-colored book and asked him, "'Carpenter, what do you think of this?'"[29] It was the first English edition of Whitman's *Leaves* (1868), edited by William Michael Rossetti, and it soon attracted a growing body of young English men who found in Whitman's poetry a language that corresponded to the notion of being "comrades," or members of a "fellowship." In contrast with the effeminate constructions of male homosexuality, Whitman's *Leaves* seemed to offer a masculinity that included same-sex affections that did not seem weak or immoral:

> A glimpse through an interstice caught,
> Of a crowd of workmen and drivers in a bar-room around the stove
> late of a winter night, and I unremark'd seated in a corner,
> Of a youth who loves me and whom I love, silently approaching
> and seating himself near, that he may hold me by the hand,
> A long while amid the noises of coming and going, of drinking and
>   oath and smutty jest,
> There we two, content, happy in being together, speaking little,
> perhaps not a word.[30]

Poems like "A Glimpse," in the "Calamus" section of *Leaves*, presented working-class social relations in the United States as less structured and more sexually permissive than the hierarchical, reserved relations of middle-class men in England. To Carpenter, Whitman seemed a harbinger of "Love's Coming-of-Age"; he possessed a fluid masculinity that seemed to dissolve the socially constructed boundaries of class and gender, placing him outside the disciplinary power of categorization. Whitman's declarations and questions were always ambiguous, but he suggested a new integration of mind and body, an authenticity of experience that resonated on so many levels that they affected some readers with the force of a religious conversion. After his first reading of Whitman, Carpenter claims, "a profound change set in within me."[31] Whitman had "spoken the word which is on the lips of God," permitting Carpenter, the former minister, to "see the new, open, life which is to come."[32]

Just as many gift books in this period describe "the language of flowers," or served as "tokens of friendship," the dissemination of Whitman's poetry and persona acquired a silent language of its own. "My friend Roden Noel gave me by token of comradeship one of two photographs signed with your own name, which you gave him," writes Symonds to Whitman in 1877; "those who love me best, make me gifts recalling you."[33] "Photographs of Whitman, gifts of Whitman's books, specimens of his handwriting, news of Whitman, admiring references to 'Whitman,'" observes Eve Sedgwick, "functioned as badges of homosexual recognition."[34] And there was no greater collection of such badges than that assembled by Bolton's Whitman Fellowship.[35]

The "Walt Whitman Fellowship," also known as "Bolton College," was organized by J. W. Wallace (1853–1926) and John Johnston (1855–1927). The Fellowship consisted of middle-class men who met informally at Wallace's house in Bolton from 1885 to the mid-1920s to read adulatory papers about Whitman, to read Whitman's poetry, to drink from the "Whitman loving cup," and to sing boisterous songs about Whitman.[36] These events, Wallace writes, "led us, by imperceptible stages, to a deepened intimacy, in which the inmost quest[ions] and experiences of the soul were freely expressed."[37] They corresponded regularly with Whitman, and Wallace and Johnston visited him in Camden, bringing back tokens of the poet's affection. They also corresponded with and occasionally met Carpenter and Symonds, along with other Whitman enthusiasts at home and abroad, which, Wallace writes, drew "them together and strengthened their comradeship."[38]

It was this participation in a community of verbal and symbolic discourse that enabled Wallace to readily engage in a homoerotically charged dialogue with Whitman when he finally visited Camden: "[Horace] Traubel told him that I wanted to take some calamus home, and that Ed. [Carpenter] was chewing the root. W[hitman] began to describe it, and I told him that we had it in England."[39] Wallace was not surprised when Traubel encouraged him to escalate this flirtation to a physical level: "'Horace asks why I don't kiss you good-bye, and I have come back to do so.' He was as tender as a mother," Wallace writes, "and as our lips met he showed unmistakable emotion."[40]

Carpenter, according to Gavin Arthur, once described sleeping with Whitman as a customary part of the pilgrimage: "he regarded it as the best way to get together with another man."[41] Arthur describes this event as a "laying on of hands," a symbolic transmission of lineage and power from Whitman to Carpenter to him. Whitman's visitors would often return to England laden with tokens. Although it is unclear whether Wallace slept with Whitman, he did bring back a trunk full of souvenirs for his friends in the Fellowship: signed editions of *Leaves*, one of Whitman's teacups, a lock of Whitman's hair, and Whitman's bird, a canary which had died during the visit and had been stuffed for Wallace. These tokens, while they may not have indicated actual homosexual activity, came to signify this "laying on of hands" from one Whitmanite to another in an expanding network whose purpose was not purely sexual or aesthetic but also political.

Whitman's writings, particularly his "Calamus" poems, are an example of a means by which working-class discourses of same-sex desire opened up new social spaces in which middle-class men like Carpenter could enact alternative subjectivities that avoided the elitism of the aristocratic style or the effeminacy of the work-ing-class fairy. Carpenter's exposure to Whitman's conception of American working-class "comradeship," facilitated his shift from the perceived artificiality of sexual rela-tionships with men of his own social standing to the perceived authenticity of rela-tionships with English working-class men. "You hardly know, I think, in America," Carpenter says in his first letter to Whitman in 1874, "what the relief is here to turn from the languid inanity of the well-fed to the clean hard lines of the workman's face."[42]

Carpenter, however, did not turn to Whitman only for his apparent celebration of same-sex relationships. As Whitman claims, "the special meaning of the *Calamus* cluster of *LEAVES OF GRASS* . . . mainly resides in its Political significance."[43] Besides the legitimization of same-sex desires, what political role could be played by those whose activities placed them outside the primary structural element of a cap-italist society: heterosexual marriage? Could men who took pleasure in non-procre-ative sexual activities—who understood the fluidity of social identity construc-tions—restore the authenticity of pre-capitalist social relations? For Carpenter, among others, Whitman seemed to provide an overwhelmingly affirmative answer:

> I will make the most splendid race the sun ever shone upon,
> I will make divine magnetic lands,
>   With the love of comrades,
>   With the life-long love of comrades.[44]

Whitman uses "comradeship" as a term to describe the complex interplay of physical and emotional relations between men ranging from the homosocial to the homosexual, "the beautiful and sane affection of man for man."[45] "Comradeship," Whitman writes, provides "the counterbalance and offset of our materialistic and vulgar American democracy."[46] Whitman implies that the revolutionary potential of comradeship is characteristic of the free, sexually ambiguous relations of working-class men, who, in contrast to middle-class men, are nearer to material reality and, by implication, unashamedly expressive of their physical desires:

> I am enamour'd of growing out-doors,
> Of men that live among cattle or taste of the ocean or woods,
> Of the builders and steerers of ships and the wielders of axes and
> mauls, and the drivers of horses,
> I can eat and sleep with them week in and week out.[47]

As portrayed by Whitman, the ambiguity of American class boundaries coincided with the ambiguity of American sexual relations. Carpenter describes Whitman's "love" as "piercing through the layers and folds of caste, through differences of race, climate, character, occupation, despising distances of space and time."[48]

Whitman's depiction of the freedom of masculine relations among the American working-classes had divergent implications for his English readers. On the one hand, Whitman seems to legitimate middle-class sexual "slumming," which implies the inferiority of the working-class partner and is based on a model of aristocratic patronage. As Eve Sedgwick observes, Whitman's poetry and his intimate relationships with young, working-class men seem to "sacralize something like the English homosexual system whereby bourgeois men had sexual contacts only with virile working-class youths."[49] On the other hand, Whitman's blurring of the boundaries of gender and class seems to use sexual contact to facilitate social revolution. It was Whitman's "fervid adhesiveness", according to Carpenter, that would draw "members of the different classes together."[50] Such relationships would not necessarily be based on the subordination of the working-class partner, for, in the poetry of both Whitman and Carpenter, the skill of the manual laborer is eroticized as the sexual domination of the poet. Carpenter describes his ideal lover as "a powerful, strongly built man, of my own age or rather younger—preferably of the working class."[51] Correspondingly, in his long, Whitmanesque poem, "Towards Democracy," Carpenter subordinates himself to a series of working-class male partners:

> The ploughman shall turn me up with his ploughshare among the
> roots of the twitch in the sweet-smelling furrow;
> The potter shall mould me, running his finger along my whirling
> edge (we will be faithful to one another, he and I);
> The bricklayer shall lay me; he shall tap me into place with the
> handle of his trowel.[52]

Ideally, Whitman inspired cross-class contacts that were not predicated on exploitation but on equal partnership, and possibly the physical subordination of the middle-class partner to the more masculine working-class youth, thus inverting the social order of capitalism.

While Whitman welcomed this attention from abroad—and used it to shame Americans for supposedly neglecting him—he became increasingly uncomfortable with his appropriation by these young Englishmen for specific sexual and political agendas. "Everybody comes here demanding endorsements," Whitman complained to Traubel in 1888, "endorse this, endorse that: each man thinks I am radical his way: I suppose I am radical his way, but I am not radical his way alone."[53] Whitman was most suspicious of the motives of affluent, cultivated English admirers, for many of them—particularly Symonds—represented abroad those (like James Russell Lowell) who had thwarted his ambitions at home.[54]

Whitman was more at ease with more casual admirers who did not try to commit him to a particular program like socialism or sex reform. "It was," Wallace and Johnston remembered, "a continual astonishment to us, and indescribably affecting, to find him writing . . . with inexhaustible kindness and consideration, and with ever-recurring messages of tender affection and blessing to us all."[55] On the other hand, Whitman was cautious, even cold with correspondents like Symonds, who tried to press him for an explanation of "Calamus," and who unwisely bragged of his wealth, influence, and university degrees.[56] Whitman would generally respond to such letters by thanking the writer for his admiration while adding some mention of *his* financial difficulties, his humble dinner, and his ongoing health problems.[57] Even less aristocratic visitors could be similarly brushed off if they presumed too much. Carpenter writes of his visit, Whitman "left us, I remember with that queer brusque manner of his which so often offended his friends—just coldly saying 'Ta-ta.'"[58] This unresponsiveness over many years caused some English admirers to suspect that they had offended the poet, which, in fact, they had when they tried to impose their vision of "Whitman" on him.

III. WHITMANITES AND WILDEANS

Having studied artistic culture of Renaissance Italy, Symonds easily recognized the significance of some of Whitman's clues and indirections. What remained unclear to Symonds was their political usefulness. Symonds responded to Whitman, in "The Song of Love and Death" for example, as a poet whose homoeroticism could be the basis for political reform:

> Thou dost establish—and our hearts receive—
> New laws of Love to link and intertwine
> Majestic peoples; Love to weld and weave
> Comrade to comrade, man to bearded man,
> Whereby indissoluble hosts shall cleave
> Unto the primal truths republican.[59]

Symonds's paramount concern was not whether Whitman was homosexual; rather, it was the applicability of Whitman's influential poetry to the political agenda of Uranianism supported by Symonds and his intellectual colleagues.

The Uranians were a loosely organized group of homosexual men in late Victorian England. In addition to Symonds, their ranks included Edward Carpenter and perhaps some members of the Bolton Fellowship. The word "Uranian" denotes something "pertaining to or befitting heaven," but, like "comrade," the word signified more to Victorian radicals. In his Whitmanesque poem, "O Child of Uranus," Carpenter identifies a Uranian as a "Woman-soul within a Man's form dwelling . . . With man's strength to perform, and pride to suffer without sign, / And feminine sensitiveness to the last fibre of being."[60] The author of several studies of homosexuality, Carpenter sometimes identified Whitman as a Uranian; he represented an "intermediate sex," whose sexuality represented "a higher development of humanity than we are accustomed to—a type supervirile, and so far above the ordinary man and woman that it looks upon both with equal eyes."[61] Carpenter's conception of Uranianism, unlike Symonds's, is theoretically bisexual rather than homosexual, and it corresponds with the inclusiveness of Whitman's poetry more than homoerotic exclusivity.

The Uranian agenda was not limited to redefining sexual categories; they wanted to change the English sex laws, for they felt sexual liberty would facilitate social change. The "most pronounced, & socially hopeful, features [of] masculine love," Symonds writes, is its "blending of Social Strata . . . . Where it appears, it abolishes class distinctions."[62] Carpenter also believed that "Homogenic Love is a valuable social force." Whitman's advocacy of "comrade love" made him the "inaugurator of a new world of democratic ideals and literature."[63] Uranian admirers of Whitman's poetry were almost universally supporters of egalitarian principles, and, in the 1890s, they became closely allied with socialism, particularly that of the Fabian Society.[64]

The British socialist movement, including the Fabians, advocated the redistribution of land and capital, placing the means of production into the hands of the workers. More specific goals included industrial reform, women's rights, environmentalism, and vegetarianism, along with protection for homosexuals. As they saw it, the best means of achieving these reforms was the solidarity of the laboring classes, which Whitman seemed to support. Wallace writes, Whitman "represented a new type, as yet rare, but which his example and influence will help to make common in the future; that of one of the average workers and mass-peoples of the world."[65]

Carpenter biographer Chushichi Tsuzuki observes that an "element of sexual attraction" was "in the fellowship of Socialism, and sustained its moral fervour."[66] Admiration for Whitman was one means by which socialism and homosexuality temporarily became interrelated. The sexual reform advocated by socialists would make homosexuality a legal option, and homosexuality would itself transform society according to socialist principles. It was the fervid "adhesiveness" exemplified by Whitman, Carpenter believed, that would draw "members of the different classes together, and none the less strongly because they are members of different classes."[67] And Symonds believed that Whitman had enabled him to break free from the confines of class prejudice: "Through him, I have been able to fraternize in comradeship with men of all classes and several races. To him I owe some of the best friends I now can claim—sons of the soil, hard-workers, 'natural and nonchalant,' 'powerful uneducated' persons."[68] "Among my own dearest friends," he continues, "are a postillion, a stevedore, a gondolier, a farm servant, a porter in a hotel."[69] Thus, in part, through the medium of Whitman's poetry, bourgeois homosexuality and socialism became intertwined, and socialist discourse blended with the iconography of homosexual fantasy of "rough trade." Uranians gave socialism an aesthetic of muscularity, youth, and athleticism. They gave socialism the term "comrade," which never lost its subversive quality. And socialist art and literature eventually became rife with homoerotic images of young, muscular, working-class men.

The socialist faction of Uranianism soon became so closely associated with Whitman that the term "Whitmanite" was applied to them by their enemies, for it was a combination of Whitman and sodomite.[70] The Uranian socialists, in time, adopted the title as their own. For the Whitmanites, Whitman came to define a new masculine ethos set in opposition to capitalism, so linked with masculinity in America, where the ability to seize property and wealth defined one's manliness. Followers like Symonds and Carpenter generated a homosexual culture of language,

Figure 8. Edward Carpenter in his late twenties. Carpenter Collection photographs 8/6, courtesy Sheffield City Council.

gesture, posture, clothing, and appearance that opposed long-existing homosexual stereotypes: beards were popular, as were "wide-awakes," a kind of broad-brimmed hat, and some formerly prim Englishmen wore their shirt collars open as Whitman did. "[S]omewhere in the early 'eighties," Carpenter writes, "*I gave my dress clothes away,* I did so without misgiving and without fear that I should need them again."[71] They put on the appearance of being "roughs" with "beards," exuding the "rugged-ness," and "nonchalance" described by Whitman, and basing their appearance on the defiant workman-poet of the frontispiece of the 1855 *Leaves* (see Figures 1, 8, and 9).[72]

As Byrne Fone observes, Whitman's concept of comradeship excludes "the effeminacy and the sexual passivity—though not the sexuality itself—of the unman-ly homosexual."[73] Whitmanites defined themselves in opposition to another faction of English homosexuals who were epitomized by—and often associated with—the flamboyant Oscar Wilde. These two antithetical homosexual discourses were close-ly related to social class and political orientation: the Whitmanites were largely mid-dle-class supporters of socialism; the other group were aristocrats by wealth and title (or presumption to such) who disdained the crudities of labor and nature for the refinements of an elite culture unrestricted by conventional morality.

Figure 9. Edward Carpenter at age 43 in 1887. Carpenter Collection photographs 8/24, courtesy Sheffield City Council.

The Whitmanites mostly considered themselves Uranians in the sense defined by Carpenter; they were an intermediate sex that represented "Love's Coming of Age," the *avant-garde* of human evolutionary development. Ideally, the male Uranian was a combination of the healthy, active male body with the "tender, sensitive, pitiful, and loving" nature of the female soul.[74] They posed as physically vigorous, and, although they were intellectual, they were not overly refined or genteel. Carpenter writes, "Anything effeminate in a man, or anything of the cheap intellectual style, repels me very decisively."[75] The Wildeans, on the other hand, represented a retrograde variety of inversion—the feminized or debased male body containing not the noble "feminine" virtues of empathy and intuition but rather the ignoble one's of pettiness, indolence, and hedonism. Unlike the rough, muscular image of Whitman imitated by his followers, the Wildean ideal was refined androgyny. Aubrey Beardsley's etchings, for example, are often sexually ambiguous: males with long, feminine hair. He depicts some bodies with breasts and penises; other bodies have vulvas but male chests.[76] While the Whitmanites were presenting homosexuality as "supervirile," heroically active and manly, the Wildeans undermined their effort by making campy, parodic displays of homosexual stereotypes—appearing as if they were, in fact, neither man nor woman.

While their approaches were different, both groups supported reforming the laws against homosexuals. Their chief difference was their relationship to socialism. While the Whitmanites advocated socialism as a means of liberating the working classes along with homosexuals, the Wildeans separated themselves from labor; they cared little for advancing a leveling socialist agenda, but they did support socialism if it would provide sexual liberty and artistic freedom.[77] To the Whitmanites "Wildean" homosexuality was undemocratic, for it represented passivity and weakness rather than individual assertion, which they viewed as the foundation of universal rights. Effeminacy was the manner of the privileged classes. It was the aristocratic decadence of the salon rather than the socialistic simplicity of Carpenter's Millthorpe; it was Art Nouveau versus Arts and Crafts.[78]

Sedgwick observes that near the end of the nineteenth century the Wildean construction of homosexuality emerged when the aristocratic construction had "been sublimated, feminized, and materially hollowed out."[79] Ellis's case studies in *Sexual Inversion*, which were compiled at this time, indicate that subjects who were from affluent backgrounds were more likely to describe themselves as effeminate, or at least possessing feminine qualities like "vanity, irritability and petty preoccupations," than those who had working class backgrounds.[80] Only a few years later W. C. Rivers, in his book *Walt Whitman's Anomaly*, identifies Whitman as a homosexual because he sometimes fitted the feminized role of aristocratic homosexual culture: "he cared nothing for sport," he delighted "in cooking," "he can talk about clothes with a woman's knowledge," he had "feminine devotion" to nursing during the Civil War. "No true man could feel like that," Rivers writes, "however full of compassion and patriotism."[81] Masculinity, for Rivers, is a prerequisite for "Manhood." Effeminate behavior, rather than sexual activity, became the predominant sign of homosexuality and the chief basis for attacks on homosexuals. The stronger and more pervasive this configuration of homosexuality became, the more men had to differentiate themselves from anything effeminate. American law officials, for example, came to identify homosexuals not by sexual acts but as those who "'affect the carriage, mannerisms, and speech of women.'"[82]

The most visible homosexuals—the ones most readily identified in elite discourses—were primarily working-class men who signified their same-sex desires by becoming "fairies," who externalized the so-called woman within by acting in ways culturally designated as "feminine." Carpenter observes with some frustration, that fairies "excite a good deal of attention" and that most people believe all homosexual men fall into this category.[83] It is unclear whether fairies were a source of the elite characterization of the homosexual as an invert or whether they were responding to this characterization; it is most likely that both processes occurred at the same time, but the visibility of fairies did increase in the late-nineteenth century as sexuality became increasingly bifurcated. In either case, like Carpenter's model of the Uranian, fairies preserved the model of opposite sex attraction. As George Chauncey observes, "fairies reaffirmed the conventions of gender even as they violated them."[84] Masculine working-class men, for example, did not regard sexual relations with fairies as feminizing; on the contrary, it made them regard themselves as more masculine.

Although fairies constituted a minority of homosexual men, even among the working classes, their effeminacy contributed to the oppression of homosexuals in general. Consequently, they were resented by many men who experienced same-sex desire, particularly those in the middle class. Although the Uranian male possesses feminine qualities, Carpenter, for example, always distances himself from the effeminacy of fairies, whom he calls "extreme and exaggerated types of the race." In contrast with the vigorous image of the Uranian, Carpenter describes the fairy as "sentimental, lackadaisical, mincing in gait and manners, something of a chatterbox, skillful at the needle and in woman's work, sometimes taking pleasure in women's clothes." Moreover, the body of the fairy was also different from that of the muscular Uranian; "his figure not infrequently betraying a tendency toward the feminine, large at the hips, supple, not muscular, the face wanting in hair, the voice inclined to be high-pitched."[85] "Straight-acting" homosexuals like Carpenter, it seems, participated in the broader cultural pattern of defining effeminate males as a separate species, even from Uranians.

The stronger and more pervasive the construction of the homosexual as a fairy became in the general culture, the more men who were unwilling to risk identification as homosexuals had to differentiate themselves from anything effeminate. This need to defend oneself from the accusation of effeminacy became endemic to middle-class men, particularly those in the professions, who were most exposed to medical and legal surveillance and who had the most to lose in terms of social status. The need to avoid the risks of effeminacy as a signifier of same-sex desire accelerated the circulation of other homosexual subjectivities between classes. Some homosexuals, as Chauncey observes, "created a place in middle-class culture by constructing a persona of highly mannered—and ambiguous—sophistication," which was based on the emulation of the English aristocratic style of connoisseurship and extreme refinement.[86] Oscar Wilde is, perhaps, the most prominent example of this style, which could obscure and dismiss anti-homosexual attacks by accusing the accuser of being uncultivated and ignorant.

Oscar Wilde's arrest for sodomy in 1895—and the explosion of publicity that followed—reinforced the Wildean type as the popular embodiment of homosexuality. His imprisonment generated an anti-homosexual shock wave.[87] In response, literary and intellectual types began to adopt a more manly pose, and the Whitmanites redoubled their effort to distinguish themselves from the homosexual stereotype of femininity, weakness, privilege. The Uranian, for Carpenter, was not a feminized man; nor was he simply homosexual. He was, like Whitman, a totality that could not be reduced to a perversion punishable in a court of law. Carpenter's efforts, however, were anticipated by similar scandal involving Whitman thirty years earlier, when the poet's American supporters set out to prove that Whitman was a man, that manhood could include homosexuality, and that they, his followers and imitators, were men as well.[88]

IV. "WELL *HE* LOOKS LIKE A MAN!"

Although it was a serious charge, comradely affection did not impugn one's manhood at the beginning of the nineteenth century in the United States the way it did later in the century. The boundaries of the masculine and feminine had not yet been so rigidly defined along the lines of heterosexual and homosexual. However, "By 1856, when Whitman wrote to Emerson," observes Fone, "Manliness had definitely begun to exclude affectional, and had rarely included the possibilities of sexual relations between men."[89] By the end of the Civil War, the expression of affection between men in the wrong context could be socially and legally dangerous.

James Harlan, who fired Whitman from his job at the Department of the Interior, justified the dismissal on the grounds of Whitman's "moral character" as the author of the obscene *Leaves of Grass*.[90] Harlan said *Leaves* was "full of indecent passages," and that Whitman was "a very bad man," a "free lover."[91] Harlan never said anything about advocating sodomy, but Whitman's supporters seem to have known that this was, in fact, the poet's offense. Just as the English Whitmanites struggled to protect themselves in the aftermath of Wilde's imprisonment with a veneer of masculinity, Whitman and his supporters rallied to prove the poet's "manliness," which had been officially impugned by this dismissal from a government post.

Under Whitman's direction, William D. O'Connor defended the poet in *The Good Gray Poet: A Vindication* (1866). O'Connor writes that Whitman's "whole form [is] surrounded with *manliness*."[92] "A better *man* in all respects, or one more irreproachable in his relations to the other sex, lives not upon this earth."[93] Another Whitman supporter wrote a letter as "A. Van Rensellaer," which O'Connor republished. The letter said that President Lincoln, upon seeing the author of *Leaves of Grass* from his White House window remarked, "Well *he* looks like a MAN!"[94] This letter was widely published both in United States and abroad as a defense against the charge of Whitman's unmanliness.

There were, however, some quarrels between English and American conceptions of manliness. In 1855 the *Critic*, a London periodical, complains that Whitman "calls his free speech the true utterance of a *man*: we, who may have been misdirected by civilization, call it the expression of a *beast*."[95] Referring to *Leaves*, an English correspondent of Thoreau writes, "I find the gentleman altogether left out of the book!"[96] In London's aptly named *Gentleman's Magazine*, Standish O'Grady writes, "the language of his [Whitman's] evangel-poems appears simply disgusting"[97] To this position the Canadian Richard Maurice Bucke responds, "Yes, 'disgusting,' to fops and artificial scholars and prim gentlemen of the clubs—but sane, heroic, full-blooded, natural men will find in it the deepest God-implanted voices of their hearts."[98] The English "gentleman," with his associations of refinement and elitism, stood at variance to the American "man" with his associations of roughness and egalitarianism.

American "manhood" had little of the English gentility and respect for hierarchy in it. The Declaration of Independence itself used the word *manly* to describe the courage to resist tyranny.[99] Ideally, American manhood was defiant, plainspoken, vigorous, skillful, and strong. The American man did not live comfortably on trust funds; he stood on his own sturdy legs and went only where they could carry him. He was not a bookworm or an aesthete; he was a laborer and an athlete. He was not vain about his appearance; he was natural and unselfconscious. He was not, in short, a conventional English poet. Whitman, perhaps best of all, defines this man in "Song of Myself":

> The boy I love, the same becomes a man not through derived
> power, but in his own right . . .
> First rate to ride, to fight, to hit the bull's eye, to sail a skiff, to sing
> a song or play a banjo,
> Preferring scars and the beard and faces pitted with small-pox
> over all latherers,
> And those well-tann'd to those that keep out of the sun.[100]

English manliness, as defined by the literary class, did not engage in labor, which was a sign of subordination to another man. For Americans, labor was a means of achieving independence, just as the laborer, in time, becomes a contractor, then a real estate speculator. It was the latter sense of masculinity in labor, as well as bodily strength, that reshaped the English socialist in accordance with "American" values via Whitman.

After Carpenter's conversion to socialism in the 1870s, he became as repelled by those who seem "glib or refined" as he was by fairies. "Anything effeminate in a man," Carpenter writes, "or anything of the cheap intellectual style, repels me very decisively."[101] As Peter Stearns observes, working-class men seemed to have "a clearer, more elementary notion of what manhood was."[102] Moreover, a pervasive belief emerged in the late nineteenth century that the middle class and its desire for "respectability" had confined sexual acts to the bedrooms of the procreative, married, heterosexual couple, and had abandoned the ancient sexual freedom—possibly descending from Classical time—of the working classes. Sex became a hushed matter, and physical needs were suppressed with dire psychological consequences. There was a belief that the working classes had somehow escaped the excesses of sexual repression endemic to the bourgeoisie; they represented a more primitive state of sexual openness. Sexual expression was not codified into "normal" and "deviant," men, women and children could wink and laugh knowingly about sex, which was not obsessively concealed. Even "homosexuality," though unnamed, was expressed in the rough play and labor of the men, whose often exposed bodies, muscular from the habit of honest toil, were free to sing, dance, and carouse with each other. Their very being seemed a rebuke to the pale, starched-collar effeminacy of their domesticated middle-class brethren. As Carpenter writes in *Towards Democracy*:

> The dressed-up man of the world eyes him curiously—
> and does not forget;

The pale student eyes him: he envies his healthy face
and unembarrassed manner.[103]

This somewhat impressionistic image of class difference is reflective of broadly based sense of alienation rather than substantial differences between classes. As
Michael Mason observes, even in the first half of the nineteenth century there was
a persistent "drive to working-class sexual respectability."[104] Nevertheless,
Carpenter's rejection of the middle-classes seems to have resulted less from homosexuality than from a desire to seek a "cure" for the hypocrisies of civilized life, "the
insuperable *feeling* of falsity and dislocation."[105] Carpenter's break with the ministry
in 1874 was, in part, precipitated by being told that "'It is all such tomfoolery . . .
it doesn't matter whether you say you believe in it, or whether you say you don't.'"[106]
Carpenter wished "To feel downwards and downwards through this wretched maze
of shams for the solid ground—to come close to the Earth itself and those that live
in direct contact with it."[107] Whitman may have given Carpenter a "ground for the
love of men," but it was the poet's apparent frankness that attracted him most;
Whitman, Carpenter writes, "made men to be not ashamed of the noblest instinct
of their nature." Unable to integrate his thoughts with his profession, Carpenter
abandoned his ministerial position at Cambridge and began a correspondence with
Whitman, sending him a manifesto that clearly equates the middle class with effeminate artificiality and the working class with masculine authenticity:

> There is no hope, almost none, from English respectability. The Church is
> effete. . . . I was in orders; but I have given that up—utterly. It was no good.
> Nor does the University do: there is nothing vital in it. Now I am going away
> to lecture to working men and women in the North. They at least desire to lay
> hold of something with a real grasp."[108]

Posing as a missionary among "the mass of the people and the manual workers," Carpenter declared to Whitman, "my work is carry on what you have begun.
You have opened the way: my only desire is to go onward with it."[109]

"One of the pathetic things of the Socialist movement," Carpenter complains,
"is the way in which it has caused not a few people of upper class birth and training
to try and leave their own ranks and join those of the workers." Most such men,
Carpenter writes, are "more or less pitied or ridiculed by both classes."[110] Perhaps
there is a redeeming hint of self-reflexive irony in Carpenter's observation, for he
never fully extricated himself from his middle-class upbringing. Although Whitman
seemed to give political legitimacy to the activity, Carpenter's turn to working-class
men for sexual partners was not predicated simply on socialist politics. In addition
to their reputation for masculinity and physical prowess, there were social and economic reasons why working-class men were sexually attractive to middle-class men
like Carpenter.

George Chauncey presents evidence to suggest that "straight-acting" working-
class men were more likely to accept homosexual propositions than middle-class

men. On the one hand, this suggests a greater tolerance for sexual variation; the pro-
hibition of all same-sex acts that had become pervasive among the middle-class had
not yet permeated working-class attitudes. Working-class men, or "rough trade,"
could engage in homosexual acts without losing status provided they assumed the
dominant or masculine role. The availability of working class men also suggests a
greater need among them for patronage and protection. There seems to be a direct
correlation between poverty and the receptiveness to homosexual advances; the most
common group to accept them, Chauncey observes, was common day laborers.[111]

This does not imply that it is simply a matter of economic exploitation of the
poor by the more affluent. A lack of secure income and propertylessness made heterosexual relationships unavailable for many working-class men. "A propertyless
man," according to Stearns, was "prevented usually from marriage, from normal sexuality."[112] For sailors, soldiers, day-laborers, prisoners, and other men at the bottom
of the labor system (all common subjects of Whitman's and Carpenter's eroticized
catalogues of labor), a sexual relationship was most often feasible with another man,
preferably a wealthier one who, because he possessed an income of his own, need
not be concerned with social status of his sex partners unless they were from his own
class (as the example of Wilde and Alfred Douglas proved). The relationship of
Carpenter and George Merrill, his partner of many years, suggests that homosexual
bonds across class lines had the potential to be mutually beneficial and democratic;
however, the economic inequality of the relationship seems to have provoked the
emergence of supposedly rejected discourses of paternalism, patronage, and slumming.

Although theoretically classless, life at Millthorpe, Carpenter's farm, was highly stratified. Merrill was twenty years younger than Carpenter and his social inferi-
or; Carpenter describes him as "Bred in the slums quite below civilization." "I knew
of course that George had an instinctive genius for housework," Carpenter writes,
"and that in all probability he would keep house better than most women would."[113]
Described by Edith Ellis as Carpenter's "factotum and friend in one," Merrill
assumed the housekeeping functions at Millthorpe and permitted Carpenter the
leisure to pursue his writing and lecturing.[114] In the numerous photographs of
Carpenter and Merrill together, Carpenter is generally depicted in the conventionally seated position of the husband, while Merrill either stands like a wife or sits on
the ground like a child or domestic animal. When Carpenter was photographed
with educated, middle-class "comrades" like Dr. John Johnston of the Bolton
Whitman Fellowship, Merrill was inevitably forced into the background (Figure
10). Merrill's dissatisfaction with these arrangements is described by Carpenter with
surprising condescension and sexism as "hysterical jealousy."[115]

While undoubtedly beneficial in many respects to both partners, Carpenter's
patronage of young, uneducated, working-class men like Merrill frequently echoes
the discourses of English bourgeois marriage and the aristocratic homosexual system
that Carpenter claimed to oppose. As such, Carpenter's *masculinities*—even after
committing himself to socialism and homosexuality—both resisted and complied

Figure 10. Edward Carpenter on right, John Johnston on left, and George Merrill Standing. Carpenter Collection photographs 8/53, courtesy of Sheffield City Council.

with the dominant models and failed to achieve the comradely ideal suggested by Whitman.

VI. CONCLUSION

Whitman writes, "I am the poet of the woman the same as the man" and, if anything, Whitman struggles against his own preferences to be balanced: "That of the male is perfect, and that of the female is perfect."[116] Despite the advocacy of many of Whitman's disciples, there is no shortage of heterosexual images in *Leaves*.[117] Whitman told Traubel that *Leaves* must not be used to support any specific sexual or political program:

> If there is anything whatever in Leaves of Grass—anything that sets it apart as a fact of importance—that thing must be its totality—its massings. . . it is never to be set down in traits but as a symphony: is no more to be stated by superficial criticism than life itself is to be so stated: is not to be caught by a smart definition or all given up to one extreme statement.[118]

The "manly love of comrades" could not be separated from other erotic forms and modes of discourse which, in sum, incarnate the poet, who, in turn, incarnates his nation. Although Whitman may have been homosexual, his poetry was sexually all-inclusive, and quite similar to the Uranian identity proposed though not enacted by Carpenter.

For nineteen years Symonds intermittently wrote to Whitman.[119] Just as Whitman had written to Ralph Waldo Emerson in 1855, Symonds sought the approval and affection of *his* "master" in the 1870s and 80s.[120] Unlike Whitman's literary correspondence with Emerson, Symonds's letters assumed a homoerotic quality that made Whitman uncomfortable: "When we meet, a comrade's hand-touch and a kiss will satisfy me, and a look into your eyes."[121] Although Whitman seems to have been openly homosexual among close friends, he scrupulously avoided placing conclusive evidence of it in writing, often burning letters and using numbers and codes to signify names and sexual acts in his own journals.[122] Symonds, on the other hand, wanted Whitman's open approval for his advocacy of homosexuality, which was just beginning to emerge as a clinically and socially classified sexual variety or "perversion." Whitman, however, came to resent Symonds' efforts to force him to make a clear, public declaration of a sexual orientation he did not comprehend in the same way. For Whitman, sexuality was part of an organic unity that included a range of behaviors that could not be so easily classified and used to support political agendas. Symonds threatened to transform the poet from an incarnation of his nation into a symbol of an emerging homosexual consciousness—a prospect from which Whitman distanced himself, particularly when he began to reach a mainstream audience in the 1880s as a patriotic poet and celebrator of Lincoln.

With increasing directness and frustration, Symonds eventually asked Whitman to clearly articulate the homoerotic meaning of the "Calamus" poems. On 3 August 1890, Symonds writes, "In your conception of Comradeship, do you contemplate the possible intrusion of those semi-sexual emotions and actions which no doubt do occur between men?" The key issue for Symonds is not whether there is a homoerotic element in Whitman's poetry, which is plain enough, but whether, Symonds writes, "*you are prepared to leave them to the inclination and the conscience of the individuals concerned?*"[123] Could homosexuality, through illegal, be productive of social good as it had been in ancient Greece, asked Symonds? Were Whitman's "Calamus" poems intended as a model for an ideal democracy, a blueprint for reform? In other words, would Whitman come out of the closet, so to speak, and step forward openly as a leader of an emerging transatlantic homosexual community?

Whitman's reply to Symonds's letter on August 19, 1890, is shocking, deceptive, and famous:

> Ab't the questions on Calamus pieces &c: they quite daze me. L of G. is only to be rightly construed by and within its own atmosphere and essential character—all of its pages & pieces so coming strictly under *that*—that the calamus part has even allow'd the possibility of such construction as mentioned is terrible . . . morbid . . . damnable . . . My life, young manhood, mid-age, times South, etc., have been jolly bodily, and doubtless open to criticism. Though unmarried, I have had six children.[124]

Symonds's was stunned by this response, which was made to appear as if it had been dashed off in a minute. He replied ironically: "It is a great relief to me to know so clearly and precisely what you feel about the question I raised."[125]

Although seemingly open about his sexuality among close friends, Whitman was understandably cautious about making the matter public, which would ruin his reputation among the growing body of mainstream readers he carefully cultivated in the United States.[126] He probably believed—or thought Symonds would believe—that evidence of frequent heterosexual intercourse would disprove his homosexuality. Symonds, of course, being a married homosexual with several children, and a scholar on the topic, knew that multiple paternity did not preclude homosexuality.[127]

While it was not necessary for Whitman to remain fully closeted about his homosexuality among friends, it was necessary, despite the "Calamus" poems, to circumscribe this aspect of his identity within a discourse of words and gestures and symbols that signified participation in a covert community that existed largely unrecognized—and, to that extent, unthreatened—by the larger society. As his Lincoln lectures and "O Captain" show, he craved acceptance by a large, popular audience, which open homosexuality would have precluded, though it might have enhanced his status as an avant-garde artist in some circles (as it surely has in our own time). Symonds, unlike Carpenter and the members of the Whitman Fellowship, threatened to remove Whitman from the private discourse of "comradeship" and to bring him into a developing public, clinical discourse of sexuality, which, in Whitman's mind, had nothing to do with his poetic sensibility.

In part, Whitman reacted strongly against Symonds's attempt to make a symbol and a martyr out of him for the wrong cause, just as Wilde would suffer five years later. Whitman's friendship for Carpenter, Wallace, and Johnston, on the other hand, was based on their respect for his privacy and their unwillingness to reduce the complexity of Whitman's poetry to suit a narrowly conceived political agenda. Whitman complained, "What Symonds admires in my books is the comradeship; he says that he had often felt it, and wanted to express it, but dared not."[128] Unlike Symonds, Carpenter viewed Whitman's poetry as a totality: "For the first time in history do we hear the voice of a prophet who really *knows* and really *accepts* the whole range of human life."[129] To label Whitman as an "invert," as Symonds wished to do, would be to reduce the poet who to "a type of life, a life form, and a morphology, with an indiscreet anatomy and possibly a mysterious physiology," making all of his poetry the result of his sexuality.[130] To decontextualize "Calamus" from the rest of *Leaves* would be to reduce the complexity of a man to a fixed sexual orientation.

Although Whitman's attempt to pass as straight in his letter to Symonds and the efforts of followers to assert his manliness now appear misguided, Whitman's articulation of his motives for maintaining the integrity of "Calamus" within *Leaves* seems consistent. Moreover, it was the only practical response to furthering the political reforms advocated by Whitman and his English admirers, as the mainstream socialists decided by 1910. Ultimately, the creation of a public, clinical homosexual identity facilitated by the behavior of the Wildeans and the research of Symonds and Ellis would break the connection between socialism and sexual reform in England, for general opposition to homosexual supporters became a millstone that slowed the pace of socialist economic reform. Meanwhile, the deceased Walt Whitman would soon be appropriated by admirers and disciples who would rewrite his texts and appropriate his persona to legitimize a series of incompatible ideologies.

Figure 11. Edgar Allan Poe, the "Ultima Thule" daguerreotype (1848). Courtesy American Antiquarian Society.

Chapter Five

A Question of "Character"

Visual Images and The Nineteenth-Century Construction of "Edgar Allan Poe"

I. "ULTIMA THULE"

O N 9 NOVEMBER 1848, NOT LONG BEFORE HIS DEATH, EDGAR ALLAN POE found himself seated uncomfortably in a heavy armchair, the back of his head braced by an iron ring, his hands clenching the arms of the chair so as to avoid the slightest movement. Overhead, a huge glass plate tilted below an open skylight, bathing him in an eerie blue light. It was the "operating room" of Samuel Masury and S. W. Hartshorn, daguerreotypists in Providence, Rhode Island; around their gallery hung silvery images of generals, politicians, and other notables. Aware of the mysterious aura of his craft, the daguerreotypist manipulated his instrument, while Poe, possibly hungover from recent drinking and tremulous from a nearly suicidal dose of laudanum taken four days earlier, struggled to remain absolutely still. The tension and pain of this moment showed clearly on his face; Poe's fiancé, the poet Sarah Helen Whitman, would later call the image that resulted the "Ultima Thule" (Figure 11).

In an 1874 letter to Poe biographer John Henry Ingram, Whitman claims she named the daguerreotype "Ultima Thule" because it suggested a passage in Poe's poem "Dream-Land":

> I have reached these lands but newly
> From an ultimate dim Thule—
> From a wild weird clime that lieth, sublime,
> Out of Space—out of Time[1]

Although "Dream-Land" describes a fearful journey from the netherworld, it is actually a hopeful narrative of emergence from mental trauma. The narrator, having safely "wandered home," may use his ordeal as a source of romantic inspiration.

Whitman's use of "Dream-Land" as the referent for the "Ultima Thule" daguerreotype, however, seems to highlight the tension between Whitman's private experience
of Poe's psychological problems and her public romanticization of him as an idealistic dreamer after his death in 1849. The phrase "Ultima Thule" does not exactly
occur in Poe's poem "Dreamland" so much as in Poe's short story, "The Pit and the
Pendulum":

> I could no longer doubt the doom prepared for me by monkish ingenuity in
> torture . . . *the pit*, whose horrors had been destined for so bold a recusant as
> myself—*the pit*, typical of hell, and regarded by rumor as the Ultima Thule of
> all their punishments.[2]

Whitman's presentation of Poe's activities on the day the "Ultima Thule"
daguerreotype was made seems to complete the parallel, for Poe arrived at
Whitman's house "in a state of wild & delirious excitement, calling upon me to save
him from some terrible impending doom." Whitman continues, evoking the "loud,
long, and final scream of despair" of "The Pit": "The tones of his voice were
appalling & rang through the house. Never have I heard anything so awful, even to
sublimity."[3]

As Hervey Allen observes, the "Ultima Thule" daguerreotype of Poe was taken
"probably at the very hour when he looked the worst that he ever looked in his life,"
but of all the images of Poe, Allen continues, it "has become the best known to the
world."[4] The "Ultima Thule" was exhibited, copied, sold, and circulated almost
immediately after it was made. For at least a decade the "Ultima Thule" hung in a
prominent place in the gallery of Masury and Hartshorne and their successor firm,
the Manchester Brothers, where some visitors bought expensive reproductions of it.
Numerous copies of the "Ultima Thule" were already in circulation when the original disappeared from the Manchester Brothers' gallery around 1860. Another
Providence firm, Coleman and Remington, was selling relatively cheap *carte-de-visite* prints of the "Ultima Thule" from a retouched photographic negative by this
time.[5] Matthew Brady also sold modified copies of the "Ultima Thule" from the
early 1860s, although he claimed, significantly, to have taken the original. Copies
were displayed Brady's galleries in New York and Washington from the 1860s until
the early 1880s, where still more *carte-de-visites*, and larger versions of the image
were sold.[6] In the nineteenth century alone, the "Ultima Thule" would become the
basis not only for numerous photographic reproductions (Manchester, Coleman
and Remington, Brady), but also for lithographs (Alexis Perrassin), engravings
(Timothy Cole), woodcuts (Félix Vallotton) and paintings (William E. Winner, and
E. C. Lewis, and F. T. L. Boyle).[7] By the early 1880s versions of the "Ultima Thule"
had been published frequently in books and periodicals, sometimes as the frontispiece for collections of Poe's works, along with several articles and a prominent
biography.[8] Although the "Ultima Thule" was not the only image of Poe in circulation, it seemed to replicate more closely than any other image the competing read-

Figure 12. Oliver Leigh's "swelled head" Poe. From Oliver Leigh, *Edgar Allan Poe: The Man, the Master, the Martyr* (Chicago, 1906).

ings of Poe's "character": on one side, Griswold's prosaic view of Poe as a literary hatchet man and rhymester ruined by moral weakness, on the other, Whitman's poetic view of Poe as a romantic dreamer doomed by personal misfortune.[9]

Many nineteenth-century biographers of Poe, including Whitman, saw their task as analyzing Poe's "character" as well as the value of his literary works, and they regularly used Poe's visual record in tandem with his writings. The apparently concealed ambivalence of Whitman's reading of the "Ultima Thule" daguerreotype is typical of Poe's biographers, who found, as one writes, a "strange diversity of character displayed in the portraits of Edgar A. Poe."[10] Another biographer, Edmund Clarence Stedman, relying on Poe's visual record as well as his writings, concluded, "Two natures in him strove / Like day with night, his sunshine and his gloom."[11] By the turn of the century Poe had become so Janus-faced that Oliver Leigh could create a transposable version of the "Ultima Thule" portrait unifying opposite sides of the image in order to test the "theory of Poe's contradictory temperament."[12] In the "sober and sane" head, Leigh saw, "The square headed *constructor* of stories and poems, the architect, builder and adorner with art." In the "swelled-head unity" (Figure 12), Leigh saw the "top-heavy brain that bred and fed on eerie fancies, strange monstrosities, grotesques and arabesques, of the unbalanced mind that 'laughs but smiles no more.'" Leigh concluded that, like the doomed "House of Usher," the "brain of Poe the Critic and Poe the Poet was a lordly house divided against itself."[13]

It is often assumed that portraits of an author are subordinate or even incidental to the text of a biography or an edition of an author's works. As this chapter will show, however, the reciprocal relationship between image and text guided the construction of "Edgar Allan Poe." By the end of the nineteenth century, photographs were the standard of objective evidence in fields like criminology and literary biography, both of which were concerned with the accurate identification of "character." The widespread analysis of Poe's visual record did not stabilize his character; quite the contrary. Images like the "Ultima Thule" were used to construct alternative readings of Poe's life and works. Moreover, such interpretations were complicated not only by the relationship between image and text, but also by the competing and overlapping discourses of poetry and prose, fiction and autobiography, and the complex intersection of meanings in the word "character" itself.

II. *MEMENTO MORI*

Like much of his fiction, the daguerreotypes of Poe are somewhat morbid. The photographic portrait is a "ghost we hold imprisoned," writes Oliver Wendell Holmes, "a latent soul, which will presently appear before its judge."[14] Walt Whitman describes photography as "a new world—a peopled world, though mute as the grave."[15] "All photographs are *memento mori*," explains Susan Sontag, "To take a photograph is to participate in another person's (or thing's) mortality, vulnerability, mutability."[16] Possession of an old photographic portrait gives the feeling of a temporal collapse, of direct contact with the physical reality of an individual who no longer exists. This is particularly the case when the photograph is an original, when it registers the light directly reflected from the face of the subject. As such, it has the quality of a relic, and the use of original daguerreotypes seems to support interpretive claims not based upon personal contact, as in the case of the late nineteenth-century biographers of Poe. As Walter Benjamin observes, photographic portraiture offered "a last refuge for the cult value of the picture."[17] Like sacred relics, photographic traces of Poe's material reality seem to confer authority on their possessors and to reinforce the faith of what Eugene Didier has rightly called, "The Poe Cult."[18]

As Walter Benjamin observes in "The Work of Art in the Age of Mechanical Reproduction," "The presence of the original is the prerequisite to the concept of authenticity."[19] Poe himself had written, "the Daguerreotype plate is *infinitely* more accurate in its representation than any painting by human hands."[20] Photography also reinforces the genre of biography, which depends upon claims of objectivity and authenticity—there must be a "real" subject, and the biographer must have the most direct contact possible. Late nineteenth-century biographers like John Henry Ingram, William F. Gill, Edmund Clarence Stedman, and George Woodberry went to great pains to collect authenticated Poe portraiture after the death of nearly all of Poe's intimate contemporaries. By the 1870s and 80s, during the rise of literary realism and scientific empiricism, a race was on to acquire "original" Poe daguerreotypes, which would provide direct access to the "real" Poe. An "original" image made by the unbiased eye of a scientific instrument could reveal more factual information about the subject than any idealized engraving. Ingram tracked down every daguerreotype of Poe available, but he was often unable to acquire originals; "copies," he complained, "are everywhere."[21] Stedman too had been collecting steadily since the 1870s, and by 1895 his edition of the *Works of Edgar Allan Poe* in ten volumes triumphantly announced it included photographic copies of the originals of all but two of Poe's portraits.[22] Didier summarizes these competitive efforts in 1909: "Nine lives of Poe have been published, each of which contains a portrait, more or less different, but all claiming to be the 'best' likeness."[23] In his *Life of Edgar Allan Poe* (1878), for example, Gill claims his frontispiece, "taken from life," "represents the poet in his later years, and by several of his most intimate friends is pronounced the best portrait extant."[24] Like Brady's claim to owning the original "Ultima Thule," Gill's claim is significant. The possession an original daguerreotype (as opposed to an infinitely reproducible photographic negative) is a more immediate appropriation of the subject; it gives the owner an interpretive authority exceeded only by those who actually "knew" the subject when he or she was alive.

Poe's long-surviving fiancée and defender, Sarah Helen Whitman (1803–1878), long claimed an interpretive privilege on the authentication of Poe's visual records based on her own "intimate" contact with him, an experience that no other biographer could claim after the late 1870s. Only those who actually "knew" Poe, she claims, could comment objectively on the authenticity and meaning of his images. She criticizes the engraving of Poe in Redfield's *Poetical Works of Edgar Allan Poe*, for example, as "clerkly and clerical" and "very unlike the original."[25] She declares the painting of Poe by Samuel Osgood "valueless as a portrait to those who remember the unmatched glory of his face."[26] And she pronounces the engraving in Gill's anthology, *Laurel Leaves,* "hideous. There is no other word that can describe it," she continues, "The expression is weak, nerveless, inane—altogether *unlike* him & *unworthy* of him." With the possible exception of the "Whitman" daguerreotype, which seems to have been an engagement present from Poe to Whitman, nearly every other image of Poe, even the one used by Gill, is an inaccurate reflection: "What malign spirit inspired him [Gill] in making this *memento mori*, it is difficult to conceive."[27] Apparently conscious of the subjectivity of visual analysis, Whitman writes of one portrait, "it is no true lens through which to peer into the wondrous, far-down depths of the mind-and-soul of him."[28] Photographic evidence, Whitman maintains, is inadequate to describe the complexities of Poe's "character, any adequate transmission of its variable and subtle moods [is] impossible."[29]

Whitman is suspicious of daguerreotypes of Poe, no doubt, because some of them tend to confirm the image of Poe as the maddened, disinherited Edgar of *King Lear* fixed by Griswold in his obituary of Poe in the New York *Daily Tribune*:

> He walked the streets, in madness or melancholy, with lips moving in indistinct curses, or with eyes upturned in passionate prayers . . . or with his glance introverted to a heart gnawed with anguish, and with a face shrouded in gloom, he would brave the wildest storms.[30]

Figure 13. Edgar Allan
Poe, the "Whitman"
daguerreotype (1848).
Brown University Library.

"Likenesses such as the 'Ultima Thule,'" observes Michael Deas, "provided a
kind of visual credence to Rufus Griswold's defamatory description of Poe, and have
been instrumental in shaping a popular image of the poet."[31] Henry S. Cornwell's
reading of the "Ultima Thule" in 1880, for example, seems to echo Griswold's darkly romantic image:

> The aspect is one of mental misery, bordering on wildness, disdain of human
> sympathy, and scornful intellectual superiority. There is also in it, I think, dread
> of imminent calamity, coupled with despair and defiance, as of a hunted soul at
> bay.[32]

In this representative comparison, the relationship between Poe's writing, his visual
record, and his personal history becomes problematically intertwined. The language
of Griswold's description of Poe is, in fact, rather Poe-esque. John Neal angrily
attacked Griswold's description of Poe as pure plagiarism: "The thoughts I have
underscored are Poe's—and so is the very language—every word of it."[33] While Poe's
fiction shades Griswold's influential portrait, Cornwell's visual reading of Poe's portrait emerges from the combined influence of Poe's fiction, Griswold's interpolation,
and the known circumstances of Poe's biography. Would Cornwell have identified

Poe's look in 1848 as "dread of imminent calamity" without knowing that Poe died miserably in 1849?

Whitman's larger project, asserting the interpretive authority of her personal contact with Poe, involved refuting "the spirit of Dr. Griswold's unjust memoir" by discrediting interpretations based upon second-hand information and visual evidence.[34] In *Edgar Poe and His Critics* (1860) Whitman not only refutes many of Griswold's positions but undermines the visual grounds on which his construction of Poe is partially based. An opening epigraph suggests that her project is, in part, to re-focus on Poe's distorted visage; she quotes Tennyson, "We cannot see thy features right; / They mix with hollow masks of night."[35] Whitman goes on to critique the engraving of Poe in Griswold's *Works of the Late Edgar Allan Poe* (1850–56) as "utterly void of character and expression; it has no sub-surface." Only by "writers personally unacquainted with Mr. Poe," she writes, has this engraving been "favorably noticed."[36] In other words, Whitman's intimate association with Poe makes her a better judge of how well any daguerreotype reflects his "character."

Given her professed interpretive authority over Poe's daguerreotypes, it is striking that Whitman's biography does not include any of them. Although she comes to regard the more relaxed "Whitman" daguerreotype of Poe (Figure 13) in her private collection as "the best likeness he ever had," she never publishes it as a refutation of the dark intensity of the "Ultima Thule." Until her own death seemed imminent in 1874, her only public display of Poe's image is a poem called "The Portrait":

Slowly I raised the purple folds concealing
    That face, magnetic as the morning's beam;
While slumbering memory thrilled at its revealing,
    Like Memnon waking from his marble dream.
Again I saw the brow's translucent pallor,
    The dark hair floating o'er it like a plume;
The sweet imperious mouth, whose haughty valor
    Defied all portents of impending doom.
Eyes planet calm, with something in their vision
    That seemed not of earth's mortal mixture born;
Strange mythic faiths and fantasies Elysian,
    And far, sweet dreams of 'fairy lands forlorn.'
Unfathomable eyes that held the sorrow
    Of vanished ages in their shadowy deeps;
Lit by that prescience of a heavenly morrow
    Which in high hearts the immortal spirit keeps.[37]

Whitman's interpretations of Poe's visual image are multi-leveled, as in the previously discussed naming of the "Ultima Thule." The language, style, and form of Whitman's "Portrait of Poe," is, perhaps appropriately, derivative of Poe's verse. As such, it conflates Poe's image with his poetry, alluding to "Ulalume," "Lenore," "The Haunted Palace," and "The Bells," just as Griswold conflates Poe's life with his prose. But, in doing so, it engages with Griswold on his own terms, for she directly refutes his depiction of Poe's madness, bitterness, introversion, and despair. Poe is not mad but, like the romantic poet John Keats, dreaming of "fairy lands forlorn"; his mouth is not cursing but "sweet" and "imperious"; he is not looking inward but to "vanished ages"; he is not "shrouded in gloom" but defying "impending doom." Such an approach to the construction of Poe's image seems consistent with Whitman's mistrust of the visual and her criticism of Griswold. Moreover, Griswold places Poe's dark fiction in a reciprocal relationship with Poe's visual image. Whatever her private understanding of Poe may have been, Whitman's public interpretation of Poe's image is interwoven with the culturally privileged genre of poetry rather than Poe's somewhat disreputable prose, with romantic idealism rather than gothic terror, with "Dream-Land" rather than "The Pit and the Pendulum."[38]

Whitman's avoidance of unfiltered visual evidence would not seem as valid to the generation of Poe interpreters writing after 1878, when nearly all of Poe's contemporaries were gone. Biographers like Stedman (1833–1908) and Woodberry (1855–1930) emerged at the moment when the general public was first trained to comprehend historical figures and events through photographs.[39] They came to know the faces of the eminent through photographic galleries, picture books, and stereoscopic cards and *carte de visites* of places and people that were traded like contemporary baseball cards. For the first time, the illustrious, people at an inaccessible distance, and the long dead, were visually accessible to almost anyone. Historical figures were subject to interpretation not in the flattering romantic portraiture that disguised character, but in the open, revealing, realistic photograph. Photography seemed to democratize biography by making it possible for those without the privilege of personal access to their subjects to view them as equals and contemporaries.

Even the former authority of personal acquaintance with the subject began to be displaced by the authority of photographic evidence. Artists like Thomas Eakins used photographic studies of motion to detect realities invisible to the human eye, and biographers began to think along similar lines. "We have learned many curious facts from photographic portraits which we were slow to learn from faces," writes Oliver Wendell Holmes; photographs reveal "the mental and emotional shapes by which his [the subject's] inner nature made itself known to us."[40] Such an approach to biography and the construction of authors led to a process in which a canon of authenticated portraits was created along with a canon of authenticated texts.

Poe existed for biographers like Stedman and Ingram not simply as a body of scripture. He was a face, and preferably not the face of the old-fashioned, idealized engraving or portrait. Rather, he was recorded by the modern, scientifically accurate perception of the photograph, which had become the standard of objective evidence. The text and the photograph of the writer became increasingly interconnected in the literary biographer's craft, each shaping the meaning of the other. Ultimately, the claims of those, like Sarah Helen Whitman, who "knew" Poe in life would be displaced by those with access to "authentic" images and texts, those validated by technological and scholarly inspection.[41] Stedman declared that readers must "drive out of mind the popular conceptions of his [Poe's] nature, and look only at the portraits of him in the flesh."[42] Stedman and Woodberry's *Works of Edgar Allan Poe* (1894–95) in ten volumes seems a triumph of empiricism and of the collecting impulse applied to the construction of Poe as an author. It includes not only the "authorized text" revised "in Poe's own hand" with an extensive scholarly apparatus, but "Contemporary Notices," a complete bibliography, and all but two of the known "portraits that were undoubtedly taken from life."[43]

It is significant that Stedman insists upon a close study of Poe "in the flesh," for visual images provided for a mediated inspection of Poe's body using so-called scientific methods like chirography, cryptography, phrenology and physiognomy. Using both literary criticism and emerging techniques for reading the body, biographers would attempt to unearth Poe's "character" from the *memento mori*—the possessions, the texts, the handwriting, the visual images, and perhaps even the physical remains of Poe, which were disinterred and examined in 1876: "Some hair yet attached the skull, and the teeth, which appeared to be white and perfect, were shaken out of the jaws."[44] By this time Poe's remains were inextricable from his identity as the author of macabre fiction, and the description of this event seems a darkly comical allusion to Poe's short story, "Berenice." Afterwards, Poe's remains were moved to a more prominent place with an appropriate monument with "a finely executed medallion bust of the poet, taken from a photograph copy of an original daguerreotype."[45] The body of Poe itself had been appropriated and reconstructed by his interpreters using visual evidence thrice-removed from the subject. "Strange, is it not," said the church sexton who unearthed the writer's remains, "that Poe will not stay put!"[46]

III. "CHARACTER"

It has been observed that it was not specifically Poe's work that Griswold had maligned in 1849 but his *character*. Griswold claims that Poe possessed "no moral susceptibility" and "little or nothing of the true point of honor."[47] Numerous other critics took their cue from Griswold in their post-mortem attacks.[48] The introduction to an early edition of Poe states that "a truthful delineation of his career would give a darker hue to his character than it has received from any of his biographers."[49] Poe's friends and admirers likewise rallied in defense of his "character." In 1850 George Graham of *Graham's Magazine* claims that Griswold's "exceedingly ill-timed and unappreciative estimate of the character of our lost friend is UNFAIR AND UNTRUE . . . so dark a picture has no resemblance to the living man" Gill's 1878 biography of Poe likewise professes to give "an impartial estimate of the true character of my subject."[50] And J. J. Moran, the physician who attended the death of Poe in Baltimore, publishes *A Defense of Edgar Allan Poe, Life, Character, and the Dying Declarations of the Poet* in 1885. In short, delineating Poe's "character" becomes an obsession for his nineteenth-century biographers; it is seldom clear, however, what these biographers mean by "character," a term that signified an unstable intersection of meanings in the nineteenth century.

In the oldest literal sense, a character is a letter of type or a symbol used in printing or engraving.[51] It can also be the mark imprinted by this character, and, by extension, character may relate to the unique quality of a person's handwriting. In a figurative sense, character may be applied to the peculiar physical or moral qualities of an individual just as they describe the physical qualities of handwriting. A face, then, may be imprinted or "characterized" with meaning as a blank sheet is imprinted by type; a face, therefore, may be "read" like a text for abstract meanings such as moral "character."

In 1856 Charles Baudelaire, for example describes Poe as one of those "who bear the words *bad luck* written in mysterious characters in the sinuous creases of their foreheads."[52] A person's "character" may also reflect the quality of his or her "type"; poor character—possibly the result of poor breeding—leaves its imprint on the face. John M. Dillon's *Edgar Allan Poe: His Genius and Character*, for example, begins, "The willful, restless spirit, the great weakness of character have also left their imprint [on Poe]."[53] In this sense, "Character" may be an "expression" rather than an "impression," it shapes the features from within; Stedman writes, for example, that Poe's "external aspects were the signs of a character within." For Stedman, the external manifestations of internal character create an interpretive framework for the construction of Poe. Stedman begins with an impression of Poe's character and observes that "The recorded facts of his [Poe's] life serve to enhance this feeling."[54] Like Stedman, many of Poe's nineteenth-century biographers have relied even more explicitly upon the "character" of Poe's appearance to defame or defend the "character" within.

The complexities of the nineteenth-century understanding of "character" are particularly apparent in the efforts of photographers to explain the incredible promise of their newly developed skills. In 1864 Marcus A. Root writes that the photographer's task is to "penetrate, by whatever means at his command, the fleshly mask, which envelops the spiritual part of his model, and ascertain his real type and character."[55] H. J. Rodgers echoes this opinion a decade later; a photographer, he writes, should recognize "character, from the lowest type and form of life to the highest grade of human excellence"; moreover, the photographer should "be able to read the faces of men and women as easily as he would an open book."[56] Both photographers maintain a species of dualism; external character signifies a hidden internal reality or "truth" to which their technology and skills give them access. The metaphors seem to multiply: the photographer is a philosopher seeking verities among shadows, a surgeon penetrating the flesh to expose internal pathologies, a critic explicating the meanings of an obscure text. Amid this kind of technological confidence, the perceptive skills of the photographer seem to promise new opportunities for the student of human nature.

Rodgers, for example, creates a lengthy visual catalogue of human types based upon their appearance. The faces of great intellects, he claims, are always similar, "the forehead is high and broad, and the lower portion of the face thin."[57] Such a description could easily be applied to the "Ultima Thule," which was probably made to be displayed in a gallery as a portrait of a conventionally hydrocephalic *auteur*. Despite the apparently lofty brows of the "Ultima Thule," Poe is described by those who knew him as possessing a receding forehead, "sloping back sharply from, the brow."[58] Rodgers explains this mystery: "A person with a small, narrow forehead could be posed to look highly intellectual by bringing the head slightly foreword."[59] Paradoxically, photographers like Rodgers who place such confidence in their ability to read internal character are also conscious that they edit their visual texts using backdrops, props, poses, lighting, composition, exposure, and darkroom techniques to achieve certain effects.

The complex negotiation of physical reality and preconceived effects suggested by Root and Rodgers seems to emerge from and run parallel to the eighteenth-century "science" of physiognomy, which interpreted abstract qualities on the basis of external features. Just as photographers used posing strategies and lighting to shape the visual personae of their sitters, James Burgh and Johann Caspar Lavater encouraged public speakers to make their facial expression and body language correspond to their words.[60] By the 1880s, however, physiognomy (along with other new "sciences" like anthropomorphic measurement) was also being used by the state as a means of identifying criminal types, by school systems for determining the educability of students, and by biographers in the analysis of Poe.[61] Stedman applies such techniques to the identification of Poe's character in his 1881 biography: "But look at some daguerreotype taken shortly before his death . . . we find those hardened lines of the chin and neck that are often visible in men who have . . . lived loosely and slept ill . . . the man was at war with his meaner self."[62]

Poe, it seems, was a recognizable "type"; the "dissipations" of his youth, his rumored gambling habits, and the destitution of his middle age, both of which were biographical circumstances known to Stedman, are clearly legible in retrospect.

Probably the most notorious nineteenth-century method of reading the body is phrenology, which determines character from the shape of one's head. According to Rodgers, a good photographer should also be a competent phrenologist, and Poe's visual record was frequently the subject of analysis by phrenologists in the nineteenth century.[63] Phrenological analysis of Poe was enthusiastically undertaken by literary critics as well. In March 1850, for example, John Moncure Daniel supports Griswold's defamation of Poe's character by subjecting Poe to a phrenological examination: "The head, as a whole, was a decidedly bad one," Daniel writes, "the coronal region was very deficient. It contained little moral sense and less reverence." Here, as in the case of physiognomy, preconceived notions of Poe's personal character are read into his visual record. What is more complicated, however, is the way Daniel then uses Poe's character as a "key to many of his literary characteristics." Daniel writes, "In Poe's writings there is despair, hopelessness; and the echoes of a melancholy extremely touching to those who read with a remembrance of his broken life."[64] Poe's fictional "characters," then, are a reflection of his "character," which can be deduced from the "character" of his appearance. An 1858 introduction to a collection of Poe's poetry puts it simply, "What he writes he is."[65]

In this last sense, "character" has a relationship to the fictional and dramatic, such as a character in a narrative or dramatic work, or the character assumed by an actor in a performance. In 1856 Charles Baudelaire unifies without explanation the characters of Poe's fiction with Poe's personal character: "The characters of Poe, or rather *the* character of Poe."[66] Fictional characterization becomes identical with personal character; the fiction, therefore, can be mined for insights into the inner character of the author, and the *Works* may supplement or substitute for the autobiography. An 1850 review by John Neal, for example, claims that *The Works of Edgar A. Poe* "give one a very just idea of his character as a writer."[67] Griswold's obituary extends this claim, asserting of Poe that "Nearly all that he wrote in the last two or three years—including much of his best poetry—was in some sense biographical."[68]

But in what "sense" does Griswold mean Poe's works were biographical? Is Poe's writing biographical in the sense that it reflects his development as a writer? Or does Griswold mean that Poe was actually mentally disturbed like Roderick Usher? E. D. Forgues, for example, concludes the latter; he writes in 1846 that in many of Poe's tales, the "protagonist is none other than Mr Poe hardly taking the trouble to hide himself."[69] As seen above, this myth of Poe as one of his own fictional characters emerges from and responds to the visual images as well as textual images. Didier, for example writes, "We turn away with a shudder from this 'sorrow-laden' face wondering what had wrought the terrible change in him." He continues, "Was the change caused by retributions of conscience, which he had described with such awful fidelity in *William Wilson*, the *Tell-Tale Heart*, and *The Man of the Crowd*?"[70] In the imagination of some critics, then, Poe had become, both physically and imaginatively, the tormented protagonists of his grotesque tales and mournful poetry.

The clearest example of this kind of interaction between fiction, visual imagery, and personal history, is the biographical response to Poe's "The Fall of the House of Usher." As Deas observes, "The physical similarities between Poe and a character such as Usher have led at times to an unfortunate blurring of the distinction between life and art."[71] The character of Roderick Usher—supersensitive, artistic, morbid, hypochondriacal, mourning the death of a beautiful woman—seems the embodiment of the biographical Poe; the visual description of Usher is even more compelling:

> Yet the character of his face had been at all times remarkable. A cadaverousness of complexion; an eye large, liquid, and luminous beyond comparison; lips somewhat thin and very pallid, but of a surpassingly beautiful curve; a nose of a delicate Hebrew model, but with a breadth of nostril unusual in similar formations; a finely molded chin, speaking, in its want of prominence, of a want of moral energy; hair of more than web-like softness and tenuity; these features, with an inordinate expansion above the regions of the temple, made up altogether a countenance not easily to be forgotten.[72]

Although she does not mention the short story, Susan Archer Weiss's analysis of Poe's features seems to repeat the description of Usher:

'Unstable as water,' is written upon Poe's every visage in characters which all might read; in the weak falling away of the outline of the jaw, the narrow, receding chin, and the sensitive, irresolute mouth. Above the soul-lighted eyes and the magnificent temple of intellect overshadowing them, we look in vain for the rising dome of *Firmness*, which, like the keystone of the arch, should strengthen and bind together the rest. Lacking this, the arch must be ever tottering to a fall.

Weiss here reads the narrative logic of "Usher" in the face of Poe, showing that Poe's character is readable simultaneously in Poe's face and fiction. Weiss continues: "In order to understand Poe, it is necessary that one should recognize the dominant trait of his character," which is, she writes, "*weakness of will* . . . To this weakness of will we may trace nearly every other defect in Poe's character."[73] Just as the fractured House of Usher collapses into oblivion, so Poe's defective moral character led to the downfall of an otherwise great artist. Weiss's reading, of course, is derived not only from her analysis of Poe's physical features, which are suggested by "Usher," but from her reading of "Ligeia," which begins with the quotation, "Man doth not yield himself up to the angels, nor unto death utterly, save only through the weakness of his feeble will."[74] Based upon such physiognomic and phrenological readings of Poe's visual character, which were themselves influenced by the character and characters of Poe's writings, Poe becomes a tragic hero doomed by a minor character flaw. Stedman, concluding his own examination of Poe's character, writes, "His will, in the primary sense, was weak from the beginning."[75]

IV. CONCLUSION

In "Some Words With a Mummy," Poe seems to predict the circumstances of his own reception; a dead author's works, he writes, are converted into "a kind of literary arena for the conflicting guesses, riddles, and personal squabbles of whole herds of exasperated commentators." The author's original meaning is "enveloped, distorted, and overwhelmed."[76] But if a would-be biographer cannot get at the meaning of the "real" Poe, what inferences can be drawn from this account of Poe's construction in the nineteenth century?

This case, in which several cultural processes converge, illuminate some of the complexities of author-reader relations in the nineteenth century. The increasing importance of the author category placed greater emphasis on the physical reality of the producer of an identifiable body of texts. This had the effect of accelerating the production of authoritative editions, biographies, and visual representations, all of which interacted with each other as elements in the construction of an "author." As photographic and printing technology improved during the shift from romanticism to realism, representations of authors in idealized engravings and portraits were gradually replaced by supposedly more realistic photographic representations. The resulting multiplication of images of authors increased the relative impact of visual evidence on the interpretation of authors. As shown in this essay, the critical methods of biography, which formerly relied more exclusively on textual evidence, began to direct more attention to records of physical evidence, to the body of the author itself. In many cases besides that of Poe, one may expect to find similar interactions between readers' interpretations of the textual and visual—even when the reader claims to be focusing on only one or the other.

This shift from engravings to photographs had significant implications in the management of the public and private spheres of author-reader relations as well. The use of photography resulted in increasing public exposure of authors and diminishing control over their private identities, particularly when infinitely reproducible (and surreptitiously taken) photographs could be used as the basis for many new forms of scientific character reading: physiognomy, phrenology, and later, psychology. The inability to control the production, distribution, and interpretation of photographs, complicated the already formidable difficulties of controlling one's publications. Predictably, such conditions created some generational conflict between 1840 and 1900. There was considerable resistance to the intrusion of the public realm of photography into the formerly private, frequently domestic sphere of genteel literary production among those born earlier in the nineteenth century. In 1865 a reviewer for *The Nation* writes that it was fortunate for one female author "that she lived in pre-daguerreotype ages," because, "she could scarcely have escaped the momentary glance of the camera that now perpetuates indiscriminately for us both the evanescent shapes of beauty and grace as well as their opposites."[77] Photography increased the difficulty of managing the distribution of personal information and disrupted the social distance between authors and readers.

The advent of photography forced some authors (or the custodians of author's reputations) into retrenchment like that of Sarah Helen Whitman, who regretted the publication of the "Ultima Thule" and preferred to publish the supposedly more representative "Whitman" daguerreotype only in a poetic form. Another strategy was to deny the ability of photographs to capture human character; photographs were merely superficial, but art could perceive inner truth. Whitman, for example, clearly preferred the idealized engravings to photographs. She writes to Ingram, "The portrait is much more like E.A.P. than the photograph from which it was taken."[78] Subsequent writers, however, embraced photography, ostensibly accepting the complete exposure of the private self while complicating the very category of selfhood. The protean Walt Whitman, for example, through circulating numerous photographs of himself in tandem with his evolving poetry, presented new visual personae to complement new literary priorities.[79] In the final edition of Walt Whitman's poems, he concludes, "I look upon 'Leaves of Grass,' now finish'd to the end of its opportunities and powers, as my definitive *carte visite* to the coming generations of New World."[80] As we move through the nineteenth century, then, we may characterize authors as engaging in an ongoing struggle with readers both textually *and* visually to negotiate the complexities of self-revelation and concealment. We may also characterize the struggle to construct and sustain a specific kind of authorial identity—aimed at a particular constituency of readers in a specific market context—as ongoing well after the death of an author by competing factions seeking to use construct and reconstruct authors to serve their own purposes.

Notes

NOTES TO THE INTRODUCTION

[1] Emerson, "Experience," *Essays and Lectures* (New York: Library of America, 1983), 473.

[2] Whitman, *Leaves of Grass: Comprehensive Reader's Edition,* eds. Harold W. Blodgett and Sculley Bradley (New York: New York University Press, 1965), 565.

[3] Horace Traubel, *With Walt Whitman in Camden,* 9 Vols. Vol. I (1905; rpt., New York: Rowman and Littlefield, 1961); Vol. II. (1907; rpt., New York: Rowman and Littlefield, 1961); Vol. III. (1912; rpt., New York: Rowman and Littlefield, 1961); Vol. IV (1953; rpt., Carbondale: Southern Illinois University Press, 1959); Vol. V (Carbondale: Southern Illinois University Press, 1964); Vol. VI (Carbondale: Southern Illinois University Press, 1982); Vol. VII (Carbondale: Southern Illinois University Press, 1992); Vols. VIII-IX (Oregon House, CA: W. L. Bentley, 1996), 1:108.

[4] For more detailed discussions of Whitman's visual self-representations see Ed Folsom, *Walt Whitman's Native Representations* (Cambridge: Cambridge University Press, 1994); Folsom, "Appearing in Print: Illustrations of the Self in *Leaves of Grass,*" *The Cambridge Companion to Walt Whitman,* ed. Ezra Greenspan (Cambridge: Cambridge University Press, 1995), 135–165; and Folsom, "Whitman's Calamus Photographs," *Breaking Bounds: Whitman and American Cultural Studies,* ed. Betsy Erkkila and Jay Grossman (New York and Oxford: Oxford University Press, 1996), 193–219.

[5] Traubel, *With Walt Whitman,* 1:108.

[6] Whitman, *Leaves of Grass* (Boston: Thayer and Eldridge, 1860–61), 455.

[7] The butterfly motif would reappear on the spines of the matching 1881–82 editions of *Leaves* and *Specimen Days,* as well in Whitman's publicity photographs in the 1880s.

[8] Lawrence Buell, "Democratic Ideology and Autobiographical Personae in American Renaissance Writing," *Amerikastudien* 35 (1990): 267–280.

NOTES TO CHAPTER ONE

¹ Franklin, *Essays, Articles, Bagatelles, and Letters, Poor Richard's Almanac, Autobiography* (New York: Library of American, 1987), 1307.

² William Matthews, *American Diaries: An Annotated Bibliography of British Autobiographies Published or Written Before 1951* (Berkeley: University of California Press, 1945); Louis Kaplan, *A Bibliography of American Autobiographies* (Madison: University of Wisconsin Press, 1961). These pioneering bibliographies have been supplemented by William Matthews, *American Diaries in Manuscript, 1580–1954: A Descriptive Bibliography* (Athens: University of Georgia Press, 1974); Mary Louise Briscoe, et al, *American Autobiography, 1945–1980* (Madison: University of Wisconsin Press, 1982); Russell Brignano, *Black Americans in Autobiography: An Annotated Bibliography of Autobiographies and Autobiographical Books Written Since the Civil War* (Durham, NC: Duke University Press, 1984); Gwen Davis and Beverly A. Joyce, *Personal Writings By Women to 1900: A Bibliography of American and British Writers* (London: Mansell, 1989).

³ Stephen A. Shapiro, "The Dark Continent of Literature: Autobiography." *Comparative Literature Studies* 5 (1968): 425–435; Roy Pascal, *Design and Truth in Autobiography* (London: Routledge and Kegan Paul, 1960); Robert F. Sayre, *The Examined Self: Benjamin Franklin, Henry Adams, Henry James* (Princeton, NJ: Princeton University Press, 1964); John Cawelti, *Apostles of the Self-Made Man* (Chicago: University of Chicago Press, 1965); Daniel B. Shea, *Spiritual Autobiography in Early America* (Madison: University of Wisconsin Press, 1968); David L. Minter, *The Interpreted Design as a Structural Principle in American Prose* (New Haven, CT: Yale University Press, 1969).

⁴ Francis R. Hart, "Notes for an Anatomy of Modern Autobiography," *New Literary History* 1 (1970): 485–511; James Olney, *Metaphors of the Self: The Meaning of Autobiography* (Princeton, NJ: Princeton University Press, 1972); William Howarth, "Some Principles of Autobiography," *New Literary History* 5 (1974): 363–381; Phillipe Lejeune, *Le Pacte Autobiographique* (Paris: Editions du Seuil, 1975); Karl J. Weintraub, "Autobiography and Historical Consciousness," *Critical Inquiry* 1 (1975): 821–848; Elizabeth Bruss, *Autobiographical Acts: The Changing Situation of a Literary Genre* (Baltimore, MD: Johns Hopkins University Press, 1976); Roland Barthes, *Roland Barthes*, trans. Richard Howard (New York: Hill and Wang, 1977); Louis Renza, "The Veto of the Imagination: A Theory of Autobiography," *New Literary History* 9 (1977): 2–26; Paul de Man, "Autobiography as De-facement," *MLN* 94 (1979): 919–930; James Olney, ed., *Autobiography: Essays Theoretical and Critical* (Princeton, NJ: Princeton University Press, 1980); William Spengemann, *The Forms of Autobiography* (New Haven, CT: Yale University Press, 1980); Janet Varner Gunn, *Autobiography: Toward a Poetics of Experience* (Philadelphia: University of Pennsylvania Press, 1982); Paul Jay, *Being in the Text: Self-Representation from Wordsworth to Roland Barthes* (Ithaca, NY: Cornell University Press, 1984); Paul John Eakin, *Fictions in Autobiography: Studies in the Art of Self-Invention* (Princeton, NJ: Princeton University Press, 1985); Linda

Peterson, *Victorian Autobiography: The Tradition of Self-Interpretation* (New Haven, CT: Yale University Press, 1986); Robert Elbaz, *The Changing Nature of the Self: A Critical Study of the Autobiographic Discourse* (Iowa City: University of Iowa Press, 1987); James Olney, ed., *Studies in Autobiography* (New York: Oxford University Press, 1988); Paul John Eakin, *Touching the World: Reference in Autobiography* (Princeton: Princeton University Press, 1992); Robert Folkenflik, ed., *The Culture of Autobiography: Constructions of Self-Representation* (Stanford, CA: Stanford University Press, 1993); John Sturrock, *The Language of Autobiography: Studies in the First Person Singular* (New York: Cambridge University Press, 1993).

⁵ James Cox, "Autobiography and America," *Virginia Quarterly Review* 47 (1971): 252–277; Lawrence Buell, "Transcendentalist Self-Examination and Autobiographical Tradition," in *Literary Transcendentalism: Style and Vision in the American Renaissance* (Ithaca, NY: Cornell University Press, 1973), 265–283; Sacvan Bercovitch, *The Puritan Origins of the American Self* (New Haven, CT: Yale University Press, 1975); Thomas Cooley, *Educated Lives: The Rise of Modern Autobiography in America* (Columbus: Ohio State University Press, 1976); Robert F. Sayre, "The Proper Study—Autobiographies in American Studies," *American Quarterly* 29 (1977): 241–262; G. Thomas Couser, *American Autobiography: The Prophetic Mode* (Amherst: University of Massachusetts Press, 1979); Albert E. Stone, *Autobiographical Occasions and Original Acts* (Philadelphia: University of Pennsylvania Press, 1982); Jeffrey Steele, *The Representation of the Self in the American Renaissance* (Chapel Hill: University of North Carolina Press, 1987); G. Thomas Couser, *Altered Egos: Authority in American Autobiography*, (New York: Oxford University Press, 1989); James Cox, *Recovering Literature's Lost Ground: Essays in American Autobiography* (Baton Rouge: Louisiana State University Press, 1989); Paul John Eakin, ed., *On Autobiography* (Minneapolis: University of Minnesota Press, 1989); Joseph Fichtelberg, *The Complex Image: Faith and Method in American Autobiography* (Philadelphia: University of Pennsylvania Press, 1989); Herbert Leibowitz, *Fabricating Lives: Explorations in American Autobiography* (New York: Knopf, 1989); Lawrence Buell, "Democratic Ideology and Autobiographical Personae in American Renaissance Writing," *Amerikastudien* 35 (1990): 267–280; Paul John Eakin, ed., *American Autobiography: Retrospect and Prospect* (Madison: University of Wisconsin Press, 1991).

⁶ John F. Bayliss, *Black Slave Narratives* (New York: Macmillan, 1970); Russell C. Brignano, *Black Americans in Autobiography* (Durham, NC: Duke University Press, 1974); Stephen Butterfield, *Black American in Autobiography* (Amherst: University of Massachusetts Press, 1974); Sidonie Smith, *Where I'm Bound: Patterns of Slavery and Freedom in Black American Autobiography* (Westport, CT: Greenwood Press, 1974); Robert Stepto, *From Behind the Veil: A Study of Afro-American Narrative* (Champaign-Urbana: University of Illinois Press, 1979); William L. Andrews, *To Tell a Free Story* (Champaign-Urbana: University of Illinois Press, 1986); Charles Davis and Henry Louis Gates, Jr., *The Slave's Narrative* (New York: Oxford University Press, 1985); Valerie Smith, *Self-Discovery and Authority in Afro-*

American Narrative (Cambridge, MA: Harvard University Press, 1987); Eric Sundquist, *To Wake the Nations* (Cambridge, MA: Harvard University Press, 1993); Francis Smith Foster, *Witnessing Slavery: The Development of Ante-bellum Slave Narratives* (Madison: University of Wisconsin Press, 1994).

⁷ Estelle Jelinek, ed., *Women's Autobiography: Essays in Criticism* (Bloomington: Indiana University Press, 1980); Estelle Jelinek, *The Tradition of Women's Autobiography: From Antiquity to the Present* (Boston: Twayne Publishers, 1986); Sidonie Smith, *A Poetics of Women's Autobiography* (Bloomington: Indiana University Press, 1987); Shari Benstock, *The Private Self: Theory and Practice of Women's Autobiographical Writings* (London: Routledge, 1988); Carolyn G. Heilbrun, *Writing a Woman's Life* (New York: Norton, 1988); Linda Anderson, *Women and Autobiography* (New York: St. Martin's Press, 1990); Margo Culley, ed., *American Women's Autobiography: Fea(s)ts of Memory* (Madison: University of Wisconsin Press, 1992); Sidonie Smith and Julia Watson, eds., *De/Colonizing the Subject: The Politics of Gender in Women's Autobiography* (Minneapolis: University of Minnesota Press, 1992); Leigh Gilmore, *Autobiographica: A Feminist Theory of Women's Self-Representation* (Ithaca, NY: Cornell University Press, 1994).

⁸ Tables 1–3 include life writings published in the United States between 1801 and 1900 listed in Louis Kaplan, *A Bibliography of American Autobiographies* (Madison: University of Wisconsin Press, 1961); Russell Brignano, *Black Americans in Autobiography: An Annotated Bibliography of Autobiographies and Autobiographical Books Written Since the Civil War* (Durham, NC: Duke University Press, 1984); and Gwen Davis and Beverly A. Joyce, *Personal Writings By Women to 1900: A Bibliography of American and British Writers* (London: Mansell, 1989). Works that do not bear an imprint date or were published outside what is now the United States are excluded. Tables 1–4 only include authors with surnames beginning with the letters "A" through "C." Inequalities of alphabetical distribution (e.g., an upsurge of autobiographies by authors whose last name begins with "Mc" in the 1890s) may reduce slightly the accuracy of these tables.

⁹ Population figures are from *Historical Statistics of the United States: Colonial Times to 1970*, 2 vols. (Washington, DC: Bureau of the Census, 1975), 1:8.

¹⁰ John Cawelti, *Apostles of the Self-Made Man* (Chicago: University of Chicago Press, 1965); Sacvan Bercovitch, *The Puritan Origins of the American Self* (New Haven, CT: Yale, 1975), and "The Ritual of American Autobiography: Edwards, Franklin, Thoreau," *Revue Française D'Ètudes Amèricaines* 7 (1982): 139–150; Lawrence Buell, "Democratic Ideology and Autobiographical Personae in American Renaissance Writing," *Amerikastudien* 35 (1990): 267–280.

¹¹ Buell, "Autobiography in the American Renaissance," in *American Autobiography: Retrospect and Prospect*, ed. Paul John Eakin (Madison: University of Wisconsin Press, 1991), 47–69; Spengemann, *The Forms of Autobiography* (New Haven, CT: Yale, 1980), 132–165; Steele, *The Representation of the Self in the American Renaissance* (Chapel Hill: University of North Carolina Press, 1987).

[12] Several scholars have examined revision in Frederick Douglass's autobiographies: William Andrews, *To Tell a Free Story* (Urbana and Chicago: University of Illinois Press), 214–239; Thomas DiPietro, "Vision and Revision in the Autobiographies of Frederick Douglass," *College Language Association Journal* 26 (1984): 384–395; Joseph Fichtelberg, "The Writer Against Himself: Child and Man in the Autobiographies of Frederick Douglass," *Mid-Hudson Language Studies* 12 (1989): 72–80; Henry Louis Gates, Jr., *Figures in Black* (New York: Oxford University Press), 98–124; David Leverenz, "Frederick Douglass's Self Refashioning," *Criticism* 29 (1987): 341–370; Robert S. Levine, *Martin Delany Frederick Douglass, and the Politics of Representative Identity* (Chapel Hill: University of North Carolina Press, 1987); Peter Ripley, "The Autobiographical Writings of Frederick Douglass," *Southern Studies* 24 (1985): 5–29; Eric J. Sundquist, *To Wake the Nations* (Cambridge, MA: Harvard University Press, 1993), 83–93; and Henry Louis Gates, Jr., in the notes to Douglass's *Autobiographies* (New York: Library of America, 1994), 1078–1107. Various aspects of Whitman's revisions are examined by Roger Asselineau, *The Evolution of Walt Whitman: The Creation of a Book* (Cambridge, MA: Harvard University Press, 1960); Mutlu Konuk Blasing, *The Art of Life* (Austin: University of Texas Press, 1977), 25–54; G. Thomas Couser, *American Autobiography: The Prophetic Mode* (Amherst: University of Massachusetts Press, 1979), 80–100; Ezra Greenspan, *Walt Whitman and the American Reader* (New York: Cambridge University Press, 1990); and Michael Moon, *Disseminating Whitman: Revision and Corporeality in* Leaves of Grass (Cambridge, MA: Harvard University Press, 1991). Barnum's revisions are discussed briefly by G. Thomas Couser, *Altered Egos: Authority in American Autobiography*, (New York: Oxford University Press, 1989), 52–69; and by A. H. Saxon, *P. T. Barnum: The Legend and the Man* (New York: Columbia University Press, 1989), 8–24. There are also essays about the revised autobiographies of Mary Chesnut (C. Vann Woodward, "Mary Chesnut in Search of Her Genre," *The Yale Review* 73 [1984]: 199–209); William Dean Howells (Marcia Jacobson, "The Mask of Fiction: William Dean Howells's Experiments in Autobiography," *Biography* 10 [1987]: 55–67); Rousseau (Eugene Stelzig, "Rousseau's Reveries: Autobiography as Revision," *A/B: Autobiography Studies* 4 [1988]: 97–106); Mark Twain (Marilyn Davis DeEulis, "Mark Twain's Experiments in Autobiography" *American Literature* 53 [1982]: 202–213; Louis Renza, "Killing Time with Mark Twain's Autobiographies," *ELH* 54 [1987]: 157–182); and Booker T. Washington (Pierre Denain, "Booker T. Washington et ses Autobiographies," *Revue Française D'Études Américaines*, 14 [1992]: 269–276). However, no effort has yet been made to address this common pattern of revision among several figures or the significance of self-refashioning as a characteristic of American authorship.

[13] Frederick Douglass, *Narrative of the Life of Frederick Douglass, an American Slave, Written by Himself* (Boston: Anti-Slavery Office, 1845); *My Bondage and My Freedom* (New York and Auburn, NY: Miller, Orton & Mulligan, 1855); *Life and Times of Frederick Douglass, Written by Himself* (Hartford, Conn.: Park Publishing

Co., 1881); *Life and Times of Frederick Douglass, Written by Himself: His early life as a slave, his escape from bondage, and his compete history to the present time* (Boston: DeWolfe, Fisk, & Co., [1892]).

¹⁴ Barnum, P. T. [Barnaby Diddleum]. "Adventures of an Adventurer" (New York *Atlas* 14 April 1841; 18 April 1841; 25 April 1841; 2 May 1841; 9 May 1841; 16 May 1841; 23 May 1841; 30 May 1841, incomplete); *The Life of P. T. Barnum, Written by Himself* (New York: Redfield, 1855); *Struggles and Triumphs; or, Forty Years' Recollections of P. T. Barnum, Written by Himself* (Hartford, CT: J. B. Burr, 1869); *Struggles and Triumphs; or, Forty Years' Recollections of P. T. Barnum, Written by Himself* (Buffalo, NY: Courier Company, 1875); *Struggles and Triumphs: or, Forty Years Recollections of P. T. Barnum. Written by Himself* (Buffalo, NY: Courier Company, 1876); *Struggles and Triumphs: or, Fifty Years Recollections of P. T. Barnum. Written by Himself* (Buffalo, NY: The Courier Company, 1884); *Struggles and Triumphs, or Sixty Years Recollections of P. T. Barnum. Including His Golden Rules for Money Making. Illustrated and Brought up to 1889* (Buffalo, NY: The Courier Company, 1889); Nancy Barnum, *"The Last Chapter": In Memoriam, P. T. Barnum* (New York: J. J. Little, 1893); Joel Benton, *Life of Hon. Phineas T. Barnum, Comprising His Boyhood, Youth, Vicissitudes of Early Years . . . His Genius, Wit, Generosity, Eloquence, Christianity, &c., &c., as Told by Joel Benton, Esq.* (Philadelphia: Edgewood, 1891). Also see the A. H. Saxon's indispensable *Barnumiana: A Select, Annotated Bibliography of Works By or Relating to P. T. Barnum and A Barnum Chronology* (Fairfield, Conn.: Jumbo's Press, 1995).

¹⁵ Other revisers include William Andrus Alcott, Nathaniel Ames, Mary Arms, Betty Beaumont, Harriet Bishop, Black Hawk, Henry Boehm, Asa Bullard, Letitia Burwell, Warren Chase, George Coles, and Caroline Dall.

¹⁶ Barnum, *Life*, 404.

¹⁷ *Hand-Book of American Literature: Historical, Biographical, and Critical* (London: W. and R. Chambers, n.d.), 263.

¹⁸ White, *The Adventures of Sir Lyon Bouse, Bart., in America, During the Civil War* (New York, 1867), 30.

¹⁹A. H. Saxon, ed., *Selected Letters of P. T. Barnum* (New York: Columbia University Press, 1983), xviii.

²⁰ Douglass, *Autobiographies: Narrative of the Life, My Bondage and My Freedom, Life and Times* (New York: Library of America, 1994), 54, 60.

²¹ Compare Whitman's 1855 frontispiece with the images shown in Michael L. Carlebach, *Working Stiffs: Occupational Portraits in the Age of Tintypes* (Washington, DC: Smithsonian Institution Press, 2002).

²² *Leaves of Grass, Comprehensive Reader's Edition* (New York: Norton, 1965), 52, 52n.

²³ Emerson, *Essays and Lectures* (New York: Library of America, 1983), 630.

²⁴ Douglass, *Autobiographies*, 132.

²⁵ William S. McFeely, *Frederick Douglass* (New York, Norton, 1991), 132.

²⁶ It is telling that the 1845 engraving is less frequently reproduced in modern editions of the *Narrative* than more confrontational images of Douglass For example, the Norton Critical Edition, edited by William L. Andrews and William S. McFeely (New York: Norton, 1997), omits the 1845 engraving and presents an early Daguerreotype of Douglass on the cover.

²⁷ William Andrews and William S. McFeely, eds. *Narrative of the Life of Frederick Douglass* (New York: Norton, 1997), 88.

²⁸ A. H. Saxon, *P. T. Barnum: The Legend and the Man* (New York: Columbia University Press, 1983), 13–14.

²⁹ *Criterion* 1 (10 November 1855), 24; Reprinted in Kenneth Price, *Walt Whitman: The Contemporary Reviews* (Cambridge: Cambridge University Press, 1996), 26–27. Griswold is probably the first critic to attack Whitman on sexual grounds in print; *Leaves*, in Griswold's viewing, was an account of "'*Peccatum illud horribile, inter Christianos non nominandum*'" (27)," The horrible crime not to be named among the Christians."

³⁰ Barnum, *Life*, n.p.

³¹ Douglass, *Autobiographies*, 81–82.

³² McFeely, *Frederick Douglass*, 109–110.

³³ Reynolds, *Walt Whitman's America: A Cultural Biography* (New York: Knopf, 1995), 70; the original source for this event is an obscure pamphlet by Katherine Molinoff, *Walt Whitman at Southhold* (1966).

³⁴ Whitman, *Leaves of Grass: Comprehensive Reader's Edition*, 52.

³⁵ Douglass, *Autobiographies*, 286.

³⁶ Barnum, *Life*, 12.

³⁷ An excellent analysis of Barnum and Joice Heth is Benjamin Reiss's *The Showman and the Slave: Race, Death and Memory in Barnum's America* (Cambridge, MA: Harvard University Press, 2001).

³⁸ Douglass, "Reply to Thomson's Letter," originally published in *The Liberator*, 27 Feb. 1846; rpt. in Andrews and McFeely, *Narrative*, 94.

³⁹ Saxon, *P. T. Barnum: The Legend and the Man*, 15.

⁴⁰ Barnum, *Selected Letters*, 134.

⁴¹ Paul DeMan, "Autobiography as De-facement," *MLN* 94 (1979): 921.

⁴² Philippe Lejeune, *Le Pacte Autobiographique* (Paris: Editions du Seuil, 1975); Elizabeth Bruss, *Autobiographical Acts: The Changing Situation of a Literary Genre* (Baltimore, MD: The Johns Hopkins University Press, 1976).

⁴³ William H. Shurr provides a detailed analysis of the composition of the work in "'Now, Gods, Stand Up for Bastards': Reinterpreting Benjamin Franklin's *Autobiography*," *American Literature* 64 (1992): 435–451.

⁴⁴ Based on the works by Benjamin Franklin listed in HOLLIS, the Harvard On-line Library Information System.

⁴⁵ Douglass, *Autobiographies*, 941.

⁴⁶ See the photographs of Whitman taken with children in the 1880s in Folsom, "'This Heart's Geography's Map': The Photographs of Walt Whitman," *Walt*

Whitman Quarterly Review 4.2–3 (1986–87): 1–72; Saxon, *P. T. Barnum: The Legend and the Man,* opposite 211.

⁴⁷ Shortly after this time, his miscellaneous prose writings were, in fact, repackaged under titles such as *Autobiography, Or, The Story of a Life* (New York: Charles Webster, 1892) and *Leaves of Grass with Autobiography* (Philadelphia: David McKay, 1900). The latter work includes a facsimile holographic manuscript of Whitman's own account of his life—a manner of creating volumes of Whitman's writings as literary reliquaries that was common in the early years of the Whitman cult.

⁴⁸ William D. O'Connor, *The Good Gray Poet: A Vindication* (New York: Bunce and Huntington, 1866); John Burroughs, *Notes on Walt Whitman as a Poet and Person* (New York: American News Company, 1867); Richard Maurice Bucke, *Walt Whitman* (Philadelphia: David McKay, 1883).

NOTES TO CHAPTER TWO

¹ Quoted in William E. Barton, *Abraham Lincoln and Walt Whitman* (Indianapolis: The Bobbs-Merrill Company, 1928), 170.

² Horace Traubel, *With Walt Whitman in Camden.* 9 Vols. Vol. I. (1905; rpt., New York: Rowman and Littlefield, 1961); Vol. II. (1907; rpt., New York: Rowman and Littlefield, 1961); Vol. III. (1912; rpt., New York: Rowman and Littlefield, 1961); Vol. IV (1953; rpt., Carbondale: Southern Illinois University Press, 1959); Vol. V (Carbondale: Southern Illinois University Press, 1964); Vol. VI (Carbondale: Southern Illinois University Press, 1982); Vol. VII (Carbondale: Southern Illinois University Press, 1992); Vols. VIII-IX (Oregon House, CA: W. L. Bentley, 1996), 38.

³ Walt Whitman, *Poetry and Prose* (New York: Library of America, 1982), 1310.

⁴ Whitman, *Poetry and Prose,* 1313–1314.

⁵ Whitman, *Poetry and Prose,* 1308.

⁶ Abraham Lincoln, *Collected Works,* ed. Roy Basler, 8 vols. (New Brunswick: Rutgers University Press, 1953), 1:112

⁷ Walt Whitman, *Leaves of Grass: Comprehensive Reader's Edition* (New York: Norton, 1965), 52.

⁸ Lincoln, *Collected Works,* 4:271.

⁹ Qtd. in Daniel Aaron, *The Unwritten War: American Writers and the Civil War* (New York: Knopf, 1973), 70.

¹⁰ Whitman, *The Correspondence of Walt Whitman,* ed. Edwin Haviland Miller, 6 vols. (New York: New York University Press, 1961–77), 1:83.

¹¹ Lincoln, *Collected Works,* 8:333.

¹² Whitman, *Leaves of Grass: Comprehensive,* 309.

¹³ Roy P. Basler, ed., *Walt Whitman's Memoranda During the War [&] Death of Abraham* Lincoln (Westport: Greenwood Press, 1962), 3.

¹⁴ William Coyle, ed., *The Poet and the President: Whitman's Lincoln Poems* (New York: Odyssey Press, 1962), 167

[15] Gay Wilson Allen, *The Solitary Singer: A Critical Biography of Walt Whitman* (New York: New York University Press, 1967), 369.

[16] Allen, *The Solitary Singer*, 68.

[17] Aaron, *Unwritten War*, 71.

[18] Barton, *Abraham Lincoln and Walt Whitman*, 150.

[19] Allen Grossman, "The Poetics of Union in Whitman and Lincoln: An Inquiry Toward the Relationship of Art and Policy," in *The American Renaissance Reconsidered*, eds. Walter Benn Michaels and Donald E. Pease (Baltimore, MD: The Johns Hopkins University Press, 1985), 187.

[20] Whitman, *Leaves of Grass: Comprehensive*, 88.

[21] Whitman, *Uncollected Poetry and Prose*, ed. Emory Holloway, 2 vols. (Garden City, NY: Doubleday, 1921), 2:286, 256.

[22] Whitman, *Uncollected Poetry and* Prose, 1:51.

[23] Lincoln, "Speech on the Sub-Treasury" (1839) in *Collected Works,* 1:178.

[24] Lincoln, *Collected Works*, 1:279.

[25] Lincoln, *Collected Works* 1:108.

[26] Lincoln, *Collected Works,* 1:112.

[27] Whitman, *Walt Whitman of the New York Aurora*, ed. Joseph Jay Rubin and Charles H. Brown (State College, PA: Bald Eagle Press, 1950), 82, 110–111.

[28] Whitman, *Walt Whitman of the New York Aurora*, 67.

[29] Whitman, *Walt Whitman of the New York Aurora*, 64.

[30] Whitman, *Walt Whitman of the New York Aurora*, 12.

[31] Joseph Jay Rubin, *The Historic Whitman* (University Park, PA: Pennsylvania State University Press, 1973), 223.

[32] Lincoln, *Collected Works*, 1:100.

[33] Lincoln, *Collected Works*, 1:178–179.

[34] Lincoln, *Collected Works*, 1:295.

[35] Lincoln, *Collected Works*, 1:301.

[36] Grossman, "Poetics of Union," 186–187.

[37] Lincoln, *Collected Works*, 2:463–464.

[38] Lincoln, *Collected Works,* 2:461.

[39] Lincoln, *Collected Works*, 1:434–435.

[40] Albert Beveridge, *Abraham Lincoln, 1809–1858* (Boston: Houghton Mifflin, 1928), 430–432, 493.

[41] Dwight G. Anderson, *Abraham Lincoln: The Quest for Immortality* (New York: Knopf, 1982), 74.

[42] Lincoln, *Collected Works*, 2:498.

[43] Whitman, *Early Poems and the Fiction*, ed. Thomas L. Brasher (New York: New York University Press, 1963), 36–37.

[44] Whitman, *Uncollected Poetry and Prose*, 40.

[45] Traubel, *With Walt Whitman*, 1:6.

[46] Arthur Golden, "Nine Early Whitman Letters, 1840–1841," *American Literature* 58.3 (1986): 350.

47 Whitman, *Leaves of Grass: Comprehensive*, 52, 41.

48 Golden, "Nine Early Whitman Letters," 351–352.

49 Lincoln, *Collected Works*, 1:115.

50 Quoted in Edmund Wilson, *Patriotic Gore: Studies in the Literature of the American Civil War* (Boston: Northeastern University Press, 1962), 119.

51 Lincoln, *Collected Works*, 1:178.

52 Both Whitman and Lincoln were also caught in a tension between their resentment of the more affluent classes and their desire to become part of this establishment, and, in addition, between their sense of belonging socially to the working class and their distaste for its vulgarity. Hence, their writing and oratory was often ineffectively directed to an ambiguous audience. The high-flown fustian and obscure literary allusions of their early rhetoric, which were nearly always too awkward and heavy-handed to attract the admiration of the well educated, alienated the working class they sought to cultivate. On the other hand, their vestigial roughness, pulpit absolutism, outlandish colloquialisms, abusive language, and egalitarian politics alienated any would-be supporters among the well-educated establishment.

53 See, for example, Allen Grossman, "The Poetics of Union," 188–189.

54 Whitman, *Leaves of Grass: Comprehensive*, 3.

55 Whitman, *Leaves of Grass: Comprehensive*, 83.

56 Whitman, *Leaves of Grass: Comprehensive*, 76.

57 Whitman, *Leaves of Grass: Comprehensive*, 77.

58 Whitman, *Leaves of Grass: Comprehensive*, 4.

59 Whitman, *Leaves of Grass: Comprehensive*, 32.

60 Whitman, *Leaves of Grass: Comprehensive*, 23–24.

61 Whitman, *Leaves of Grass: Comprehensive*, 62.

62 Whitman, *Leaves of Grass: Comprehensive*, 77.

63 Ralph Waldo Emerson, *Essays and Lectures* (New York: Library of America, 1983), 40.

64 Whitman, *Leaves of Grass: Comprehensive*, 1.

65 Whitman, *Leaves of Grass: Comprehensive*, 76.

66 Justin Kaplan, *Walt Whitman, A Life* (New York: Simon and Schuster, 1980), 228.

67 Whitman, *Leaves of Grass: Comprehensive*, 29.

68 Richard Maurice Bucke, ed., *Notes and Fragments* (London, Ontario, Canada, 1899), 57.

69 Whitman, *Leaves of Grass: Comprehensive*, 33.

70 Milton Hindus, ed. *Walt Whitman: The Critical Heritage* (London: Routledge and Kegan Paul, 1971), 22–23.

71 Hindus, *Critical Heritage*, 32

72 Quoted in Allen, *Solitary Singer*, 178

73 I do not mean to suggest that Whitman's poetry influenced Lincoln's style, although it is a remote possibility. According to alleged law student Henry B. Rankin, in *Personal Recollections of Abraham Lincoln* (New York: G. P. Putnam's Son,

1916), Lincoln actually read *Leaves of Grass* in 1857 in his Springfield law office. He apparently liked it so much that he read it aloud regularly to his associates: "he commended the new poet's verses for their virility, freshness, unconventional sentiments, and unique forms of expression, and claimed that Whitman gave promise of a new school of poetry" (qtd. in Allen, *Solitary Singer,* 175).

[74] Gaber Borrit, ed., *The Historian's Lincoln: Pseudohistory, Psychohistory, and History* (Urbana: University of Illinois Press, 1988), 9.

[75] Wilson, *Patriotic Gore,* 103.

[76] Lincoln, *Collected Works,* 4:190.

[77] Wilson, *Patriotic Gore,* 123.

[78] Stephen B. Oates, *With Malice Towards None* (New York: Harper and Row, 1977), 176.

[79] Whitman, *Comprehensive Reader's Edition,* 29.

[80] William E. Gienapp, "Who Voted for Lincoln" in *Abraham Lincoln and American Political* Thought, ed. John Thomas (Amherst: University of Massachusetts Press, 1986), 58.

[81] Lincoln, *Collected Works,* 4:265–271.

[82] Lincoln, *Collected Works,* 4:271.

[83] Anderson, *Abraham Lincoln,* 9.

[84] Lincoln, *Collected Works,* 4:190.

[85] Anderson, *Abraham Lincoln,*194.

[86] Quoted in Geoffrey C. Ward, *The Civil War* (New York: Knopf, 1990), 174.

[87] Lincoln, *Collected Works,* 8:333.

[88] Whitman, Leaves of Grass: Comprehensive, 311.

[89] Whitman, Correspondence, 1:232.

[90] Whitman, *Leaves of Grass: Comprehensive,* 322.

[91] Barton, *Abraham Lincoln and Walt Whitman,* 154.

[92] Grossman, "Poetics of Union," 203.

[93] Lincoln, *Collected Works,* 5:537.

[94] Traubel, *With Walt Whitman,* 1:14.

[95] Basler, *Memoranda,* 65.

[96] Whitman, *Leaves of Grass: Comprehensive,* 281.

[97] Whitman, *Correspondence,* 1:92.

[98] Whitman, *Leaves of Grass: Comprehensive* 286, 291.

[99] Whitman, *Prose Works 1892,* 2 vols., Ed. Floyd Stovall (New York: New York University Press, 1964), 1:24–25.

[100] Whitman, *Leaves of Grass: Comprehensive,* 284.

[101] Kaplan, *Walt Whitman,* 262.

[102] Whitman, *Leaves of Grass: Comprehensive,* 305.

[103] Whitman, *Prose Works 1892,* 1:26, 27.

[104] Charles I. Glicksberg, ed., *Walt Whitman and the Civil War* (Philadelphia: University of Pennsylvania Press, 1933), 125.

[105] Whitman, *Leaves of Grass: Comprehensive,* 308.

[106] Whitman, *Leaves of Grass: Comprehensive*, 309.

[107] Whitman, *Leaves of Grass: Comprehensive*, 226.

[108] Basler, *Memoranda*, 6.

[109] Whitman, *Correspondence*, 1:114.

[110] Whitman, *Leaves of Grass: Comprehensive*, 309.

[111] Glicksberg, *Walt Whitman and the Civil War*, 89.

[112] Whitman, *Leaves of Grass: Comprehensive*, 311.

[113] Basler, *Memoranda*, 5.

[114] Whitman, *Leaves of Grass: Comprehensive*, 313.

[115] *Whitman the Political Poet* (New York: Oxford University Press, 1989), 201.

[116] Whitman, *Leaves of Grass: Comprehensive*, 321.

[117] Whitman, *Leaves of Grass: Comprehensive*, 327.

[118] Traubel, *With Walt Whitman*, 1:14.

[119] Traubel, *With Walt Whitman*, 1:14,13.

[120] Basler, *Memoranda*, 42, 43.

[121] Lincoln, *Collected Works*, 8:333.

[122] Lincoln, *Collected Works*, 3:550.

[123] Lincoln, *Collected Works*, 4:240.

[124] Lincoln, *Collected Works*, 5:527.

[125] Lincoln, *Collected Works*, 7:23.

[126] Ward, *Civil War*, 334, 345.

[127] Lincoln, *Collected Works*, 8:332.

[128] Lincoln, *Collected Works*, 8:333.

[129] Lincoln, *Collected Works*, 8: 154.

[130] Lincoln, *Collected Works*, 4:270.

[131] Lincoln, *Collected Works*, 1:333.

[132] Ward, *Civil War*, 382.

[133] Glen Thurow, *Abraham Lincoln and the American Political Religion* (Albany: State University of New York Press, 1976), 116.

[134] Lincoln, *Collected Works*, 8:333, 400–401.

[135] The shift in Lincoln's rhetoric from inflexibility to compromise is reflected by parallel changes in the military policy of Lincoln's generals. During the siege of Atlanta, months before the outcome of the war was certain, William Tecumseh Sherman said, "War is the remedy our enemies have chosen, and I say let us give them all they want" (qtd. in Ward, *Civil War*, 321). U. S. Grant, whose nicknames were "Unconditional Surrender" and "Unspeakable Slaughter," became unusually restrained at the surrender of Robert E. Lee at Appomattox. Years later, when describing the event, Grant adopted the rhetorical stance of Lincoln's "Second Inaugural": "I felt like anything rather than rejoicing at the downfall of a foe who had fought so long and valiantly, and had suffered so much for a cause, though that cause was, I believe, one of the worst for which a people ever fought." Unlike the celebration of Lincoln at the Confederate capital, Grant carefully refrained from violating the terms of reconciliation articulated by the chief executive: "When news of

the surrender first reached our lines our men commenced firing a salute of a hundred guns in honor of the victory. I at once sent word, however, to have it stopped . . . we did not want to exult over their downfall" in *Personal Memoirs* (New York: Library of America, 1990), 739, 741.

   [136] Lincoln, *Collected Works*, 8:356.

   [137] Whitman, *Correspondence*, 1:246–247.

   [138] Barton, *Abraham Lincoln and Walt Whitman*, 155.

NOTES TO CHAPTER THREE

   [1] "Incidents of Walt Whitman," *Conservator* 23.1 (1912): 8–9.

   [2] Pierre Bourdieu, *The Field of Cultural Production*, ed., Randall Johnson (New York: Columbia University Press, 1993), 41, 40.

   [3] Although copyright protects authors and publishers from the unlawful republication of their texts, there is a tendency for literary canonicity to increase at the moment when an author's estate loses its right to demand royalties for the republication of works. Following an inverse bell-curve, many "literary" works, after a brief popularity (and cost-reducing economies of scale), fall into a period of neglect, only regaining attention in the more restricted economies of cultural institutions when the copyright ceases to raise the costs of republication above what the institutional markets will bear.

   [4] Such a comparative strategy is deployed repeatedly in, for example, Jane Tompkins's *Sensational Designs: The Cultural Work of American Fiction, 1790–1860* (New York: Oxford, 1985), which reasserts the value of the sentimental tradition by direct comparison with the so-called masculinist tradition that once replaced it: "If the tradition of American criticism has not acknowledged the value of *Uncle Tom's Cabin*, it has paid even less attention to the work of Stowe's contemporaries. . . . The writer I am concerned with is Susan Warner, who was born in the same year as Herman Melville" (146). Though there is no causal link between the co-nativity of Melville and the displacement of Warner, Tompkins's rhetoric suggests that the consecration of one requires the desecration of the other as if the canon is a zero-sum game, which it often can be.

   [5] Lowell was certainly not regarded in the nineteenth century as *the* greatest American poet. That title surely belongs to Longfellow, but Lowell was certainly ranked near the top, while Whitman was nearly always seen, when noticed at all, as a minor poet.

   [6] Whitman was born on 31 May 1819 and died on 26 March 1892; Lowell was born on 22 February 1819 and died on 12 August 1891. Late in life, Whitman observed the coincidence of their age: "Did you notice, Horace, how close his [Lowell's] age and mine correspond? He is about three months younger" (Traubel, *With Walt Whitman*, 8:405).

   [7] See, for example, the influential *Cambridge History of American Literature*, edited by William Peterfield Trent, John Erskine, Stuart P. Sherman, and Carl Van Doren (New York: Macmillan, 1917).

[8] Quoted in Harold Blodgett, *Walt Whitman in England* (Ithaca, NY: Cornell University Press, 1934), 1.

[9] "The Glittering Metropolis," *Poetry: A Magazine of Verse* 14.1 (1919): 32.

[10] "The Week," *The New Republic* 67 (27 May 1931): 30.

[11] Richard Ruland, *The Rediscovery of American Literature* (Cambridge, MA: Harvard University Press, 1967), 47.

[12] Percy H. Boynton, "Lowell in His Times," *The New Republic* 18 (22 February 1910): 112.

[13] Marjorie Kaufman, ed., *The Poetical Works of James Russell Lowell* (Boston: Houghton Mifflin, 1978), xxxiii.

[14] Stuart Merrill, *Walt Whitman,* trans. Leon Bazelgette (Toronto: Henry S. Saunders, 1922), 3.

[15] See, for example, the following: "A Poet in Penury," in the *Daily News* [London] (16 December 1886): 5; "Occasional Notes," *Pall Mall Gazette* (16 December 1886): 3; "Walt Whitman's Purse," *New York Times* (17 December 1886): 5; and Jeanette Gilder, "The Lounger," *The Critic* n.s. 6 (25 December 1886): 319.

[16] J. H. Johnston, "In Re Walt Whitman," in *Walt Whitman as Man, Poet and Friend,* ed. Charles N. Elliot (Boston: Richard G. Badger, 1915), 155–158.

[17] According to Justin Kaplan in *Walt Whitman, A Life* (New York: Simon and Schuster, 1980), 29; Johnston claims that "the house was packed," in "In Re Walt Whitman," 157; Merrill supports Kaplan's estimate, writing that the audience was "thinly scattered," in *Walt Whitman,* 2. See Higginson, "Women and Men. War Pensions for Women," *Harper's Bazar* 20 (5 March 1887): 162.

[18] There are numerous accounts of the audience; one of the most detailed is "A Tribute from a Poet: Walt Whitman Tells of Lincoln's Death," *New York Times* (15 April 1887): 1–2.

[19] Merrill, *Walt Whitman,* 3; Martí's account is reprinted in Gay Wilson Allen and Ed Folsom, eds., *Walt Whitman and the World* (Iowa City: University of Iowa Press, 1995), 96–106.

[20] Horace Traubel, *With Walt Whitman in Camden.* 9 Vols. Vol. I. (1905; rpt., New York: Rowman and Littlefield, 1961); Vol. II. (1907; rpt., New York: Rowman and Littlefield, 1961); Vol. III. (1912; rpt., New York: Rowman and Littlefield, 1961); Vol. IV (1953; rpt., Carbondale: Southern Illinois University Press, 1959); Vol. V (Carbondale: Southern Illinois University Press, 1964); Vol. VI (Carbondale: Southern Illinois University Press, 1982); Vol. VII (Carbondale: Southern Illinois University Press, 1992); Vols. VIII-IX (Oregon House, CA: W. L. Bentley, 1996), 1:127.

[21] Traubel, *With Walt Whitman,* 8: 515, 433.

[22] Richard Maurice Bucke, *Walt Whitman: A Contemporary Study* (Philadelphia: David McKay, 1883), 100n; Traubel, *With Walt Whitman* 3:126.

[23] Traubel, *With Walt Whitman,* 4:74.

[24] Traubel, *With Walt Whitman,* 6:95.

[25] Traubel, *With Walt Whitman,* 4:74.

26 James Russell Lowell, Letter to Richard Watson Gilder, 13 April 1887, Ms. AM765(31), 53, Houghton Library, Harvard University.

27 Traubel, *With Walt Whitman*, 4:273; Johnston, "In Re," 157.

28 *Letters of James Russell Lowell*, ed. Charles Eliot Norton, 2 vols. (New York: Harper and Brothers, 1894), 1:242; Norton reviewed *Leaves of Grass* in *Putnam's Monthly* 6 (September 1855): 321–323. This review and Norton's Whitmanesque poetry is reprinted in *A Leaf of Grass from Shady Hill*, ed. Kenneth B. Murdock (Cambridge: Harvard University Press, 1928).

29 Eggleston had dedicated his novel, *The Hoosier Schoolmaster* (1871) to Lowell, "Whose cordial encouragement to my early studies of American dialect is gratefully remembered." Although Howells is missing from other inventories of the audience, the correspondent for the *New York Tribune* has him collecting tickets at the door in "Hearty Cheers for Whitman. He Speaks on Abraham Lincoln" (15 April 1887): 2. Jeanette Gilder corrects this misconception in "The Lounger," *The Critic* n.s. 7 (7 May 1887): 232.

30 "An Old Poet's Reception," reprinted in Walt Whitman, *Daybooks and Notebooks*, ed. William White, 3 vols. (New York: New York University Press, 1978), 2:418n. Burroughs had exchanged pleasantries with Lowell and Norton earlier that day at the office of the *Century*. In addition to many mutual friends, they shared a publisher, Houghton Mifflin, and had appeared alongside each other in the *Atlantic*. Burroughs took an immediate liking to Norton, whom he found similar in nature to Whitman: "sweet," "gentle," "a man to make fast friends with and to love." But Burroughs had attacked Lowell in print, which Lowell remembered. Burroughs was intimidated by Lowell, whom he described as a "pretty strong-looking man, more than a mere scholar; a man of affairs, and of the world." Although Burroughs dared not attack the elder statesman and critic face-to-face, his devoted friendship for Whitman and political beliefs caused him to continue privately to regard Lowell as an enemy: "I can't endure the man," he later wrote. Burroughs continues, Lowell "seems to me one of those minds that never get ripe, but are crude and puckery to the last. . . . It is a kind of torture to me to read him." Burroughs softened this statement in 1914: "That is pretty severe—an exaggerated truth." See *The Heart of Burroughs Journals*, ed. Clara Barrus (Boston: Houghton Mifflin, 1928), 140, 120.

31 Johnson, Robert Underwood, *Remembered Yesterdays* (Boston: Little, Brown, 1923), 329.

32 *Letters of Richard Watson Gilder*, ed. Rosamond Gilder (Boston: Houghton Mifflin, 1916), 412.

33 *Letters of Richard Watson Gilder*, 410.

34 Gilder was also an authority on Lincoln. It was he who rediscovered the plaster life mask of Lincoln made by Leonard Volk in 1860 and who had written a sonnet about it. Gilder's *Century Magazine* often published reminiscences of Lincoln, and Gilder serialized Nicolay and Hay's *Abraham Lincoln: A History;* See *Letters of Richard Watson Gilder*, 173–179.

35 James Russell Lowell, Letter to Richard Watson Gilder, 21 January 1887, Ms. AM765(31), 46, Houghton Library, Harvard University.

36 *The Works of James Russell Lowell,* 10 vols. (Boston: Houghton Mifflin, 1890), 5:153–209, 189.

37 Lowell, *Works,* 10:22–24.

38 Merrill Peterson provides a thorough contextualization of impact of Lowell's ode in *Lincoln in American Memory* (New York: Oxford University Press, 1994), 32–33.

39 "Old Poet's Reception," 417n.

40 Roy P. Basler, ed., *Walt Whitman's* Memoranda During the War [&] *Death of Abraham Lincoln* (Westport, CT: Greenwood Press, 1962), 123.

41 Whitman, *Prose Works, 1892,* 2 vols., ed. Floyd Stovall (New York: New York University Press, 1963), 2:503.

42 Merrill, *Walt Whitman,* 2.

43 Whitman, *Prose Works, 1892,* 2:509.

44 Whitman, *Daybooks,* 2:418n.

45 Merrill, *Walt Whitman,* 5.

46 William Sloane Kennedy, *Reminiscences of Walt Whitman* (London: Alexander Gardner, 1896), 27.

47 Quoted in Henry C. Beck, Letter, *Sunday Star Ledger* (4 March 1956): 28.

48 Stedman, *Poets of America* (Boston: Houghton Mifflin, 1885), 364. For Whitman's comments on Stedman's comparison, see Traubel, *With Walt Whitman,* 1:156.

49 Whitman, Leaves of Grass, Comprehensive, 337–338.

50 Stedman, *Poets of America, 392.*

51 Charles B. Willard charts the rapid canonization of "O Captain! My Captain!" and finds that it had been anthologized "more often than any other poem of Whitman's" between 1892 and 1950; see *Walt Whitman's American Fame: The Growth of His Reputation in America after 1892* (Providence, RI: Brown University, 1950), 217.

52 Johnston, "In Re," 157.

53 Traubel, *With Walt Whitman,* 8:406.

54 Burroughs, "Walt Whitman and His Recent Critics," in *In Re Walt Whitman,* eds. Horace Traubel, Richard Maurice Bucke, and Thomas B. Harned (Philadelphia: David McKay, 1893), 17.

55 Clara Barrus, *Whitman and Burroughs: Comrades* (Boston: Houghton Mifflin, 1931), 264.

56 Jeanette Gilder, "The Lounger," *The Critic* n.s. 8 (23 July 1887), 43.

57 Traubel, *With Walt Whitman,* 8:509.

58 Traubel, *With Walt Whitman,* 8:172.

59 Traubel, *With Walt Whitman,* 8:515.

60 Whitman, *Correspondence,* 5:214n.

⁶¹ Kennedy, *The Fight of a Book for the World* (West Yarmouth, Mass.:Stonecraft Press, 1926), 288.

⁶² Thayer, "James Russell Lowell as a Teacher: Recollections of His Last Pupil," *Scribner's* 68.4 (1920): 480.

⁶³ "New Biglow Papers," *The Nation* 3 (15 November 1886): 386–387.

⁶⁴ H. L. Mencken writes, "Lowell and Walt Whitman, in fact, were the first men of letters, properly so called, to give specific assent to the great changes that were firmly fixed in the national speech during the half century between the War of 1812 and the Civil War," *American Language* (New York: Knopf, 1919), 73.

⁶⁵ Quoted in Thomas Wortham, "William Cullen Bryant and the Fireside Poets," in *The Columbia Literary History of the United States*, ed. Emory Elliott (New York: Columbia University Press, 1988): 287.

⁶⁶ Zweig, *Walt Whitman: The Making of a Poet* (New York: Basic Books, 1984), 141.

⁶⁷ See an account of Whittier's reading in Traubel, *With Walt Whitman*, 1:127.

⁶⁸ Buell, *New England Literary Culture: From Revolution Through Renaissance* (Cambridge: Cambridge University Press, 1986), 379–380.

⁶⁹ Lowell, *Letters*, 1:161.

⁷⁰ Lowell, *Letters*, 1:60.

⁷¹ Martin Duberman, *James Russell Lowell* (Boston: Houghton Mifflin, 1966), 402.

⁷² Lowell, *Letters*, 1:63.

⁷³ See the *North American Review* (April 1841), Boston *Morning Post* (20 February 1841), *Brownson's Quarterly Review* (April 1841), the *Dial* (July 1841), and *Graham's Magazine* (April 1842).

⁷⁴ Review of *A Year's Life* by James Russell Lowell, *The Dial* 2 (July 1841): 133.

⁷⁵ Charvat, *Literary Publishing in America* (Philadelphia: University of Pennsylvania Press, 1959), 34.

⁷⁶ Duberman, *James Russell Lowell*, 45–46.

⁷⁷ Lowell, *Letters*, 1:69–70.

⁷⁸ Lowell, *Works* 10:244.

⁷⁹ Charvat, *Literary Publishing*, 33.

⁸⁰ Whitman, *Uncollected Poetry and Prose*, 1:69–72.

⁸¹ Traubel, *With Walt Whitman*, 6:563.

⁸² Traubel, *With Walt Whitman*, 1:193.

⁸³ Raymond Williams, in *The Sociology of Culture* (New York: Schocken Books, 1982), 44–51, describes four market situations: the artisanal, "the independent producer . . . offers his work for direct sale"; the post-artisanal, "the producer sells his work not directly but to a *distributive* intermediary, who then becomes, in a majority of cases, his factual if often occasional employer"; the market professional, the writer negotiates a contract, involving royalties and copyright with a publisher; and the corporate professional, the artist is an employee of a literary organization such as a magazine or newspaper.

[84] Golden, "Nine Early Whitman Letters," 347–348.

[85] Bourdieu, *Field*, 70.

[86] Quoted in Alice Felt Tyler, *Freedom's Ferment: Phases of American Social History to 1860* (Minneapolis: University of Minnesota Press, 1944), 212–213.

[87] Traubel, *With Walt Whitman*, 8:406.

[88] Lowell, *Letters*, 1:242.

[89] See David Reynolds, *Beneath the American Renaissance: The Subversive Imagination in the Age of Emerson and Melville* (Cambridge, MA: Harvard University Press, 1990), 165.

[90] Whitman, *Leaves of Grass, Comprehensive*, 56.

[91] Whitman, *Leaves of Grass, Comprehensive*, 54.

[92] Whitman was apparently not so offended by Lowell's indifference that he sought to oppose him as a poet; still hoping to curry favor, Whitman later published some of Lowell's poetry in the *Brooklyn Daily Eagle*, when he was editor from 1846–48; see Thomas L. Brasher, ed., *Whitman as Editor of the* Brooklyn Daily Eagle (Detroit, MI: Wayne State University Press, 1970), 199.

[93] Milton Hindus, ed., *Walt Whitman: The Critical Heritage* (London: Routledge and Kegan Paul, 1971), 66.

[94] Charvat, *Literary Publishing*, 64.

[95] Hindus, *Walt Whitman: The Critical Heritage*, 66.

[96] Bourdieu, *Field*, 67.

[97] Bourdieu, *Field*, 42.

[98] Bourdieu, *Field*, 54.

[99] Bourdieu, *Field*, 42.

[100] Traubel, *With Walt Whitman*, 1:127.

[101] *New Letters of James Russell Lowell*, ed. M. A. DeWolfe Howe (New York: Harper's, 1932), 115–116.

[102] AL 4159.35.

[103] Pages 331, 304.

[104] Duberman, *James Russell Lowell*, 169.

[105] E. H. House, "A First Interview with Lowell," *James Russell Lowell Magazine Articles, Etc., 1885–99* (Volume of clippings, Harvard College Library), n.p.

[106] House, "A First Interview," n.p;"Bardic Symbols" later became "As I Ebb'd with the Ocean of Life" in the third edition of *Leaves of Grass*.

[107] Whitman, "Bardic Symbols," *Atlantic Monthly* 5 (April 1860): 445.

[108] Traubel, *With Walt Whitman*, 3:126–127.

[109] There is some evidence that Whitman was periodically a heavy drinker, which would have been a serious impediment to his admission to respectable society in Boston, stricken as it was by stereotypes of working-class alcoholism (particularly among the recent Irish immigrants), if not so much in other cities (such as New York and Philadelphia) where the German tradition of social drinking was more common. In 1884 the critic Richard Grant White parodied Whitman with the following: "I glorify schnapps; I celebrate gin./ In beer I revel and welter. I shall liquor./

Ein lager!/I swear there is no nectar like lager. I swim in it; I float upon it; it heaves me up to heaven . . ." (Henry S. Saunders, *Parodies on Walt Whitman* [New York: American Library Service, 1923], 48). Curiously, in the late 1950s (near the time of the well-publicized centenary of *Leaves*), Whitman appeared in a series of print advertisements for Old Crow Kentucky Bourbon, which, the advertisers claim, the poet endorsed (personal collection).

¹¹⁰ John T. Trowbridge, "Reminiscences of Walt Whitman," *Atlantic Monthly* 89 (102), 164.

¹¹¹ Whitman, *Leaves of Grass, Comprehensive*, 131–132.

¹¹² Howells, *Literary Friends and Acquaintance: A Personal Retrospect of American Authorship* (New York: Harper and Brothers, 1902), 76.

¹¹³ Whitman, *Leaves of Grass, Comprehensive*, 729.

¹¹⁴ Kenneth Price, *Walt Whitman: The Contemporary* Reviews (Cambridge: Cambridge University Press, 1990), 8.

¹¹⁵ Kennedy, *Fight*, 86.

¹¹⁶ Hindus, *Walt Whitman: The Critical Heritage*, 183.

¹¹⁷ Whitman, *Leaves of Grass, Comprehensive*, 731; *Whitman* seems to have been recalling the approximate sales figures of his temperance novel *Franklin Evans* (1842).

¹¹⁸ Price, *Walt Whitman: The Contemporary* Reviews, 22.

¹¹⁹ Allen, *Solitary Singer*, 188.

¹²⁰ Kennedy describes "Traubel in a not very polite way quizzing and terebrating Walt about his (Walt's) assertion to Emerson that the first edition of Leaves of Grass 'readily sold.'" Backed against the wall Whitman admitted that he would not now say the book readily sold . . . there were no sales, they came back" from consignment; see Kennedy, *Fight*, 117.

¹²¹ Traubel, *With Walt Whitman*, 4:20.

¹²² David Reynolds, *Walt Whitman's America, A Cultural Biography* (New York: Knopf, 1995), 352–3.

¹²³ Quoted in Reynolds, *Walt Whitman*, 356.

¹²⁴ Price, *Walt Whitman: The Contemporary Reviews*, 81.

¹²⁵ Whitman, *A Child's Reminiscence*, eds. Thomas O. Mabbott and Rollo G. Silver (Seattle: University of Washington Book Store, 1930), 19–21.

¹²⁶ Quoted in Reynolds, *Walt Whitman*, 382.

¹²⁷ Whitman, *Correspondence*, 1:52.

¹²⁸ Clifton Joseph Furness, ed., *Walt Whitman's Workshop: A Collection of Unpublished Manuscripts* (Cambridge: Harvard University Press, 1928), 245.

¹²⁹ Larson, *Whitman's Drama of Consensus* (Chicago: University of Chicago Press, 1988), 43.

¹³⁰ Whitman, *Prose Works 1892*, 1:31.

¹³¹ Charles Glicksberg, ed., *Walt Whitman and the Civil War* (Philadelphia: University of Pennsylvania Press, 1933), 175.

¹³² Whitman, *Prose Works 1892*, 2:499.

[133] Whitman, *Prose Works 1892*, 2:501.

[134] Lincoln, *Collected Works* 4:232–233.

[135] Whitman, *Prose Works 1892*, 1:100.

[136] Traubel, *With Walt Whitman*, 5:362.

[137] Anderson, *Abraham Lincoln*, 199.

[138] See, for example, *Poetical Tributes to the Memory of Abraham Lincoln* (Philadelphia: J. B. Lippincott, 1865), which, incidentally, does not include any poems by Whitman.

[139] Oates, *With Malice Towards None*, 434.

[140] John Harmon McElroy, ed., *The Sacrificial Years: A Chronicle of Walt Whitman's Experiences in the Civil War* (Boston: David R. Godine, 1999), 136–137.

[141] Aaron, *Unwritten War*, 71.

[142] Whitman, *Correspondence*, 1:171. Whitman is probably referring to Louisa May Alcott's successful first book, *Hospital Sketches* (1863), also published by James Redpath.

[143] Whitman, *Correspondence*, 1:208.

[144] Quoted in Reynolds, *Walt Whitman's America*, 457.

[145] Whitman, *Leaves of Grass, Comprehensive*, 329.

[146] Whitman, *Leaves of Grass, Comprehensive*, 331, 329.

[147] Whitman, *Leaves of Grass, Comprehensive*, 337.

[148] Whitman, *Prose Works 1892*, 2:508.

[149] Whitman, *Leaves of Grass, Comprehensive*, 328.

[150] Kaplan, *Walt Whitman*, 309.

[151] Whitman, *Correspondence*, 1:350.

[152] Whitman, *Leaves of Grass, Comprehensive*, 49.

[153] Price, *Contemporary Reviews*, 112–113.

[154] Coyle, *The Poet and the President*, 144.

[155] Allen, *Solitary Singer*, 345.

[156] Kaplan, *Walt Whitman*, 304.

[157] There were comparable theories afloat concerning Lincoln's assassination at this time; some suggested that he was murdered in a conspiracy hatched by Northern businessmen who were eager to pillage the South after the war.

[158] Victimization (and foreign admiration coupled with domestic shaming) was also becoming a basis for Poe's canonization. Whitman was perhaps the only major poet to attend the dedication of the Poe memorial in Baltimore on 17 November, 1875. According to O'Connor: "our prosperous and popular literary people stayed away or were not there, few of them even sending messages" with the exception of Whitman, "our loftiest poet, broken with his hospital service to the wounded and dying of both sides of the war, and grand in his age and infirmity, like a crippled eagle" in Jerome Loving, *Walt Whitman's Champion: William Douglas O'Connor* (College Station: Texas A&M University Press, 1978), 106. Significantly, O'Connor mentions that Lowell had attacked Poe's sufferings as "self-caused."

[159] Loving, *Walt Whitman's Champion*, 203.

[160] Loving, *Walt Whitman's Champion*, 198.

[161] Price, *Contemporary Reviews*, 137.

[162] William D. O'Connor, William D., *The Good Gray Poet: A Vindication* (New York: Bunce and Huntington, 1866), 32.

[163] Aaron, *Unwritten War*, 70.

[164] Lowell, Review of *Venetian Life*, by W. D. Howells, *North American Review* 103 (October 1866): 611.

[165] Lowell, Review of *Poems* by John James Piatt, *North American Review* 107 (October 1868): 660–661.

[166] Traubel, *With Walt Whitman*, 8:500.

[167] Traubel, *With Walt Whitman*, 4:273.

[168] Anonymous, "Notes," *The Nation* 8 (28 January 1869): 69.

[169] Winchester, "Lowell as Man of Letters," *The Review of Reviews* 4.21 (October 1891): 291.

[170] Matthews, *Introduction to American Literature* (New York: American Book Company, 1896), 225.

[171] Perry, *Walt Whitman, His Life and Work* (Boston: Houghton Mifflin, 1906), 157.

[172] Macy, *The Spirit of American Literature* (Garden City: Doubleday, Page and Company, 1913), 191.

[173] Traubel, *With Walt Whitman*, 6:486.

[174] Traubel, *With Walt Whitman*, 1:156.

[175] Bartlett, "Incidents of Walt Whitman," *Conservator* 23 (March 1912), 9.

[176] Quoted in Basler, *Memoranda*, 11–12.

[177] Whitman, *Daybooks and Notebooks*, 1061.

[178] Furness, *Walt Whitman's Workshop*, 245.

[179] Quoted in Loving, *Walt Whitman's Champion*, 113.

[180] Whitman typically earned considerably more than the average income, which was around $800 in 1875; his average income from 1876–91 was around $1270 a year, see Reynolds, *Walt Whitman's America*, 524.

[181] Loving, *Walt Whitman's Champion*, 204.

[182] Loving, *Walt Whitman's Champion*, 211.

[183] Robert Buchanan, "Mr. Walt Whitman," London *Daily News* (16 March 1876): 6.

[184] Traubel, *With Walt Whitman* 3:126.

[185] Traubel, *With Walt Whitman*, 3:126.

[186] John T. Trowbridge, "Reminiscences of Walt Whitman," *Atlantic Monthly* 89 (102): 170.

[187] Hillard, "Poetry, Prose and Whitman," *New York Times Saturday Review* (12 May 1906): 312.

[188] Quoted in Robert Scholnick, "Whitman and the Magazines: Some Documentary Evidence," in *On Whitman: The Best from* American Literature, eds. Edwin H. Cady and Louis J. Budd (Durham: Duke University Press, 1987), 168.

¹⁸⁹ Reynolds, *Walt Whitman's America*, 528.

¹⁹⁰ Quoted in Barton, *Abraham Lincoln and Walt Whitman*, 192–193.

¹⁹¹ Quoted in Basler, *Memoranda*, 27.

¹⁹² Quoted in Barton, *Abraham Lincoln and Walt Whitman*, 195.

¹⁹³ Quoted in Basler, *Memoranda*, 34–35.

¹⁹⁴ See Ed Folsom, "'This Heart's Geography's Map': The Photographs of Walt Whitman." *Walt Whitman Quarterly Review* 4.2–3 (1986–87): 54.

¹⁹⁵ Whitman, *Correspondence*, 3:224.

¹⁹⁶ Ellen B. Ballou, *The Building of the House: Houghton Mifflin's Formative Years* (Boston: Houghton Mifflin, 1970), 282.

¹⁹⁷ Whitman, *Correspondence*, 3:267, 273.

¹⁹⁸ Whitman, *Correspondence* 3:271.

¹⁹⁹ Robert Pearsall Smith, a glass manufacturer and Quaker evangelist, visited Whitman in Camden at the encouragement of his daughter, Mary Whitall Smith, and the poet soon became a guest at their house in Germantown. About this time Whitman also was a frequent guest of Thomas Donaldson, a Philadelphia lawyer who provided Whitman with free ferry passes and organized a collection to buy him a horse and buggy in 1885. During the 1880s Whitman acquired other notable allies among the elites of Philadelphia: two on the faculty of the University of Pennsylvania, Horace Howard Furness, a Shakespearean scholar, and Daniel Garrison Brinton, an anthropologist; George Henry Boker, a dramatist, poet, and diplomat; Charles Godfrey Leland, a writer and translator of Heine; Elizabeth Robbins, a journalist; Joseph Pennell, a magazine illustrator; and Thomas Eakins, former director of the Academy of Fine Arts.

²⁰⁰ Traubel, *With Walt Whitman*, 1:18.

²⁰¹ Kennedy, *Fight*, 119.

²⁰² Whitman, *Specimen Days & Collect* (Philadelphia: David McKay, 1882), 375.

²⁰³ A photograph of this advertisement is in Loving, *Walt Whitman's Champion*, n.p.

²⁰⁴ From 1882 until his death, most of Whitman's American publications were handled in Philadelphia by David McKay, the successor of Rees Welsh, including *November Boughs* and a new edition of *Leaves* in 1888, *Good-Bye My Fancy* in 1891, and the "Deathbed Edition" of *Leaves* in 1891–1892. McKay also published Richard M. Bucke's adulatory biography, *Walt Whitman*, in 1883, and *Camden's Compliment to Walt Whitman* in 1889.

²⁰⁵ Traubel, *With Walt Whitman*, 4:61.

²⁰⁶ Whitman, Leaves of Grass, Comprehensive, 562.

²⁰⁷ Whitman, *Prose Works 1892*, 2:480.

²⁰⁸ Traubel, *With Walt Whitman*, 1:213.

²⁰⁹ Traubel, *With Walt Whitman* 4:74–75.

²¹⁰ Traubel, *With Walt Whitman*, 2:316–317.

²¹¹ See, for example, *Poems of American Patriotism*, ed. J. Brander Matthews (New York: Scribner's, 1882); *Bugle-Echoes*, ed. Francis Browne (New York: White, Stokes & Allen, 1886); *Reminiscences of Abraham Lincoln*, ed. Allen Thorndike Rice (New York: North American, 1886); *Representative Poems of Living Poets*, ed. Jeannette Gilder (New York: Cassell, 1886); *Harper's Fifth Reader*, ed. James Baldwin (New York: Harper, 1889); and especially *A Library of American Literature*, eds. E.C. Stedman and Ellen Hutchinson (New York: Webster, 1889).

²¹² See, for example, the following poems in addition to "O Captain!": "After All, Not to Create Only" (1871), "Death-Sonnet for Custer" or "From Far Dakota's Cañons" (1876), "Death of Carlyle" (1881), "By Emerson's Grave" (1882), "Death of Longfellow" (1882), "The Dead Tenor" (1884), "Ah, Not This Granite, Dead and Cold" (1885), "As One by One Withdrew the Lofty Actors ['Death of General Grant']" (1885), "The Dying Veteran" (1888), "Bravo, Paris Exhibition" (1889), "A Christmas Greeting" (1889), "Death's Valley" (1889), "A Voice from Death" (1889), "A Death-Bouquet" (1890), "The Pallid Wreath" (1891). One looks in vain, however, for the "Ode To Stephen Dowling Bots, Dec'd."

²¹³ Traubel, *With Walt Whitman*, 1:62.

²¹⁴ Whitman, *Daybooks*, 2:417n.

²¹⁵ Folsom, "*Leaves of Grass, Junior*: Walt Whitman's Compromise with Discriminating Tastes," *American Literature* 63 (1991): 663.

²¹⁶ Allen, *Solitary Singer*, 542.

²¹⁷ "Contributor's Club," *Atlantic Monthly* 40 (December 1878): 749.

²¹⁸ Among the reporters at the Whitman benefit were Henry Tyrell of *Frank Leslie's*, Mr. Metcalf of the *Forum*, Mr. Learned of the *Evening Post*, Wolcott Calestier of *Tid Bits*, Henry Walsh of *Catholic World*, Mr. Mabie of the *Christian Union*, Lawrence Hutton of *Harper's*, R. W. Bowker of *Publisher's Weekly*, and Dr. Holbrook of the *Herald of Health*.

²¹⁹ Carpenter, *Chants of Labour: A Songbook of the People* (London: Swan Sonnenshein, 1888), 56–58.

²²⁰ "The New Biglow Papers," *The Nation* 3 (15 November 1866): 386.

²²¹ [Henry James], "Mr. Walt Whitman, *Nation* 1 (16 November 185): 626.

²²² Traubel, "Lowell-Whitman: A Contrast," *Poet-Lore* 4 (1892): 22.

²²³ Traubel, *With Walt Whitman*, 9:158.

²²⁴ Traubel, *With Walt Whitman*, 2:372.

²²⁵ Traubel, *With Walt Whitman*, 1:246.

²²⁶ Perry, *Walt Whitman*, 262.

NOTES TO CHAPTER FOUR

¹ Edward Carpenter, *Selected* Writings, 3 vols., ed. Noel Grieg (London: GMP Publishers, 1984), 1:289; Traubel, *With Walt Whitman in Camden*, 9 Vols., Vol. I. (1905; rpt., New York: Rowman and Littlefield, 1961); Vol. II. (1907; rpt., New York: Rowman and Littlefield, 1961); Vol. III. (1912; rpt., New York: Rowman and Littlefield, 1961); Vol. IV (1953; rpt., Carbondale: Southern Illinois University

Press, 1959); Vol. V (Carbondale: Southern Illinois University Press, 1964); Vol. VI (Carbondale: Southern Illinois University Press, 1982); Vol. VII (Carbondale: Southern Illinois University Press, 1992); Vols. VIII-IX (Oregon House, CA: W. L. Bentley, 1996), 1:160

2 Whitman, *Leaves of Grass: Comprehensive Reader's Edition*, ed. Harold W. Blodgett and Sculley Bradley (New York: New York University Press, 1965), 52; Edward Carpenter, *Days with Walt Whitman* (New York: Macmillan, 1908), 5.

3 Carpenter, *Days*, 3–7; Clara Barrus, ed., *Whitman and Burroughs: Comrades* (Boston: Houghton Mifflin, 1931), 339.

4 Carpenter, *Days*, 8–9.

5 Carpenter, *Days*, 11, 15–16, 14, 31.

6 Carpenter, *Days*, 7.

7 Quoted in Randall Waldron, "Whitman as the Nazarene: An Unpublished Drawing," *Walt Whitman Quarterly Review* 7.4 (1990): 192–195.

8 The relationship between Carpenter and Whitman was certainly physical on some level; whether it was sexual or not is unclear. According to Charley Shively, Whitman performed oral sex on Carpenter during this visit, but there is little evidence to prove this assertion. Carpenter says he left Whitman with "real reluctance" after falling under "the added force of bodily presence" and admired that "wonderful genius of his for human affection and love." Whitman later said that Carpenter "is ardently my friend—ardently." Shively, ed., *Calamus Lovers: Walt Whitman's Working-Class Camderados* (San Francisco: Gay Sunshine Press, 1987), 146, Carpenter, *Days*, 32; Traubel, *With Walt Whitman*, 1:104.

9 Whitman, *Leaves of Grass: Comprehensive*, 710–712.

10 Traubel, *With Walt Whitman*, 1:234.

11 Whitman, *Leaves of Grass: Comprehensive*, 47.

12 Henry S. Saunders, *Parodies on Walt Whitman* (New York: American Library Service, 1923), 18.

13 Richard Maurice Bucke, *Walt Whitman: A Contemporary Study* (Philadelphia: David McKay, 1883), 219.

14 Higginson, "Unmanly Manhood," *Woman's Journal* 13 (4 February 1882), 1.

15 By "identity" I mean the total construction of an individual's relationship to social structures. I am also fixing the terms "masculine" and "feminine" as they are generally denoted, although these meanings cover a range of connotations, and do not intend to essentialize the categories.

16 This chapter is intended, in particular, to reassess Harold Blodgett's foundational study, *Walt Whitman in England* (Ithaca: Cornell University Press, 1934). Although Blodgett demonstrates how English followers of Whitman were political and literary "non-conformists," he minimizes the central importance of sexual orientation to Whitman's English reception.

17 Gay Wilson Allen, *The Solitary Singer: A Critical Biography of Walt Whitman* (New York: New York University Press, 1967),169.

[18] Thoreau, *Correspondence*, ed. Walter Harding and Carl Bode (New York: New York University Press, 1958), 481.

[19] Shively, 11; The horrible crime not to be named among the Christians."

[20] Allen, *Solitary Singer*, 177.

[21] The Calamus or "sweet flag" has a large, flowering seed spike that resembles an erect penis.

[22] Whitman, *Leaves of Grass: Comprehensive*, 117.

[23] "Homosexuell" is used in Westphal's essay, "Die contrare Sexualempfindung, Symptom eines neuropathischen psychopathischen Zustandes," *Archiv fur Psychiatrie and Nervenkrankheiten* 2(1870): 73–108.

[24] Carpenter, *Homogenic Love*, (London: Redundancy Press, n .d.), 3–4.

[25] Whitman, *Leaves of Grass: Comprehensive*, 135.

[26] Whitman, *Leaves of Grass: Comprehensive*, 116, 132.

[27] Allen, 467.

[28] *The Letters of John Addington Symonds,*. 3 vols., ed. Herbert Schueller and Robert Peters (Detroit: Wayne State University Press, 1969), 2:201–202.

[29] Carpenter, *My Days and Dreams: Being Autobiographical Notes* (London: Allen and Unwin, 1916), 64.

[30] Whitman, *Leaves of Grass: Comprehensive*, 131–132.

[31] Carpenter, *My Days*, 64.

[32] Traubel, *With Walt Whitman*, 1:159.

[33] Symonds, *Letters*, 2:446–447.

[34] Sedgwick, *Between Men: English Literature and Male Homosocial Desire* (New York: Columbia University Press, 1985), 206.

[35] A complete listing of the collection is in Hamer's *Catalogue of Works by and Relating to Whitman in the Reference Library, Bolton*, 1955.

[36] The membership of the Whitman Fellowship included William Broadhurst, R. Curwin, Henry Dearden, Wentworth Dixon, W. A. Ferguson, R. K. Greenhalgh, Samuel Hodgkinson, G. Humphreys, F. R. C. Hutton, John Johnston, Fred Nightingale, John Ormrod, William Pimblett, Thomas Shorrock, C. F. Sixsmith, James William Wallace, and Fred Wild. The best account of their activities is Johnston and Wallace's *Visits to Walt Whitman, 1890–1891*. Carpenter discusses their importance in *My Days and Dreams* (250), and Blodgett gives them a cursory treatment in *Walt Whitman in England* (213–215). Also see the following more recent accounts: Paul Salveson, "Loving Comrades: Lancashire's Links to Walt Whitman," *Walt Whitman Quarterly Review* 14.2-3 (1996–97): 57–84; Joann P. Krieg, "Without Walt Whitman in Camden," *Walt Whitman Quarterly Review* 14.2-3 (1996–97): 85–113.

[37] John Johnston and J. W. Wallace, *Visits to Walt Whitman in 1890–91 by Two Lancashire Friends* (Allen and Unwin, 1917), 19.

[38] Johnston, 177; Their correspondents among Whitman admirers included Richard Bucke, John Burroughs, Edward Carpenter, Edward Dowden, Herbert

Gilchrist, Warren Fritzinger, Thomas Harned, Henry Saunders, John Addington Symonds, and Horace Traubel.

[39] Johnston, 158–159.

[40] Johnston, 216.

[41] Arthur, "The Gay Succession." *Gay Roots: Twenty Years of Gay Sunshine*, ed. Winston Leyland (San Francisco: Gay Sunshine Press, 1991), 324.

[42] Traubel, *With Walt Whitman*, 1:160.

[43] Whitman, *Leaves of Grass: Comprehensive*, 751.

[44] Whitman, Leaves of Grass: Comprehensive, 117.

[45] Whitman, *Leaves of Grass: Comprehensive*, 751.

[46] Whitman, *Prose Works, 1892*, ed. Floyd Stovall, 2 vols. (New York: New York University Press, 1963), 2:414.

[47] Whitman, *Leaves of Grass: Comprehensive*, 41.

[48] Carpenter, *Days*, 58.

[49] Sedgwick, *Between Men*, 204.

[50] Carpenter, *Homogenic*, 24.

[51] Carpenter, *Selected Writings*, 1:290.

[52] Carpenter, *Towards Democracy*, (London: Swan Sonnenschein, 1905), 73.

[53] Traubel, *With Walt Whitman*, 1:65.

[54] Ironically, it was the classical education these men received that enabled them to recognize and articulate much of the homoerotic significance of Whitman's poetry.

[55] Johnston, 23.

[56] See, for example, his letter of 7 Feb 1872 in which he writes, "I have pored for continuous hours over Calamus . . . longing to hear you speak, *burning* for a revelation of your more developed meaning, panting to ask—is this what you would indicate?" Symonds made his education clear on 7 October 1871: "I first took up Leaves of Grass in a friend's rooms at Trinity College Cambridge." Symonds, *Letters*, 2:202, 167.

[57] See, for example, Whitman's typical 30 March 1891, letter to Symonds ("Nothing special to write about") or his 28 May 1887, letter to William Sloane Kennedy: "Showery & coolish . . .have had my dinner, eaten with relish." Whitman, *The Correspondence*, ed. Edwin Haviland Miller, 6 vols., (New York: New York University Press, 1961–77), 4: 95, 5:182.

[58] Carpenter, *Days*, 42.

[59] Arthur Reade, *Poems of Love and War* (London: Allen and Unwin, 1915), 5.

[60] Carpenter, *Towards Democracy*, 410.

[61] Carpenter, *Days*, 152.

[62] Symonds, *Letters* 3:808.

[63] Carpenter, *Homogenic*, 25, 23.

[64] The Fabian Society was an English socialist organization founded in 1884. While they were advocates of labor reform, they did not support revolution. Instead, they attempted to influence government policy by infiltration, disseminating their

ideas through the population in the form of pamphlets and tracts. Carpenter's *Civilization: Its Cause and Cure, England's Ideal, Desirable Mansions* were listed the "What to Read" section of London's *Fabian Tracts* 29 (1896): 36. Works by Symonds and Ellis were also frequently listed until English socialism abandoned its controversial advocacy of sexual liberty in order to concentrate on economic issues around 1910.

[65] Johnston, 223.

[66] Tsuzuki, *Edward Carpenter 1844–1929, Prophet of Human Fellowship* (Cambridge: Cambridge University Press, 1980), 199.

[67] Carpenter, *Homogenic,* 24.

[68] Symonds, *Letters* 1:160. Almost none of the Whitmanites—with the exception of a few members of the Bolton Whitman Fellowship—were working class. And, although they sometimes slept with each other, the sexual ideal of the Uranians was liaisons with working class youths, often on jaunts to the Mediterranean. As the next chapter, examines, these relationships, being based on social, educational, economic, and age-related inequalities, did not foster the kind of democratic ideals they advocated, although it created the self-satisfying illusion that were being egalitarian.

[69] Symonds, *Letters,* 3:799.

[70] Algernon Charles Swinburne called them "Calamites," which combined the words "Calamus" and "catamite." See Gregory Woods, "'Still on My Lips': Walt Whitman in Britain," *The Continuing Presence of Walt Whitman,* ed. Robert K. Martin (Iowa City, Iowa: University of Iowa Press, 1992), 130.

[71] Carpenter, *My Days and Dreams: Being Autobiographical Notes* (London: Allen and Unwin, 1916), 149.

[72] Whitman, *Leaves of Grass: Comprehensive,* 709.

[73] Fone, *Masculine Landscapes: Walt Whitman and the Homoerotic Text,* (Carbondale: Southern Illinois University Press, 1992), 24.

[74] Carpenter, *Love's Coming of Age: A Series of Papers on the Relations of the Sexes,* (Manchester, 1896), 197.

[75] Ellis and Symonds, *Sexual Inversion,* 47.

[76] See, for example, the title page by Beardsley for Oscar Wilde's *Salome* and *Enter Herodias* from *Salome.*

[77] See Oscar Wilde, *The Soul of Man Under Socialism.*

[78] The writings of both Whitman and Carpenter were used to support the Arts and Crafts movement. See John Spargo's essay, "Edward Carpenter, the Philosopher: His Gospel of Friendship and Simplicity," *The Craftsman* (October 1906): 44–56.

[79] Sedgwick, *Between Men,* 217.

[80] Ellis and Symonds, *Sexual Inversion,* 76.

[81] Rivers, *Walt Whitman's Anomaly,* (London: George Allen, 1913), 20, ibid, 21, 22, 22–23.

[82] E. Anthony Rotundo, *American Manhood: Transformations in Masculinity from the Revolution to the Modern Era* (New York: Basic Books, 1993), 276.

[83] Carpenter, *An Unknown People* (London: n.p., 1897), 23.

[84] Chauncey, *Gay New York: Gender, Urban Culture, and the Making of the Gay Male World, 1890–1940* (New York: HarperCollins, 1994), 57.

[85] Carpenter, *An Unknown People*, 21.

[86] Chauncey, 106.

[87] Beardsley was fired from the *Yellow Book*, Carpenter was forced to exclude *Homogenic Love* from *Love's-Coming of Age* and his publisher, Fisher Unwin, ended publication of *Towards Democracy*; see Carpenter, *Homogenic Love*, 2.

[88] On the other side, many of Whitman's American biographers Holloway and Binns have struggled—often against reason—to prove that Whitman was completely "straight." See Jerome Loving, "Emory Holloway and the Quest for Whitman's 'Manhood,'" *Walt Whitman Quarterly Review* 11.1 (Summer 1993): 1–17.

[89] Fone, 179.

[90] Allen, *Solitary Singer*, 345.

[91] Reprinted in Jerome Loving, *Walt Whitman's Champion*, (College Station: Texas A&M University Press, 1978), 160.

[92] Loving, *Walt Whitman's Champion*, 158.

[93] Loving, *Walt Whitman's Champion*, 161.

[94] Loving, *Walt Whitman's Champion*, 159; the line is repeated on 201.

[95] Quoted in Richard Maurice Bucke, *Walt Whitman: A Contemporary Study* (Philadelphia: David McKay, 1883), 197.

[96] Thoreau, *Correspondence*, ed. Walter Harding and Carl Bode (New York: New York University Press, 1958), 481.

[97] O'Grady, "The Poet of Joy," *Gentleman's Magazine* (December 1875), 167.

[98] Bucke, *Walt Whitman: A Contemporary Study*, 166.

[99] "[The King] has dissolved Representative Houses repeatedly, for opposing with manly firmness his invasions on the rights of the people."

[100] Whitman, *Leaves of Grass: Comprehensive*, 84–85.

[101] Carpenter, *Selected Writings*, 1:290.

[102] Stearns, *Be a Man!: Males in Modern Society*, 2nd ed. (New York and London: Holmes and Meier, 1990), 81.

[103] Carpenter, *Towards Democracy*, 43.

[104] Mason, *The Making of Victorian Sexuality* (Oxford and New York: Oxford University Press, 1994), 139.

[105] Carpenter, *My Days and Dreams*, 58.

[106] Carpenter, *My Days and Dreams*, 74.

[107] Carpenter, *Towards Democracy*, 28.

[108] Traubel, *With Walt Whitman* 1:160.

[109] Carpenter, *My Days*, 77; Traubel, *With Walt Whitman* 3:416.

[110] Carpenter, *My Days*, 170.

[111] Chauncey 108, 118.

[112] Chauncey 81.

[113] Carpenter, *My Days*, 159, 161.

114 Ellis, *Personal Impressions of Edward Carpenter* (Berkeley Heights, New Jersey: Free Spirit Press, 1922), 11.

115 Gilbert Beith, *Edward Carpenter: In Appreciation* (Boston: Houghton Mifflin, 1931), 67.

116 Whitman, *Leaves of Grass: Comprehensive*, 48, 94.

117 Take, for example, "A Woman Waits for Me": "I will go and stay with her who waits for me, and with those women that are warm-blooded and sufficient for me . . . I will be the robust husband of those women," *Leaves of Grass: Comprehensive*, 102. Or "I Sing the Body Electric": "This is the female form . . . It attracts with fierce undeniable attraction," *Leaves of Grass: Comprehensive* 96. Overall, however, there are more homoerotic images in Whitman's poetry than het-ero-erotic ones. Whitman's efforts to include heterosexuality, however, demonstrates the inclusiveness of his poetics in direct proportion to the degree of his actual homosexual exclusivity in life.

118 Traubel, *With Walt Whitman*, 2:373.

119 Symonds wrote to Whitman eleven times between 1871 and 1890: 7 Oct. 1871 (*Letters* 1:166–167), 7 Feb. 1872 (2:201–203), 25 Feb. 1872 (2:205), 13 June 1875 (2: 374–375), 23 Jan. 1877 (2:446–447), 12 July 1877 (2:484–485), 28 Nov. 1884 (2:972–973), 29 Jan. 1889 (3:343–344), 9 Dec. 1889 (3:424–425), 3 Aug. 1890 (3:481–484), 5 Sept. 1890 (3:492–494). Symonds also corresponded with Horace Traubel, J. W. Wallace, John Johnston, Edward Carpenter, and Havelock Ellis.

120 In his letter of 29 Jan. 1889 Symonds writes, "Believe me, dear Master, to be, though a silent and uncommunicative friend, your respectful and loving disciple," *Letters*, 3: 344. In 1855 Whitman wrote to Emerson, "Receive, dear Master, these statements and assurances through me," *Leaves of Grass: Comprehensive*, 739. It seems clear that Symonds sought an endorsement for his work on homosexuality comparable to the one given by Emerson to Whitman in 1855: "I greet you at the beginning of a great career."

121 Symonds, *Letters*, 3:424.

122 Perhaps the most famous example of this is Whitman's use of 16.4 to represent Peter Doyle in his private notes. Charley Shively speculates at length in *Calamus Lovers* on the significance of Whitman's other codes.

123 Symonds, *Letters*, 3:482; Homosexual acts were punishable by death in England until 1861, but a life sentence remained possible until the 1960s. The Labouchere Amendment to the Criminal Law Amendment Act of 1885 made all male homosexual acts illegal. Homosexuality was rarely prosecuted in the United States before the Civil War, but, by the 1880s prosecutions became common in major cities, see Rotundo, *American Manhood*, 275.

124 Whitman, *Correspondence*, 5:72–73.

125 Symonds, *Letters*, 3:492–493.

[126] He was right to suspect Symonds, for Whitman's response was forwarded by Symonds to Ernest Rhys, Edward Carpenter, and Havelock Ellis, and it was reprinted in Ellis and Symonds's *Sexual Inversion* after Whitman's death.

[127] No reliable evidence of Whitman's children has ever surfaced, although such evidence would not constitute proof of Whitman's heterosexuality, only that he had engaged in heterosexual acts. Whitman may not have thought Symonds would be fooled by his claim, but he may have hoped his assertion would deceive his growing body of heterosexual readers, who frequently used the letter to defend Whitman against the charge of "perversion." See particularly Emory Holloway's *Free and Lonesome Heart: The Secret of Walt Whitman* (New York: Vantage Press, 1960); and Jerome Loving's essay, "Emory Holloway and the Quest for Whitman's Manhood," *Walt Whitman Quarterly Review* 11.1 (1993): 1–17. Other biographers who deny Whitman's homosexuality include Richard Maurice Bucke, William D. O'Connor, William Sloane Kennedy, Horace Traubel, Henry B. Binns, Bliss Perry, and Leon Bazalgette. It is safe to say that proving Whitman's sexual normality was the major theme of Whitman biography until the 1970s, just as proving his homosexuality has been a major theme since then.

[128] Quoted in Allen, *Solitary Singer*, 467.

[129] Carpenter, *Days*, 65–66.

[130] Michel Foucault, *The History of Sexuality, Volume 1: An Introduction*, trans. Robert Hurley (New York: Pantheon, 1978), 43.

NOTES TO CHAPTER FIVE

[1] John Carl Miller, ed., *Poe's Helen Remembers* (Charlottesville: University Press of Virginia, 1979), 22; *Collected Works of Edgar Allan Poe*, 3 vols., ed. Thomas O. Mabbott (Cmabridge: Harvard University Press, 1969–1978), 1:344; Also quoted in Sarah Helen Whitman, *Edgar Poe and His Critics* (1860, New Brunswick, NJ: Rutgers University Pres, 1949), 81.

[2] Poe, *Collected Works*, 2:690.

[3] Poe, *Collected Works*, 2:697; Miller, *Poe's Helen*, 348.

[4] Hervey Allen, *Israfel: The Life and Times of Edgar Allan Poe*, 2 vols. (New York: George H. Doran, 1926), 2:782; also see Michael Deas, *The Portraits and Daguerreotypes of Edgar Allan Poe* Charlottesville: University Press of Virginia, 1988), 6, 36; and Amanda Pogue Schulte and James Southall Wilson, *Facts About Poe: Portraits & Daguerreotypes of Edgar Allan Poe* (Charlottesville: University of Virginia Records Extension Series, 1926), 56–57.

[5] Miller, *Poe's Helen*, 319–321; Deas 40–41.

[6] Deas 87–90.

[7] Reprinted in Deas 39–41, 101, 105, 135, 138.

[8] Among the versions of the "Ultima Thule" published in the nineteenth century are the following: *Scribner's Monthly* 20 (May 1880); E. C. Stedman, *Edgar Allan Poe* (Boston: Houghton Mifflin, 1881); *Poems of Edgar Allan Poe* (New York: Hurst, 1882); *Harper's New Monthly Magazine* 78 (March 1889); Edmund Clarence

Stedman and George Woodberry, ed., *Works of Edgar Allan Poe*, vol. 6 (Chicago, 1894–95).

[9] I. M. Walker, *Edgar Allan Poe: The Critical Heritage* (London and New York: Routledge and Kegan Paul, 1986), 294–302; originally published by Rufus Griswold ["Ludwig"] as "Death of Edgar Allan Poe," New York *Tribune* (9 October 1849), 2.

[10] Eugene L. Didier, *The Poe Cult and Other Papers* (New York: Broadway Publishing Company, 1909), 202

[11] Stedman, *Edgar Allan Poe* (Boston: Houghton Mifflin, 1881), 14.

[12] Oliver Leigh ["Geoffrey Quarles"], *Edgar Allan Poe: The Man: The Master: The Martyr* (Chicago: Frank M. Morris, 1906), 11.

[13] Leigh, 11–12; Leigh seems to have been unique in his view of Poe's face as an allegory of the impending national crisis.

[14] Oliver Wendell Holmes, "Doings of the Sunbeam," *Atlantic Monthly* 12 (1863): 5.

[15] Whitman, *The Gathering of the Forces*, 2 vols., eds. Cleveland Rodgers and John Black (New York: Putnam, 1920), 2:116.

[16] Sontag, *On Photography* (New York: Farrar, Straus, and Giroux, 1973), 15.

[17] Benjamin, "The Work of Art in the Age of Mechanical Reproduction." *Illuminations: Essays and Reflections.* Ed. Hannah Arendt. Trans. Harry Zohn. (New York: Schocken Books), 1968, 226.

[18] Didier, 75–86.

[19] Benjamin, 220.

[20] Poe, "The Daguerreotype," *Classic Essays on Photography*, ed. Alan Trachtenberg (New Haven, Conn.: Leete's Island Books, 1980), 38.

[21] Miller, *Poe's Helen*, 455.

[22] Stedman and George Woodbury, eds., *Works of Edgar Allan Poe*, 10 vols. (New York: Scribner's, 1894–95), 10:269.

[23] Didier, 199–200.

[24] William F. Gill, *The Life of Edgar Allan Poe* (London: Chatto and Windus, 1878), vi.

[25] Quoted in Didier, 195.

[26] Whitman, *Edgar Poe and His Critics*, 35.

[27] Miller, *Poe's Helen*, 378.

[28] Miller, *Building Poe Biography,* 223.

[29] Whitman, *Edgar Poe and His Critics*, 35.

[30] Walker, Critical Heritage, 299.

[31] Deas, 6.

[32] Quoted in Stedman, *Edgar Allan Poe*, 13.

[33] Walker, *Critical Heritage*, 390.

[34] Whitman, *Edgar Poe and His Critics*, "Preface," n.p.

[35] Whitman, *Edgar Poe and His Critics*, "Preface," n.p.

[36] Whitman, *Edgar Poe and His Critics*, 35.

[37] Quoted in Didier, 227–228.

[38] Whitman was not alone in preferring poetry to photography as a representation of Poe's character. N. P. Willis, upon examining the frontispiece of the *Poetical Works of Edgar Allan Poe* (1858), comments, "'The picture is from a daguerreotype, and gives no idea of the beauty of Edgar Poe. . . . After reading 'The Raven,' 'Ulalume,' 'Lenore,' and 'Annabel Lee,' the luxuryast in poetry will better conceive what his face might have been'" (qtd. in Whitman, *Edgar Poe and His Critics*, 38).

[39] According to Robert Taft, the daguerreotype was introduced in the United States around 1840. There were 938 photographers in the United States by 1850, 3,154 by 1860, 7,558 by 1870, 9,990 by 1880, and 20,040 by 1890. *Photography and the American Scene: A Social History, 1839–1889* (New York: Macmillan Company, 1938), 61.

[40] Holmes, "Doings," 9–10.

[41] Striking frontispiece portraits appear to be valuable marketing tools as well. Whitman writes that one examiner of the frontispiece to the Ingram edition "pronounced it 'good, very good.'" Afterwards, she writes, "He said he must have the book." Miller, *Poe's Helen*, 226.

[42] Quoted in Didier,193.

[43] Stedman and Woodberry, 10:v, 243, 269.

[44] *Notes and Queries*, 5th ser., 5 (May 13, 1876): 386–387.

[45] Didier, 190.

[46] Mary E. Phillips, *Edgar Allan Poe: The Man*, 2 vols. (Chicago: John C. Winston, 1926), 2:1513.

[47] Walker, *Critical Heritage*, 300.

[48] See Dudley R. Hutchinson, "Poe's Reputation in England and America, 1850–1909," *American Literature* 14 (1942): 211–223.

[49] *The Poetical Works of Edgar Allan Poe* (New York: J. S. Redfield, 1858), xix.

[50] Quoted in Gill, 249, vii.

[51] All of the following definitions are based on those in the *Oxford English Dictionary*, 2d ed. (Oxford: Clarendon Press, 1989), 3:30–32.

[52] Baudelaire, *Baudelaire on Poe*, ed. And trans. Lois and Francis E. Hyslop, Jr., (State College, Penn.: Bald Eagle Press, 1952), 89.

[53] Dillon, *Edgar Allan Poe: His Genius and Character* (New York: Knickerbocker Press, 1911), 3.

[54] Stedman, *Edgar Allan Poe*, 14.

[55] Root, *The Camera and the Pencil, or The Heliographic Art* (1864, Pawlet, Vermont: Helios, 1971), 439.

[56] Rodgers, *Twenty-three Years Under a Sky-Light, or Life and Experience of a Photographer* (Hartford, CT: American Publishing Compnay, 1873), 98.

[57] Rodgers, 113.

[58] Deas, 5.

[59] Rodgers, 99.

⁶⁰ See James Burgh, *The Art of Speaking* (Danbury, 1775); and Johann Caspar Lavater, *Essays on Physiognomy* (Boston, 1794).

⁶¹ See Philippe Ariès and Georges Duby, ed., *A History of Private Life*. Vol. 4, *From the Fires of Revolution to the Great War*, ed. Michelle Perrot, trans. Arthur Goldhammer (Cambridge, MA, and London: Belknap Press of Harvard University Press, 1990), 468–475.

⁶² Stedman, *Edgar Allan Poe*, 12–13.

⁶³ See Rodgers, 98–102; "Edgar Allan Poe," *Phrenological Journal*, 12 (March 1850): 87–89; O.S. Fowler, *New Illustrated Self-Instructor* (New York, 1859), 34–37; "Edgar Allan Poe. Mental Temperament," *Phrenological Journal*, 97 (September 1893): 126; H. S. Drayton, "Phrenotypes and Side-Views: The Vindication of 'Poe,'" *Phrenological Journal*, 104 (October 1897): 157–158; See Madeleine B. Stern, comp., *A Phrenological Dictionary of Nineteenth-Century Americans*, (Westport, Ct., and London: Greenwood Press, 1982), 66–69. For more detailed treatments see Edward Hungerford, "Poe and Phrenology," *American Literature* 2 (1930): 208–231; and Madeleine B. Stern, "Poe: 'The Mental Temperament' for Phrenologists," *American Literature* 40 (May 1968): 155–163.

⁶⁴ Walker, *Critical Heritage*, 362.

⁶⁵ *Poetical Works of Edgar Allan Poe* (New York: J. S. Redfield, 1858), xx.

⁶⁶ Walker, *Critical Heritage*, 411.

⁶⁷ Walker, *Critical Heritage*, 387.

⁶⁸ Walker, *Critical Heritage*, 301.

⁶⁹ Walker, *Critical Heritage*, 209.

⁷⁰ Didier, 200.

⁷¹ Deas, 6.

⁷² Poe, *Collected Works*, 2:401–402.

⁷³ Weiss, *The Home Life of Edgar Allan* Poe (New York: Broadway Publishing Company, 1907), 219.

⁷⁴ Poe, *Collected Works*, 2:310.

⁷⁵ Stedman, *Edgar Allan Poe*, 102.

⁷⁶ Poe, *Collected Works*, 3:1189.

⁷⁷ "Literary Notes," *The Nation*, 1.15(Oct. 12, 1865), 468.

⁷⁸ Miller, *Poe's Helen*, 226.

⁷⁹ See Ed Folsom, *Walt Whitman's Native Representations* (Cambridge: Cambridge University Press, 1994); Folsom, "Appearing in Print: Illustrations of the Self in *Leaves of Grass*," *The Cambridge Companion to Walt Whitman*, ed. Ezra Greenspan (Cambridge: Cambridge University Press, 1995), 135–165; and Folsom, "Whitman's Calamus Photographs," *Breaking Bounds: Whitman and American Cultural Studies*, ed. Betsy Erkkila and Jay Grossman (New York and Oxford: Oxford University Press, 1996), 193–219.

⁸⁰ Whitman, *Leaves of Grass: Comprehensive Reader's Edition*, eds. Harold Blodgett and Sculley Bradley (New York: Norton, 1965), 562.

Selected Bibliography

Aaron, Daniel. *The Unwritten War: American Writers and the Civil War*. New York: Alfred A. Knopf, 1973.

Adams, Bluford. *E Pluribus Barnum: The Great Showman & U.S. Popular Culture*. Minneapolis: University of Minnesota Press, 1997.

Allen, Gay Wilson. *The Solitary Singer: A Critical Biography of Walt Whitman*. New York: New York University Press, 1967.

———, and Ed Folsom, eds. *Walt Whitman and the World*. Iowa City: University of Iowa Press, 1995.

Allen, Hervey. *Israfel: The Life and Times of Edgar Allan Poe*. 2 vols. New York: George H. Doran, 1926.

Anderson, Benedict. *Imagined Communities*. New York: Verso, 1991.

Anderson, Douglas D. *A House Undivided: Domesticity and Community in American Literature*. Cambridge: Cambridge University Press, 1990.

Anderson, Dwight G. *Abraham Lincoln: The Quest for Immortality*. New York: Knopf, 1982.

Andrews, William L. *To Tell a Free Story: The First Century of African-American Autobiography, 1760–1865*. Champaign-Urbana: University of Illinois Press, 1986.

Arch, Stephen Carl. *After Franklin: The Emergence of Autobiography in Post-Revolutionary America, 1780–1830*. Hanover: University of New Hampshire, 2001.

Ariès, Philippe, and Georges Duby, eds. *A History of Private Life*. Vol. 4. *From the Fires of Revolution to the Great War*. Ed. Michelle Perrot. Trans. Arthur Goldhammer. Cambridge, MA: Harvard University Press, 1990.

Arthur, Gavin. "The Gay Succession." *Gay Roots: Twenty Years of Gay Sunshine*. Ed. Winston Leyland. San Francisco: Gay Sunshine Press, 1991. 323–325.

Baker, Portia. "Walt Whitman and the *Atlantic Monthly*." *American Literature* 63 (1934): 283–301.

Bakhtin, M. M. *The Dialogic Imagination.* Ed. Michael Holquist. Trans. Caryl Emerson and Michael Holquist. Austin: University of Texas Press, 1981.

Ballou, Ellen B. *The Building of the House: Houghton Mifflin's Formative Years.* Boston: Houghton Mifflin, 1970.

Barnum, P. T. [Barnaby Diddleum]. *Adventures of an Adventurer.* New York *Atlas* 14 April 1841; 18 April 1841; 25 April 1841; 2 May 1841; 9 May 1841; 16 May 1841; 23 May 1841; 30 May 1841, continues.

——. *The Humbugs of the World: An Account of Humbugs, Delusions, Impositions, Quackeries, Deceits and Deceivers Generally, In All Ages.* New York: Carleton, 1866.

——. *The Life of P. T. Barnum, Written by Himself.* New York: Redfield, 1855.

——. *Selected Letters of P. T. Barnum.* New York: Columbia University Press, 1983.

——. *Struggles and Triumphs; or, Forty Years' Recollections of P. T. Barnum, Written by Himself.* Hartford, CT: J. B. Burr, 1869.

——. *Struggles and Triumphs: or, Forty Years Recollections of P. T. Barnum. Written by Himself.* Buffalo, NY: Courier Company, 1876.

——. *Struggles and Triumphs, or Sixty Years Recollections of P. T. Barnum. Including His Golden Rules for Money Making. Illustrated and Brought up to 1889.* Buffalo, NY: The Courier Company, 1889.

——. *Struggles and Triumphs; or, The Life of P. T. Barnum, Written by Himself.* Ed. George S. Bryan. 2 vols. New York: Alfred A. Knopf, 1927.

Barreca, Regina, ed., *Desire and Imagination: Classic Essays in Sexuality.* New York: Meridian, 1995.

Barrus, Clara. *Whitman and Burroughs: Comrades.* Boston and New York: Houghton Mifflin, 1931.

Barton, William E. *Abraham Lincoln and Walt Whitman.* Indianapolis: Bobbs-Merrill Company, 1928.

Barua, D. K. "Where Two Visions Met: Whitman and Carpenter." *Modern Studies and Other Essays in Honour of Dr. R. K. Sinha.* New Delhi: Vikas, 1987. 122–140.

Basler, Roy P., ed. *Walt Whitman's* Memoranda During the War [&] *Death of Abraham Lincoln.* Westport: Greenwood Press, 1962.

Baudelaire, Charles. *Baudelaire on Poe.* Ed. and Trans. Lois and Francis E. Hyslop, Jr. State College, Pennsylvania: Bald Eagle Press, 1952.

Baxter, Sylvester. "Walt Whitman in Boston." *New England Magazine* 6.6. (1892): 714–721.

Beach, Christopher. *The Politics of Distinction: Whitman and the Discourses of Nineteenth-Century America.* Athens: University of Georgia Press, 1996.

Benton, Joel. *Life of the Hon. Phineas T. Barnum.* New York: Union Publishing House, 1891.

Bercovitch, Sacvan. *The American Jeremiad.* Madison: University of Wisconsin Press, 1978.

————. *The Puritan Origins of the American Self.* New Haven, CT, and London: Yale University Press, 1975.

————. "The Ritual of American Autobiography: Edwards, Franklin, Thoreau." *Revue Française D'Ètudes Amèricaines* 7 (1982): 139–150.

Binns, Henry Bryan. *A Life of Walt Whitman.* London: Methuen, 1905.

Bjorklund, Diane. *Interpreting the Self: Two Hundred Years of American Autobiography.* Chicago: University of Chicago Press, 1998.

Blanchard, Mary Warner. *Oscar Wilde's America: Counterculture in the Gilded Age.* New Haven, CT: Yale University Press, 1998.

Blodgett, Harold. *Walt Whitman in England.* Ithaca, NY: Cornell University Press, 1934.

Borritt, Gabor, ed. *The Historian's Lincoln: Pseudohistory, Psychohistory, and History.* Urbana: University of Illinois Press, 1988.

Bourdieu, Pierre. *The Field of Cultural Production.* Ed. Randall Johnson. New York: Columbia University Press, 1993.

Brignano, Russell C. *Black Americans in Autobiography: An Annotated Bibliography of Autobiographies and Autobiographical Books Written Since the Civil War.* [1974]. Rev. ed. Durham, NC: Duke University Press, 1984.

Bristow, Joseph. *Effeminate England: Homoerotic Writing After 1865.* New York: Columbia University Press, 1995.

Bruss, Elizabeth. *Autobiographical Acts: The Changing Situation of a Literary Genre.* Baltimore, MD: Johns Hopkins University Press, 1976.

Bucke, Richard Maurice. *Walt Whitman: A Contemporary Study.* Philadelphia: David McKay, 1883.

Buell, Lawrence. "American Literary Emergence as a Postcolonial Phenomenon." *American Literary History* 4.3 (1992): 411–442.

————. "Autobiography in the American Renaissance." *American Autobiography: Retrospect and Prospect.* Ed. Paul John Eakin. Madison: University of Wisconsin Press, 1991. 47–69.

————. "Democratic Ideology and Autobiographical Personae in American Renaissance Writing." *Amerikastudien* 35 (1990): 267–280.

————. *Literary Transcendentalism: Style and Vision in the American Renaissance.* Ithaca, NY: Cornell University Press, 1973. 265–283.

————. *New England Literary Culture: From Revolution Through Renaissance.* Cambridge: Cambridge University Press, 1986.

Burke, Seán. *Authorship: From Plato to the Postmodern, A Reader.* Edinburgh: Edinburgh University Press, 1995.

Burroughs, John. *Notes on Walt Whitman as Poet and Person.* New York, 1867.

————. *The Writings of John Burroughs: Walt Whitman.* Vol. 10. Boston: Houghton Mifflin, 1904.

Carpenter, Edward. *Chants of Labour: A Songbook of the People.* London: Swan Sonnenshein, 1888.

————. *Days with Walt Whitman.* New York: Macmillan, 1908.

————. *England's Ideal, and Other Papers on Social Subjects*. London: Swan Sonnenschein, 1887.

————. *Homogenic Love*. London: Redundancy Press, n.d.

————. *Love's Coming of Age: A Series of Papers on the Relations of the Sexes*. Manchester, 1896.

————. *My Days and Dreams: Being Autobiographical Notes*. London: Allen and Unwin, 1916.

————. *Selected Writings*. Vol. 1. *Sex*. Ed. Noel Grieg. London: Gay Men's Press, 1984.

————. *Towards Democracy*. London: Swan Sonnenschein, 1905.

————. *An Unknown People*. London: n.p., 1897.

Casper, Scott E. *Biography and Culture in Nineteenth-Century America*. Chapel Hill: University of North Carolina Press, 1999.

————, Joanne D. Chaison, and Jeffrey D. Groves, eds. *Perspective on American Book History: Artifacts and Commentary*. Amherst and Boston: University of Massachusetts Press, 2002.

Cawelti, John. *Apostles of the Self-Made Man*. Chicago: University of Chicago Press, 1965.

Charvat, William. *Literary Publishing in America, 1790–1850*. Philadelphia: University of Pennsylvania Press, 1959.

————. *The Profession of Authorship in American, 1800–1870*. Ed. Matthew J. Bruccoli. New York: Columbia University Press, 1992.

Chauncey, George. *Gay New York: Gender, Urban Culture, and the Making of the Gay Male World, 1890–1940*. New York: HarperCollins, 1994.

Cmiel, Kenneth. "Whitman the Democrat." *A Historical Guide to Walt Whitman*. Ed. David S. Reynolds. New York and Oxford: Oxford University Press (2000), 205–233.

James Cook. *The Arts of Deception: Playing with Fraud in the Age of Barnum*. Cambridge, MA: Harvard University Press, 2001.

Cooley, Thomas. *Educated Lives: The Rise of Modern Autobiography in America*. Columbus: Ohio State University Press, 1976.

Couser, G. Thomas. *Altered Egos: Authority in American Autobiography*. New York: Oxford University Press, 1989.

————. *American Autobiography: The Prophetic Mode*. Amherst: University of Massachusetts Press, 1979.

————. "Prose and Cons: The Autobiographies of P. T. Barnum." *Southwest Review* 70.4 (1985): 451–469.

Coyle, William, ed. *The Poet and the President*. New York: Odyssey Press, 1962.

Cox, James M. *Recovering Literature's Lost Ground: Essays in American Autobiography*. Baton Rouge: Louisiana State University Press, 1989.

Dauber, Kenneth. *The Idea of Authorship in America: Democratic Poetics from Franklin to Melville*. Madison: University of Wisconsin Press, 1990.

Davis, Gwenn, and Beverly A. Joyce. *Personal Writings by Women to 1900: A Bibliography of American and British Women Writers.* London and New York: Mansell, 1989.

Deas, Michael. *The Portraits and Daguerreotypes of Edgar Allan Poe.* Charlotteville: University Press of Virginia, 1988.

De Man, Paul. "Autobiography as De-facement." *MLN* 94 (1979): 919–930.

Didier, Eugene L. *The Poe Cult and Other Papers.* New York: Broadway Publishing Company, 1909.

Dillon, John M. *Edgar Allan Poe: His Genius and Character.* New York: Knickerbocker Press, 1911.

DiPietro, Thomas. "Vision and Revision in the Autobiographies of Frederick Douglass," *College Language Association Journal* 26 (1984): 384–395.

Douglass, Frederick. *Autobiographies: Narrative of the Life, My Bondage and My Freedom, Life and Times.* New York: Library of America, 1994.

Dowling, Linda. *Hellenism and Homosexuality in Victorian Oxford.* Ithaca, NY: Cornell University Press, 1994.

Duberman, Martin. *James Russell Lowell.* Boston: Houghton Mifflin, 1966.

Eakin, John Paul, ed. *American Autobiography: Retrospect and Prospect.* Madison: University of Wisconsin Press, 1991.

———. *Fictions in Autobiography: Studies in the Art of Self Invention.* Princeton: Princeton University Press, 1992.

———, ed. *On Autobiography.* Minneapolis: University of Minnesota, 1989.

———. *Touching the World: Reference in Autobiography.* Princeton, NJ: Princeton University Press, 1992.

Eliot, Charles Norton, ed. *Walt Whitman as Man, Poet, and Friend.* Boston: Richard Badger, 1915.

Emerson, Ralph Waldo. Essays and Lectures. Ed. Joel Porte. New York: Library of America, 1983.

Erkkila, Betsy. *Whitman the Political Poet.* New York: Oxford University Press, 1989.

———, and Jay Grossman, eds. *Breaking Bounds: Whitman and American Cultural Studies.* Oxford: Oxford University Press, 1996.

Fehrenbacher, Don E. *Lincoln in Text and Context.* Stanford, CA: Stanford University Press, 1987.

Fichtelberg, Joseph. "The Writer Against Himself: Child and Man in the Autobiographies of Frederick Douglass," *Mid-Hudson Language Studies* 12 (1989): 72–80.

Fink, Steven, and Susan S. Williams, eds. *Reciprocal Influences: Literary Production, Distribution, and Consumption.* Columbus: Ohio State University Press, 1999.

Folkenflik, Robert, ed. *The Culture of Autobiography: Constructions of Self-Representation.* Stanford, CA: Stanford University Press, 1993.

Folsom, Ed. "Appearing in Print: Illustrations of the Self in *Leaves of Grass*." *The Cambridge Companion to Walt Whitman.* Ed. Ezra Greenspan. New York and Oxford: Cambridge University Press, 1995. 135–165.

———. "'This Heart's Geography's Map': The Photographs of Walt Whitman." *Walt Whitman Quarterly Review* 4.2–3 (1986–87): 1–72.

———. "*Leaves of Grass, Junior.* Walt Whitman's Compromise with Discriminating Tastes." *American Literature* 63 (1991): 641–663.

———. *Walt Whitman's Native Representations.* Cambridge: Cambridge University Press, 1994.

Fone, Byrne R. S. *Masculine Landscapes: Walt Whitman and the Homoerotic Text.* Carbondale: Southern Illinois University Press, 1992.

Foucault, Michel. *The History of Sexuality. Volume 1: An Introduction.* Trans. Robert Hurley. New York: Pantheon, 1978.

———. "What is an Author?" *Textual Strategies: Perspectives in Post-Structuralist Criticism.* Trans. Josué V. Harari. Ithaca, NY: Cornell University Press, 1979. 141–160.

Frederickson, George M. *The Inner Civil War.* New York: Harper and Row, 1965.

Freedman, Florence Bernstein. *William Douglas O'Connor: Walt Whitman's Chosen Knight.* Athens, Ohio: Ohio University Press, 1985.

Furness, Clifton Joseph, ed. *Walt Whitman's Workshop: A Collection of Unpublished Manuscripts.* Cambridge, MA: Harvard University Press, 1928.

Garman, Bryan K. *A Race of Singers: Whitman's Working-Class Hero from Guthrie to Springsteen.* Chapel Hill: University of North Carolina Press, 2000.

Giantvalley, Scott. *Walt Whitman, 1940–1975: A Reference Guide.* Boston: G. K. Hall, 1981.

Gilder, Richard Watson. *Letters of Richard Watson Gilder.* Ed. Rosamond Gilder. Boston and New York: Houghton Mifflin, 1916.

Glicksberg, Charles I., ed. *Walt Whitman and the Civil War.* Philadelphia: University of Pennsylvania Press, 1933.

Golden, Arthur. "Nine Early Whitman Letters, 1840–1841." *American Literature* 58.3 (1986): 342–360.

Greenspan, Ezra. *Walt Whitman and the American Reader.* Cambridge: Cambridge University Press, 1990.

Griswold, Rufus, ed. *Poets and Poetry of America.* Philadelphia: A. Hart, 1853.

Grosskurth, Phyllis. *John Addington Symonds, A Biography.* New York: Arno Press, 1975.

Grossman, Allen. "The Poetics of Union in Whitman and Lincoln: An Inquiry toward the Relationship of Art and Policy." *The American Renaissance Reconsidered.* Ed. Walter Benn Michaels and Donald E. Pease. Baltimore, MD: The Johns Hopkins University Press, 1985. 183–208.

Hamer, Harold. *A Catalogue of Works By and Relating to Walt Whitman.* Bolton, England: Libraries Committee, 1955.

Harkness, David J., and Gerald McMurty. *Lincoln's Favorite Poets.* Knoxville: University of Tennessee Press, 1959.

Harris, Neil. *Humbug: The Art of P. T. Barnum.* Boston: Little, Brown and Company, 1973.

Hart, James D. *The Popular Book: A History of America's Literary Taste.* New York: Oxford University Press, 1950.

Higginson, T. W. *Contemporaries.* Boston: Houghton Mifflin Company, 1899.

Hilkey, Judy. *Character is Capital: Success Manuals and Manhood in Gilded Age America.* Chapel Hill and London: University of North Carolina Press, 1997.

Hindus, Milton, ed. *Walt Whitman: The Critical Heritage.* London: Routledge and Kegan Paul, 1971.

Howells, William Dean. *Literary Friends and Acquaintance: A Personal Retrospect of American Authorship.* New York and London: Harper and Brothers, 1902.

Hutchinson, George B. "Whitman's Confidence Game: The 'Good Gray Poet' and the Civil War." *South Central Review* 7 (1990): 20–35.

Hyde, H. Montgomery. *The Love That Dared Not Speak Its Name: A Candid History of Homosexuality in Britain.* Boston: Little, Brown and Company, 1970.

Jay, Paul. *Being in the Text: Self-Representation from Wordsworth to Roland Barthes.* Ithaca, NY: Cornell University Press, 1984.

Johnston, John, and J. W. Wallace. *Visits to Walt Whitman in 1890–91 by Two Lancashire Friends.* Allen and Unwin, 1917.

Kaplan, Louis, et al. *A Bibliography of American Autobiographies.* Madison: University of Wisconsin Press, 1961.

Katz, Jonathan, ed. *Gay American History.* New York: Thomas Y. Crowell Company, 1976.

Kaufman, Marjorie, ed. *The Poetical Works of James Russell Lowell.* Boston: Houghton Mifflin, 1978.

Kennedy, William Sloane. *The Fight of a Book for the World.* West Yarmouth, MA: Stonecraft Press, 1926.

———. *Reminiscences of Walt Whitman.* London: Alexander Gardner, 1896.

Killingsworth, M. Jimmie. "Whitman and the Gay American Ethos." *A Historical Guide to Walt Whitman.* Ed. David S. Reynolds. New York and Oxford: Oxford University Press (2000), 121–151.

———. *Whitman's Poetry of the Body.* Chapel Hill: University of North Carolina Press, 1989.

Krieg, Joann P. "Without Walt Whitman in Camden," *Walt Whitman Quarterly Review* 14.2–3 (1996–97): 85–113.

Kuebrich, David. *Minor Prophecy: Walt Whitman's New American Religion.* Bloomington: Indiana University Press, 1989.

Kummings, Donald. *Walt Whitman, 1940–1975: A Reference Guide.* Boston: G. K. Hall, 1982.

Kunhardt, Philip B., et al. *P. T. Barnum: America's Greatest Showman.* New York: Knopf, 1995.

Leigh, Oliver ["Geoffrey Quarles"]. *Edgar Allan Poe: The Man: The Master: The Martyr.* Chicago: Frank M. Morris, 1906.

Lejeune, Phillipe. *Le Pacte Autobiographique.* Paris: Editions du Seuil, 1975.

LeMaster, J. R., and Donald Kummings, eds. *Walt Whitman: An Encyclopedia.* New York: Garland Publishing, 1998.

Leverenz, David. "Frederick Douglass's Self Refashioning." *Criticism* 29 (1987): 341–370.

Levine, Robert S. *Martin Delany, Frederick Douglass, and the Politics of Representative Identity.* Chapel Hill: 1997.

Lincoln, Abraham. *Collected Works.* Ed. Roy P. Basler. 8 vols., index, and supplement. New Brunswick, NJ: Rutgers University Press, 1953.

Losey, Jay, and William D. Brewer. *Mapping Male Sexuality: The Nineteenth Century.* Madison, NJ: Fairleigh Dickinson University Press, 2000.

Loving, Jerome. "The Political Roots of *Leaves of Grass.*" *A Historical Guide to Walt Whitman.* Ed. David S. Reynolds. New York and Oxford: Oxford University Press (2000), 97–119.

———. *Walt Whitman's Champion: William Douglas O'Connor.* College Station: Texas A&M University Press, 1978.

———. *Walt Whitman: The Song of Himself.* Los Angeles: University of California Press, 1999.

Lowell, James Russell. *Letters of James Russell Lowell.* Ed. Charles Eliot Norton. 2 vols. New York: Harper and Brothers, 1894.

———. *The Works of James Russell Lowell,* 10 vols. Boston: Houghton Mifflin, 1890.

Loving, Jerome. "Emory Holloway and the Quest for Whitman's 'Manhood.'" *Walt Whitman Quarterly Review* 11.1 (1993): 1–17.

———. *Walt Whitman: The Song of Himself.* Los Angeles: University of California Press, 1999.

Marki, Ivan. *The Trial of the Poet: An Interpretation of the First Edition of* Leaves of Grass. New York: Columbia University Press, 1976.

Mason, Michael. *The Making of Victorian Sexuality.* Oxford and New York: Oxford University Press, 1994.

Matthiessen, F. O. *American Renaissance: Art and Expression in the Age of Emerson and Whitman.* New York: Oxford University Press, 1941.

McCracken, Scott. "Writing the Body: Edward Carpenter, George Gissing and Late-Nineteenth-Century Realism." *Edward Carpenter and Late Victorian Radicalism.* Ed. Tony Brown. London: Frank Cass, 1900. 178–200.

McElroy, John Harmon. *The Sacrificial Years: A Chronicle of Walt Whitman's Experiences in the Civil War.* Boston: David R. Godine, 1999.

McPherson, James M. *Abraham Lincoln and the Second American Revolution.* New York: Oxford University Press, 1991.

Merrill, Stuart. *Walt Whitman.* Trans. Leon Bazelgette. Toronto: Henry S. Saunders, 1922.

Miller, Edwin Haviland, ed. *The Artistic Legacy of Walt Whitman.* New York: New York University Press, 1970.

Miller, F. DeWolfe. "The 'Long Foreground' of Whitman's Elegies on Lincoln." *Lincoln Herald* LVIII (Spring-Summer 1956): 3–7.

Moon, Michael. *Disseminating Whitman: Revision and Corporeality in* Leaves of Grass Cambridge: Harvard University Press, 1991.

Morris, Roy, Jr. *The Better Angel: Walt Whitman in the Civil War.* Oxford: Oxford University Press, 2000.

Mott, Frank Luther. *Golden Multitudes: The Story of Best Sellers in the United States.* New York: Macmillan Company, 1947.

Nicolay, John G. and John Hay. *Abraham Lincoln: A History.* 10 vols. New York: The Century Company, 1890.

Norton, Charles Eliot. *A Leaf of Grass from Shady Hill.* Ed. Kenneth B. Murdock. Cambridge, MA: Harvard University Press, 1928.

O'Connor, William D. *The Good Gray Poet: A Vindication.* New York: Bunce and Huntington, 1866.

Olney, James, ed. *Autobiography: Essays Theoretical and Critical.* Princeton, NJ: Princeton University Press, 1980.

———. *Metaphors of Self: The Meaning of Autobiography.* Princeton, NJ: Princeton University Press, 1972.

———, ed. *Studies in Autobiography.* New York: Oxford University Press, 1988.

Parkinson, Thomas. "'When Lilacs Last in the Door-yard Bloom'd' and the American Civil Religion." *The Southern Review* 19 (1983): 1–16.

Pascal, Roy. *Design and Truth in Autobiography.* New York: Garland, 1960.

Perry, Bliss. *Walt Whitman: His Life and Work.* Boston: Houghton Mifflin, 1906.

Peterson, Linda H. *Victorian Autobiography: The Tradition of Self-Interpretation.* New Haven, CT: Yale University Press, 1986.

Peterson, Merrill D. *Lincoln in American Memory.* New York and Oxford: Oxford University Press, 1994.

Poe, Edgar Allan. *Collected Works of Edgar Allan Poe.* 3 vols. Cambridge, MA: Belknap Press of Harvard University Press, 1969–1978.

Pollak, Vivian R. *The Erotic Whitman.* Berkeley: University of California Press, 2000.

Pond, James. B. *Eccentricities of Genius: Memories of Famous Men and Women of the Platform and Stage.* New York: G. W. Dillingham, 1900.

Price, Kenneth M, ed. *Walt Whitman: The Contemporary Reviews.* Cambridge: Cambridge University Press, 1996.

———. *Whitman and Tradition: The Poet in His Century.* New Haven, CT, and London: Yale University Press, 1990.

Reiss, Benjamin. *The Showman and the Slave: Race, Death, and Memory in Barnum's America* Cambridge, MA: Harvard University Press, 2001.

Renza, Louis. "The Veto of the Imagination: A Theory of Autobiography." *New Literary History* 9 (1977): 2–26.

Reynolds, David. *Beneath the American Renaissance: The Subversive Imagination in the Age of Emerson and Melville.* Cambridge: Harvard University Press, 1990.

————. *Walt Whitman's America: A Cultural Biography.* New York: Knopf, 1995.

Rivers, W. C. *Walt Whitman's Anomaly.* London: George Allen, 1913.

Root, Marcus Aurelius. *The Camera and the Pencil, or The Heliographic Art* [1864]. Pawlet, VT: Helios, 1971.

Rose, Mark. *Authors and Owners: The Invention of Copyright.* Cambridge, MA: Harvard University Press, 1993.

Rotundo, E. Anthony. *American Manhood: Transformations in Masculinity from the Revolution to the Modern Era.* New York: Basic Books, 1993.

Rourke, Constance. *Trumpets of Jubilee: Henry Ward Beecher, Harriet Beecher Stowe, Lyman Beecher, Horace Greely, P. T. Barnum.* New York: Harcourt, Brace & Company, 1927.

Rowbotham, Sheila, and Jeffrey Weeks. *Socialism and the New Life: The Personal and Sexual Politics of Edward Carpenter and Havelock Ellis.* London: Pluto Press, 1977.

Rugg, Linda Haverty. *Picturing Ourselves: Photography and Autobiography.* Chicago: University of Chicago Press, 1998.

Salveson, Paul. "Loving Comrades: Lancashire's Links to Walt Whitman." *Walt Whitman Quarterly Review* 14.2–3 (1996–97): 57–84.

Saunders, Henry S. *Parodies on Walt Whitman.* New York: American Library Service, 1923.

Saxon, A. H., *Barnumiana: A Select, Annotated Bibliography of Works By or Relating to P. T. Barnum and A Barnum Chronology.* Fairfield, CT: Jumbo's Press, 1995.

————. *P. T. Barnum: The Legend and the Man.* New York: Columbia University Press, 1989.

————, ed. *Selected Letters of P. T. Barnum.* New York: Columbia University Press, 1983.

Sayre, Robert F. *The Examined Self: Benjamin Franklin, Henry Adams, Henry James.* Princeton, NJ: Princeton University Press, 1964.

Schmidgall, Gary. *Walt Whitman, A Gay Life.* New York: Plume, 1998.

Sedgwick, Eve Kosofsky. *Between Men: English Literature and Male Homosocial Desire.* New York: Columbia University Press, 1985.

Shapiro, Stephen A. "The Dark Continent of Literature: Autobiography." *Comparative Literature Studies* 5 (1968): 425–435.

Shea, Daniel. *Spiritual Autobiography in Early America.* [1968]. Rev. ed. Madsion: University of Wisconsin Press, 1988.

Shively, Charley, *Calamus Lovers: Walt Whitman's Working-Class Camderados.* San Francisco: Gay Sunshine Press, 1987.

Smith, F. Lannom. "The American Reception of *Leaves of Grass*: 1855–1882." *Walt Whitman Review* 22 (1976): 137–156.

Sontag, Susan. *On Photography.* New York: Farrar, Straus, and Giroux, 1973.

Spengemann, William C. *The Forms of Autobiography: Episodes in the History of a Literary Genre.* New Haven, CT: Yale University Press, 1980.

Stedman, Edmund Clarence. *Edgar Allan Poe.* Boston: Houghton Mifflin, 1881.

————. *Poets of America.* Boston: Houghton Mifflin, 1885.

————, and George Woodbury, eds. *Works of Edgar Allan Poe.* Chicago, 1894–95.

Steele, Jeffrey. *The Representation of the Self in the American Renaissance.* Chapel Hill: University of North Carolina Press, 1987.

Stern, Madeleine B., comp. *A Phrenological Dictionary of Nineteenth-Century Americans.* Westport, CT, and London: Greenwood Press, 1982.

Stone, Albert E. *Autobiographical Occasions and Original Acts: Versions of American Identity from Henry Adams to Nate Shaw.* Philadelphia: University of Pennsylvania Press, 1982.

Sundquist, Eric. *To Wake the Nations: Race in the Making of American Literature.* Cambridge, MA: Harvard University Press, 1993.

Symonds, John Addington. *The Letters of John Addington Symonds.* 3 vols. Ed. Herbert Schueller and Robert Peters. Detroit, MI: Wayne State University Press, 1969.

————. *Walt Whitman, A Study.* London: John C. Nimmo, 1893.

Taft, Robert. *Photography and the American Scene: A Social History, 1839–1889.* New York: Macmillan Company, 1938.

Tarbell, Roberta K. "Whitman and the Visual Arts." *A Historical Guide to Walt Whitman.* Ed. David S. Reynolds. New York and Oxford: Oxford University Press (2000), 153–204.

Thomas, John L. *Abraham Lincoln and the American Political Tradition.* Amherst: University of Massachusetts Press, 1986.

Thomas, M. Wynn. *The Lunar Light of Whitman's Poetry.* Cambridge, MA: Harvard University Press, 1987.

Thurow, Glen E. *Abraham Lincoln and the American Political Religion.* Albany: State University of New York Press, 1976.

Traubel Horace. "Lowell-Whitman: A Contrast." *Poet-Lore* 4 (1892): 22–31.

————. *With Walt Whitman in Camden.* 9 Vols. Vol. I. (1905; rpt., New York: Rowman and Littlefield, 1961); Vol. II. (1907; rpt., New York: Rowman and Littlefield, 1961); Vol. III. (1912; rpt., New York: Rowman and Littlefield, 1961); Vol. IV (1953; rpt., Carbondale: Southern Illinois University Press, 1959); Vol. V (Carbondale: Southern Illinois University Press, 1964); Vol. VI (Carbondale: Southern Illinois University Press, 1982); Vol. VII (Carbondale: Southern Illinois University Press, 1992); Vols. VIII-IX (Oregon House, CA: W. L. Bentley, 1996).

Tsuzuki, Chushichi. *Edward Carpenter 1844–1929, Prophet of Human Fellowship.* Cambridge: Cambridge University Press, 1980.

Waldron, Randall. "Whitman as the Nazarene: An Unpublished Drawing." *Walt Whitman Quarterly Review* 7.4 (1990): 192–195.

Ward, Geoffrey C. *The Civil War.* New York: Alfred A. Knopf, 1990.

Weeks, Jeffrey. *Coming Out: Homosexual Politics in Britain from the Nineteenth Century to the Present.* London: Quartet Books, 1977.

Weisbuch, Robert. *Atlantic Double-Cross: American Literature and British Influence in the Age of Emerson*. Chicago: University of Chicago Press, 1986.

Weiss, Susan Archer. *The Home Life of Edgar Allan Poe*. New York: Broadway Publishing Company, 1907.

Whitman, Sarah Helen. *Edgar Poe and His Critics* [1860]. New Brunswick, New Jersey: Rutgers University Press, 1949.

Whitman, Walt. *Autobiographia; or, The Story of a Life, Selected from the Prose Writings of Walt Whitman*. Ed. Arthur Stedman. Philadelphia: David McKay, 1892.

———. *The Correspondence*. Ed. Edwin Haviland Miller. 6 vols. New York: New York University Press, 1961–77.

———. *Daybooks and Notebooks*. Ed. William White. 3 vols. New York: New York University Press, 1977.

———. *The Early Poems and the Fiction*. Ed. Thomas L. Brasher. New York: New York University Press, 1963.

———. *The Gathering of the Forces*. Eds. Cleveland Rodgers and John Black. New York: Putnam, 1920.

———. *Gems from Walt Whitman*. Ed. Elizabeth Porter Gould. Philadelphia: David McKay, 1889.

———. *The Journalism*. Vol. 1. Ed. Herbert Bergman, et al. New York: Peter Lang, 1998.

———. *Leaves of Grass, Including a Facsimile Autobiography*. Philadelphia: David McKay, 1900.

———. *Leaves of Grass: A Textual Variorum of the Printed Poems*. Ed. Sculley Bradley, Harold W. Blodgett, Arthur Golden, William White. 3 vols. New York: New York University Press, 1980.

———. *Leaves of Grass: Comprehensive Reader's Edition*. Ed. Harold W. Blodgett and Sculley Bradley. New York: New York University Press, 1965.

———. *Memoranda During the War [&] Death of Abraham Lincoln*. Ed. Roy P. Basler. Westport, Connecticut: Greenwood Press, 1962.

———. *Notebooks and Unpublished Prose Manuscripts*. Ed. Edward F. Grier. 6 vols. New York: New York University Press, 1984.

———. *Prose Works, 1892*. Ed. Floyd Stovall. 2 vols. New York: New York University Press, 1963.

———. *Whitman as Editor of the* Brooklyn Daily Eagle. Ed. Thomas L. Brasher. Detroit, MI: Wayne State University Press, 1970.

Willard, Charles B. *Walt Whitman's American Fame: The Growth of His Reputation in America After 1892*. Providence, RI: Brown University, 1950.

Wills, Garry. *Lincoln at Gettysburg: The Words That Remade America*. New York: Simon and Schuster, 1992.

Wilson, Edmund. *Patriotic Gore: Studies in the Literature of the American Civil War*. Boston: Northeastern University Press, 1962.

Woods, Gregory. "'Still on My Lips': Walt Whitman in Britain." *The Continuing Presence of Walt Whitman.* Ed. Robert K. Martin. Iowa City, Iowa: University of Iowa Press, 1992. 129–140.

Wortham, Thomas. "William Cullen Bryant and the Fireside Poets." *The Columbia Literary History of the United* States. Ed. Emory Elliott. New York: Columbia University Press, 1988. 278–288.

Zboray, Ronald J. *A Fictive People: Antebellum Economic Development and the American Reading Public.* New York and Oxford: Oxford University Press, 1993.

Zuckerman, Michael. "The Selling of the Self: From Franklin to Barnum." *Benjamin Franklin, Jonathan Edwards, and the Representation of American Culture.* Ed. Barbara S. Oberg and Harry S. Stout. New York and Oxford: Oxford University Press, 1993. 152–167.

Index

Aesthetes (*See Wildeans*)
alienation, xvi, 12, 70
American Renaissance 4, 5
American Revolution 19–21, 24, 25, 33, 35–37, 40, 41, 44
Atlantic Monthly, (Boston) 54, 61, 62, 74, 77, 83, 93, 102
Aurora, the (New York) 25, 26, 69
authorial identity xiv-xvi, xviii, 6, 7, 10, 11, 13, 16, 50, 51, 53, 140–142
autobiography xv, xvi, 3–6, 11–17, 35
  religious roots of, xvii, 3, 4
  types,
    African-American, 3, 5, 11, 16
    conversion narrative, xvii
    'high,' xviii, 13–15
    'low,' xviii, 11, 14, 16
    slave narrative, (*See* 'African-American)
    'success' narrative, xviii, 3, 20
Autobiography of Benjamin Franklin 3, 5, 15

Barnum, P. T. xv, 5–7, 9–12, 17, 33, 50, 54, 82
  personas of,
    showman, 6, 9, 11, 12, 16, 50, 80
    'Universal Yankee,' 6, 7, 11, 16
Baudelaire, Charles 138, 140
Beardsley, Aubrey xviii, 108, 117
Bolton Whitman Fellowship xviii, 108, 111, 114, 123

Boston Globe, The (Boston)49
Boston, Massachusetts
  censorship of Whitman in, 54, 76, 77, 83, 96, 98–100
  elitism of, xvii, 53, 56, 61, 62, 65, 66, 71, 73, 76, 79, 83, 99, 101
  literary center, xvii, 53, 61, 64, 71, 75, 79, 101, 102
Bourdieu, Pierre 49, 50, 53, 70, 73
Brady, Matthew 130
Buchanan, Robert 92, 94, 95
Burroughs, John 49, 56, 59–61, 97, 103, 106

Calamus 40, 99, 108–113, 125, 126, 127
Carnegie, Andrew 17, 55, 62
Carpenter, Edward xviii, 102, 105–119, 121–126
  apostasy of, 105, 107, 110, 122
  reverence for Whitman, xviii, 91, 102, 107, 110, 115
  sexual identity of, xviii, 105, 107, 109, 110, 112, 114, 121–126
  socialism of, 105, 108, 112, 114, 115, 121, 122, 124
  works, *Chants of Labour*, 102; *Towards Democracy*, 121, 122
Camden, New Jersey xviii, 55, 87, 94, 95, 97, 99, 105, 106, 110, 111
Century Magazine (New York) 54, 61
Christianity xvii, 32, 33, 35, 51, 84, 106
civil religion xvii, xviii, 20, 24–29, 35, 37,

38, 40, 43, 44, 47, 50, 54, 57, 87
Civil War xiv, xvii, 4, 19, 21, 36–42, 46,
    54, 83, 93

Davis, Jefferson 30, 36, 45
Daily Tribune, the (New York) 29, 34
Death of Abraham Lincoln, The 23, 54, 58,
    62, 85, 89, 94, 97, 102
Declaration of Independence 10, 11, 33, 37,
    43, 44
Dickens, Charles 68, 96
Dickinson, Emily 56, 61, 81
Douglass, Frederick xv, 5–17
    abolitionism of, 9, 10
    daguerreotypes of, 7–9
    slave identity, 5–8, 10–12, 14, 16
    "Manhood" of 6–8, 12, 16

Douglass, Stephen 27, 28
Doyle, Peter 58, 105, 106
Drum-Taps 21, 38–41, 43, 45, 46, 60, 85,
    88–92, 102

Education of Henry Adams, The 5, 6
Eggleston, Edward 55, 56
Emerson, Ralph Waldo xiii, 5, 7, 20, 31,
    32, 56,60, 62, 72, 75, 76, 82, 83,
    88, 96, 102, 103, 120, 125
    literary figure, 5, 7, 31, 32, 66, 71, 82,
        103
    mentor to Whitman, 20, 31, 60, 72,
        75, 76, 83, 88, 125
    works, "The American Scholar," 31;
England
    constructions of masculinity in, (*See*
        'masculinity')
    cultural superiority of, 61–63, 65, 94
    homosexuality in, (*See* 'homosexuality')
    popularity of Whitman in, 54, 95, 97,
        106, 109, 113
    social progressivism in, xvii, 102,
        112–115, 121, 122, 127

Fabian Society, 115
fairies (*See* 'homosexuality')
Fireside Poets 76, 79, 103
Founding Fathers, The 23, 24, 27, 28, 43

Genteel Tradition, The 51, 53, 60, 102

Gilder, Richard Watson 54–56, 60, 97,
    101, 102
Gill, William F. 132, 133, 137
Griswold, Rufus 9, 10, 34, 69, 131,
    133–137, 139, 140
    works,
        Works of the Late Edgar Allan Poe,
        135

Harper's Weekly (New York) 39, 77, 78, 94
Harvard University 55–57, 62, 64, 67, 73,
    74
    Houghton Library 74
Hay, John 55, 56
Holmes, Oliver Wendell 66, 76, 96, 132,
    136
homosexuality 71, 107–119, 121–127
    classism within, 107, 108, 110–113,
        115–117, 119, 121–123
    constructions of identity within, 109,
        110, 115–118
    constructions of masculinity within,
        (*See* 'masculinity')
    connection to socialism, 109, 114, 115
    "fairies," 112, 118, 119, 121
    significance of Whitman in, 109–111,
        114, 115

Howells, William Dean 6, 22, 55, 56, 61,
    77, 78, 90
    works,
        Literary Friends and Acquaintance,
        77; *Poems of Two Friends*, 77;
        Venetian Life, 92

Ingram, John Henry 132, 133, 136, 142

Jackson, Andrew 19, 23, 24
James, Henry 103
Johnston, John H. 54, 56, 59, 60, 97, 101,
Johnston, Dr. John 111, 113, 123, 126

Lafayette, Marquis de 23, 24, 33
Leaves of Grass xv, 6, 17, 21, 22, 25, 29,
    31, 32, 40, 47, 55, 60, 63, 74, 79,
    88, 92, 101, 102, 105–109, 112,
    120, 124–127, 142
    design of, xiv, 33, 72, 79, 82, 83, 84
    1855 edition 7, 9, 10, 33, 34, 64, 72,

73, 78, 80–85, 106, 108, 116
1856 edition 34, 72, 76, 82, 83
1860–1861 edition xiv, 38, 39, 74, 75, 76, 83, 84, 96, 98, 108
1867 edition xiv, 90, 91
1868 edition 98, 99, 110
1876 edition xiv, 92, 97
1880–1881 edition xiv, 92, 97, 100, 104
1889 edition xiv
1892 'Deathbed' edition xiv, 103
Life of P. T. Barnum 5, 10–12, 17
alternate versions of, 5, 16
Lincoln, Abraham xv-xviii, 6, 19–29, 34–37, 42, 43, 44, 47, 53–57, 77, 84–89, 93, 94, 102, 107, 120
assassination of, 21, 43, 54, 80, 86–89, 97
"captain" of nation, 19, 86–88
martyrdom of, 22, 27, 31, 35, 47, 54, 58, 86–89
meetings with Whitman, 21, 42, 43, 86, 107, 120
nicknames for, 20, 21, 35–37, 44
speeches of, 6, 20, 21, 24, 25–28, 30, 31, 35–37, 42–46
works,
    "Address Before the Young Men's Lyceum," 20, 24, 25, 30; "Annual Message to Congress," 44; "Farewell Address at Springfield, IL," 35; "First Inaugural Address," 20, 21, 36, 37, 43, 45; "Gettysburg Address," 37, 44, 45; "House Divided Speech," 27, 28, "Letter to the Sangamo Journal," 27; "Second Inaugural Address," 21, 36, 37, 42, 43–46; "Speech Before the House of Representatives," 28; "Speech on the Sub-Treasury," 20, 26, 31; "Temperance Address," 27
literary marketplace, United States xiii, xviii, 12, 33, 50, 53, 68, 79–81, 85, 88, 90, 94, 101, 104
Longfellow, Henry Wadsworth 65–67, 76, 79, 82, 83, 95, 103, 105
works,
    Song of Hiawatha, 82

Lowell, James Russell xvii, xviii, 22, 49, 51–55, 59–66, 68, 70, 74–78, 80, 81, 92, 93, 98–105, 113
celebrator of Lincoln, 56, 57
criticism of Whitman, 56, 60, 63, 73, 80, 92, 93, 96
decline in reputation, 51–53, 61, 62, 101, 104
works,
    Biglow Papers, 63, 69; "Commemoration Ode," 57, 58, 63, 92, 93; *Pioneer, The*, 66; *Year's Life, A*, 65, 66; *Vision of Sir Lawnfall*, 69

Madison Square Theater benefit 23, 54, 57, 61, 62, 97, 101
martyrdom 21, 25, 28, 44, 57
masculinity xviii, 106–110, 112, 115–118, 120, 121
American conceptions of, 107, 110, 112, 115, 116, 120, 121
connection to social class, 113, 115, 116, 119, 122, 123
English conceptions of, 107, 108, 110, 116, 118, 120, 121
Whitman's, (*See* 'Whitman, sexuality')
Merrill, George, 123, 124
middle-class, attitudes toward Whitman, xviii, 80, 85, 90, 101, 104
influence on literature xvii, 4, 11, 15, 49, 50, 79, 80, 85, 94, 101
Milnes, Monckton (Lord Houghton) 54, 96
Myth of America, xiii, 5

Narrative of Frederick Douglass 5–10, 14, 16
alternate versions of, 5, 8, 10, 16
New Republic, The (New York) 52
New York City, New York
developing cultural center, xvii, 53, 54, 60–62, 68, 71, 77, 79, 97, 99, 101, 102
New York Times, The (New York) 52, 96
Norton, Charles Eliot 55, 56, 59, 60, 72, 73, 76

O Captain! My Captain! 22, 40, 57–59, 63,

85, 89, 93, 97, 99–102, 126
O'Connor, William P. 46, 91–93, 97, 120
    works,
        *The Good, Grey Poet: A
            Vindication,* 91, 92
Osgood, James 98, 99

Park Theater (New York) 71, 72
Pfaff's Cellar, 40, 77
Perry, Bliss 56, 93, 103
photography xv, xviii, 12, 132, 133,
    136–138, 142
phrenology xviii, 82, 138, 139, 142
physiognomy xviii, 139, 142
Poe, Edgar Allan xvi, 91, 129–142
    controversy over character of, xviii,
        137–141
    psychological instability of, 130, 131,
        133, 136
    visual images of, (see *also* 'Ultima Thule
        Daguerreotype') 130–134, 136
    works,
        "Bells, The," 135; "Bernice," 137;
            "Dream Land," 129, 130, 136;
            "Fall of the House of Usher," 131,
            140, 141; "Haunted Palace, The,"
            135; "Lenore," 135; "Man of the
            Crowd, The," 135; "Pit and the
            Pendulum, The," 130, 136; "Tell-
            Tale Heart," 140; "Some Words
            With a Mummy," 141; "William
            Wilson," 140
political religion (*See* 'civil religion')

'rags-to-riches' (*See* 'autobiography, success
    narrative')
reader communities xiii, xv
'Representative Men' (*See also* 'Authorial
    Identity) xvii, 6–9, 20, 30, 34, 35,
    51
rhetoric of exclusion 23, 28–31, 46, 51,
    53, 82, 97, 100
rhetoric of reconciliation xvii, 20, 21, 37,
    42, 43, 45–47
Rodgers, H. J. 138, 139
Rossetti, William Michael 89, 90, 94, 95,
    99, 110

Saturday Club, The 76, 77, 83, 96, 98

Schoolroom Poets, the (*See* 'Fireside Poets')
self-refashioning (*See also* 'self-representa-
    tion') xvi–xix, 3, 5, 7, 10, 53
self-representation xv, xvii–xix, 6, 7, 11, 13,
    16, 17
self-made man 5–7, 16, 84
'slumming' 30, 77, 113
'Song of Myself' 7, 23, 31, 32, 56, 76, 84,
    90, 108, 121
Stafford, Harry 105, 106
Stedman, Edmund Clarence 23, 54, 56,
    58, 59, 97, 132, 133, 136, 137,
    138, 141
    works,
        Works of Edgar Allan Poe, 137
Springfield, Illinois 26, 28, 35, 37, 86, 87
Symonds, John Addington 49, 102,
    109–111, 113–16, 125–127
    works,
        "Song of Love and Death, The",
            114
symbolic capital 81, 101

Thoreau, Henry David 5, 81, 100, 108,
    120
    works,
        Walden 5
Transcendentalism, 31, 32, 63, 71
Traubel, Horace xiv, 42, 55, 60–62, 71,
    99–103, 111, 113, 124
Trowbridge, John Townsend 95, 96
Twain, Mark 6, 54, 55, 79

Ultima Thule daguerreotype xviii, 128–135,
    138, 139, 142
Uncle Tom's Cabin 9, 82, 83
Uranians 114–119, 125

Vanity Fair 107
Washington, George 23, 24, 26, 28, 33,
    35, 37, 43, 44, 88
West, U.S. 79, 83
When Lilacs Last in the Dooryard Bloom'd
    22, 58, 59, 63, 89, 90, 92, 93, 101
Whitman, George 23, 41, 90
Whitman, Sarah Helen 129–131, 133,
    135, 136, 142
    works,
        Edgar Poe and His Critics, 135; "The

Portrait," 135
Whitman, Walter
censorship of, xvii, 17, 59, 74, 94,
  98–100
Civil War service, 38, 41, 85, 88
hatred of Lowell, 55, 63, 70, 94, 98,
  100, 103
journalism career, 20, 23, 25–27, 29,
  33, 64, 69, 81
martyrdom of, xvii, 29, 59, 63, 95
nativism of, 25, 26, 30, 69
personas of,
American Bard, xiii, 6, 7, 32, 54, 81,
  90, 103
Christ figure, 33, 91, 93–95, 106
celebrator of Lincoln xviii, 19, 21, 22,
  54, 85–94
Good, Grey, Poet, xiv, 21, 47, 54,
  56–59, 61, 63, 87, 91, 92, 102,
  107, 109
Comrade, 83, 102, 105, 106, 112–115
One of the Roughs 10, 19–21, 30, 35,
  85, 102, 105, 106
political poet, 19, 32
workman, xiv, 57, 72, 81, 82, 85
'Wound-Dresser,' xiv, 21, 38, 41–43,
  46
political appropriation of, xv, xviii, 52,
  54, 62, 102, 106, 108, 113–115,
  125–127
'poverty' of, 54, 92–95, 99–101, 104
publishers of, 34, 74, 82, 83, 88, 90,
  98
self-promotion of, 22, 33, 34, 39, 40,
  53, 85, 86, 101
sexuality of, 10, 34, 54, 71, 74, 76, 81,
  98, 104, 108–111, 120, 124–127
visual images of, xiii, xv, 33, 69, 72, 83,
  106, 116, 142
works,
  An American Primer, 63; "An Army
    Corps on the March," 40;
  *Backward Glance O'er Well-
    Traveled Roads, A*, 17, 100;
  "Bardic Symbols," 75, 76, 83;
  "Beat! Beat! Drums!," 39, 40;
  "Bivouac on a Mountain Side,"
    40; "Blood Money," 29; *Brooklyn
    Freeman* (New York), 26; "Calvary

Crossing a Ford," 40; "Child and
  the Profligate, The," 69; "Children
  of Adam, The," 99; *Eighteenth
  Presidency, The*, 19; *Franklin Evans*
  25, 69, 80; "First O' Songs for a
  Prelude," 20; "Give Me the
  Splendid Silent Sun," 42; "Good-
  Bye My Fancy," 17; "Hush'd Be
  the Camps To-day," 87, 89; *Idle
  Days and Nights of a Half-
  Paralytic*, 94; "Last of the Sacred
  Army," 68; *Memoranda During the
  War*, xv, 38, 94, 97; *Memories of
  President Lincoln*, 22, 73; "My
  Canary Bird," 17; "Prayer of
  Columbus," 17, 94; "Poem of
  Faith," 82; "Poem of Procreation,"
  82; "Poem of Women," 82; "Poem
  of You, Whoever You Are," 82;
  "Quicksand Years," 40;
  "Reconciliation," 42, 43, 89;
  "Resurgemus," 29; "Reuben's Last
  Wish," 69; "Song for a Certain
  Congressman," 29; "Song O' the
  Banner at Daybreak," 39;
  Specimen Days, xiii, xv, 99; "Vigil
  Strange I Kept One Night," 40;
  "The Wound-Dresser," 41;
  "Wounded in the House of
  Friends," 29; "Year That Trembled
  and Reel'd Beneath Me," 41; "The
  Young Grimes," 69
Whitmanites xviii, 17, 52, 56, 92, 103,
  108, 111, 115–119
Whittier, John Greenleaf 64, 72, 79, 81,
  103
Wilde, Oscar xviii, 103, 107, 108, 116,
  119, 123, 126
Wildeans xviii, 52, 108, 116–119, 127
Wallace, J. W. 111, 113, 126
Woodberry, George 132, 136, 137
works,
  Works of Edgar Allan Poe, 137
Woodbury, New York 30, 70, 77